THE PACIFIC RIM: INVESTMENT, DEVELOPMENT AND TRADE

THE PACIFIC RIM

Investment, Development and Trade

edited by
PETER N. NEMETZ

UNIVERSITY OF BRITISH COLUMBIA PRESS
VANCOUVER 1987

THE PACIFIC RIM: INVESTMENT, DEVELOPMENT AND TRADE

© 1986 The Journal of Business Administration

Canadian Cataloguing in Publication Data

Main entry under title:
The Pacific Rim : investment, development and
trade

Also issued as The journal of business
administration, v. 16, nos. 1–2.

Bibliography: p.
ISBN 0–7748–0266–9

1. Pacific Area - Commerce. 2. Pacific
Area - Economic conditions. 3. Investments,
Foreign - Pacific Area. 4. Power resources -
Pacific Area. I. Nemetz, Peter N., 1944-
HC681,P33 1986   338.99   C87–091011–6

INTERNATIONAL STANDARD BOOK NUMBER 0-7748-0266-9

Printed in Canada

Contents

Tables

Figures

Introduction and Overview

PETER N. NEMETZ

One of the world's most diverse geographic areas, the Asia-Pacific, has been transformed within the last two decades into a global centre of large-scale investment, development and trade. Manifesting a remarkable diversity of area, population and wealth (see Table I.1), the twenty-four countries which comprise this region can be divided into at least seven distinct national subgroupings: (i) Oceana, (ii) ASEAN, (iii) the newly industrializing states (NICs), (iv) Japan, (v) the People's Republic of China, (vi) island states, and (vii) two smaller independent communist countries, North Korea and Vietnam. The economic vitality of the Pacific Rim is demonstrated by the dramatic increase in gross domestic product, trade, and industrial activity characteristic of the region's twelve most prominent nations (see Tables I.2, I.3 and I.4).

The central issues of trade, investment and development—their past patterns and prognosis for the future—provide the focus for the first half of this book. What is perhaps most remarkable about this impressive record of economic activity is that it came in a period marked by global economic disruption caused to a large degree by the energy crises of 1973 and 1979. Yet it would be incorrect to assume that energy is incidental to the economic vitality of this region. As such, the second half of this book examines in closer detail the critical role of energy supply and demand in the future development of the Pacific Rim and its interdependence with other global regions.

A significant proportion of the economic vitality associated with the Pacific Basin has been attributable both directly and indirectly to one nation, Japan. Viewed by some as the next, and perhaps preeminent,

Table I.1

Basic Economic, Geographic and Demographic Data by Country (1982)

GROUPING	POPULATION (million)	GDP (billion US$)	GDP/ CAPITA (US$)	AREA (km²)	POPULATION/ km²
I. OCEANA					
Australia	15.17	169.6	11,362	7,692,300	1.97
New Zealand	3.16	25.1	8,017	269,063	11.74
II. ASEAN					
Indonesia	153.03	85.0	564	1,906,240	80.28
Malaysia	14.77	24.8	1,717	332,556	44.41
Philippines	50.74	38.9	785	300,440	168.89
Singapore	2.47	13.4	5,502	618	3,996.76
Thailand	48.49	36.0	759	514,820	94.19
Brunei	0.218[d]	19.8	27,000	5,765	37.81
III. NICs					
South Korea	39.33	64.6	1,668	98,913	397.62
Taiwan	19.117[d]	49.8[c]	2,673	35,981	531.31
Hong Kong	5.394[d]	24.144[b]	4,900	1,064	5,069.55
IV. JAPAN	118.45	1,141.8	9,705	381,945	310.12

	1,020.67	313c	308	9,600,000	106.32
V. CHINA					
VI. ISLAND STATES					
Fiji	0.66	1.2	1,940	18,376	35.92
Kiribati	0.06	0.02	400	690	86.96
Nauru	0.008	0.155	21,400	20.7	386.47
Papua New Guinea	3.09	2.5	831	475,369	6.50
Western Samoa	0.14	0.045	300	2,934	47.72
Solomon Islands	0.25	0.141	613	29,785	8.39
Tonga	0.101	0.061	610	997	101.30
Tuvalu	0.008	0.004[a]	570	26	307.69
Vanuatu	0.126	?	?	14,763	8.53
VII. SMALL COMMUNIST COUNTRIES					
North Korea	18.75	16.2	786	121,730	154.03
Vietnam	56.21	10.7	189	329,707	170.48

<u>Sources:</u> United Nations, 1983, 1985; U.S. CIA, 1984

a.1980, b.1981, c.1983, d.1984. Not included: Cook Islands, French Polynesia, Macao, New Caledonia, American Samoa, Christmas Island, Guam, Wake Island, Pacific Islands Trust

Table I.2
Annual Growth Rate in GDP for Major Asia-Pacific Nations (%)

COUNTRY	1970	1977	1982	1970–1975	1975–1981
Australia	6.5	2.9	3.1	3.5	2.6
New Zealand	3.6a	7.6	4.0d	2.2c	
Indonesia	3.6	8.0	7.9	8.5	7.9
Malaysia	5.8a	9.2	7.8	10.3	8.2
Philippines	5.1	6.3	5.5	6.2	6.0
Singapore	10.0	8.6	9.6	9.8	9.0
Thailand	8.4	6.9	6.8	6.4	7.4
South Korea	10.4	10.2	4.6	9.8	7.2
Taiwan	12.9i	9.9	7.2e	9.0f	10.5g
Hong Kong	5.0a	1.2	2.4	7.7	12.0
Japan	11.5	4.6	4.8	5.0	5.0
China	—	12.0h	3.0d	5.6	5.1b

Sources: United Nations, 1983, 1985; World Bank, 1983; U.S. CIA, 1984;
Republic of China, 1985; U.S. Department of Commerce, 1982

a) 1970/71
b) 1975-79
c) 1971-81
d) 1980/81 [Note: China's growth rate has risen sharply since 1981. The U.S. CIA reports real GNP increase of 11-12 percent in both 1984 and 1985 (U.S. CIA, 1986, p. 4).]
e) 1983
f) 1971-75
g) 1976-80
h) 1978
i) 1971

Sources: United Nations, 1983, 1985; World Bank, 1983; U.S. CIA, 1984; Republic of China, 1985, 1986; U.S. Department of Commerce, 1982

Table I.3
Total Industrial Activity as Percentage of GDP of Major Asia-Pacific Nations

COUNTRY	1970	1977	1982
Australia	33	30	30
New Zealand	26	26	27
Indonesia	15	29	36
Malaysia	24/13.4[d]	20.0[d]	21.3[d]
Philippines	26	28	29
Singapore	23	27	32
Thailand	19	22	23
South Korea	24	30	32
Taiwan	37	44	43
Hong Kong	33	27[a]	27[b]
Japan	39	33	34
China	40[e]	44.2[a, d]	42.3[c, d]

Sources: United Nations, 1983, 1985; Republic of China, 1985;
World Bank, 1983
a) 1978
b) 1980
c) 1981
d) manufacturing only [Source: World Bank, 1983]
e) percentage of net material product

Table I.4
Exports From Major Asia-Pacific Countries (million US$)

COUNTRY	1970	1977	1982
Australia	4,770	13,351	22,002
New Zealand	1,225	3,198	5,524
Indonesia	1,108	10,853	22,293
Malaysia	1,687	6,081	11,189
Philippines	1,142	3,151	4,852
Singapore	1,554	8,241	20,788
Thailand	710	3,482	6,882
South Korea	835	10,046	21,853
Taiwan	1,481	9,361	22,870
Hong Kong	2,514	9,626	20,985
Japan	19,319	80,493	138,911
China	2,260	7,590	21,474

Sources: United Nations, 1983, 1985; U.S. CIA, 1984; Republic
of China, 1985

Table I.5
Japan's Reliance on Offshore Resources

COMMODITY	RELIANCE	DATE	REFERENCE
Columbium	100%	1984	Morgan
Mica (sheet)	100%	1984	"
Strontium	100%	1984	"
Bauxite and Alumina	100%	1984	"
Cobalt	100%	1984	"
Tantalum	100%	1984	"
Potash	100%	1984	"
Nickel	100%	1984	"
Silicon	100%	1984	"
Phosphate	100%	1984	"
Wool	100%	1980	JETRO
Cotton	100%	1980	"
Corn	100%	1983	Keizai Koho
Oranges	100%	1986	Hitachi
Coffee beans	100%	1986	"
Bananas	100%	1986	"
Oil	99.7%	1983	Keizai Koho
Iron Ore	99%	1984	Morgan
Chromium	99%	1984	"
Tin	98.5%	1984	Keizai Koho
Platinum group	98%	1984	Morgan
Asbestos	98%	1984	"
Molybdenum	98%	1984	"
Copper	96.8%	1984	Keizai Koho
Manganese	96%	1984	Morgan
Soybeans	96%	1986	Hitachi
Gold	94%	1984	Morgan
Natural Gas	92.4%	1983	Keizai Koho
Tomatoes	90%	1986	Hitachi
Wheat	89%	1986	Hitachi
Lead	87.5%	1984	Keizai Koho
Honey	83%	1986	Hitachi
Coal	81.4%	1983	Keizai Koho
Aluminum	81%	1984	Morgan
Buckwheat	81%	1986	Hitachi
Tungsten	80%	1984	Morgan
Mercury	79%	1984	"
Lobsters/Shrimp	74%	1986	Hitachi
Octopus	72%	1986	Hitachi
Zinc	67.4%	1984	Keizai Koho
Wood and Lumber	64.3%	1982	Keizai Koho
Barite	39%	1984	Morgan
Salmon	37%	1986	Hitachi
Meat	20%	1983	Keizai Koho
Squid	17%	1986	Hitachi
Cow's milk	14%	1983	Keizai Koho
Textiles and clothing	9.4%	1977-9	Bunge
Fats and oils	9%	1983	Keizai Koho
Chemicals	6.8%	1977-9	Bunge
Rice	6%	1983	Keizai Koho
Iron and steel	5.7%	1977-9	Bunge
Rubber	4%	1977-9	"
Gypsum	4%	1984	Morgan
Hen eggs	2%	1983	Keizai Koho

Sources for Table I.5
Bunge, 1982, p. 409; JETRO, 1982, p. 65; Keizai Koho, 1985, pp. 17, 68;
Hitachi. 1986, p. 5; Morgan, 1986, p. 248.

global superpower (Brown et al., 1986, Vogel, 1979), Japan has, in the postwar period, built a dynamic and resilient economic system despite a considerable reliance on imports for basic necessities (see Table I.5).

Japan has become, and will continue to be in the indefinite future, the most significant driving force in the development and integration of the Western Pacific. In many respects, the process of Japanese industrial development and concomitant trade has had a profound influence on the evolution of other major developing countries in the Far East such as Korea and Taiwan. This chain of influence, or "ladder of development," extends downward to encompass the ASEAN nations of Indonesia, Malaysia, the Philippines, Singapore, and Thailand. The effect of Japanese development has been pervasive, also contributing significantly to the expansion of Australia's resource industries and, more recently, playing a central role in the international participation in Chinese industrial expansion. This is a remarkable accomplishment given Japan's relative scarcity of many important resource commodities, most notably energy.

Much analytical research has been generated in the past few years in an attempt to explain the Japanese phenomenon, attributing its success in whole or in part to such internal variables as cultural homogeneity, an excellent educational system, close government-business cooperation, the provision of low-cost capital to selected industries, long-term business strategy, a preoccupation with labour peace, consensus decision-making and quality control in the industrial system, a low level of defence expenditures, a high rate of personal savings, postwar industrial reconstruction, extensive participation by banks in the industrial sector, various tariff and non-tariff barriers, and a pronounced need to compensate for domestic deficiencies of vital foodstuffs and raw materials.[1]

Understanding the Japanese experience requires, in addition, however, a clear knowledge of external factors, particularly the pattern of Japan's investment and trade with other nations. It is this task which Professor Yoko Sazanami of Keio University undertakes in this volume. What is especially instructive in Professor Sazanami's research is how her analysis of Japanese economic interdependence with other Pacific nations describes the remarkably dynamic phasing of economic activities among groups of countries within the region. Professor Sazanami records several shifts in the pattern of Japanese foreign investment and trade from the late 1960s: first, a focus on investment in offshore resource development to guarantee a supply of relatively inexpensive raw materials; second, a shift to investment in foreign manufacturing to take advantage of low wages of production and to avoid trade barriers in developing countries; third, a growth in investment in specific foreign energy projects and a shifting of energy-intensive manufacturing offshore in the period following the 1973 oil crisis; and, more recently, a diversified strategy which sees, for example, a shift of investment from resource development in such areas as ASEAN to materials processing.

As recognized by Professor Sazanami, the lack of corporate data frequently increases the difficulty of assessing the impact of investment patterns on the changing Japanese import mix. Clearly, however, such an impact exists and it is potentially very large. The broad linkage between investment and trade is indisputable and, as Sazanami concludes: "The development of Japanese direct investment in Pacific Rim countries between 1973 and 1983 generally corresponded to the development of trade interdependence.''

The nature of export composition and performance of Japan's trading partners is the subject of a complementary study by Rodney Tyers and Prue Phillips, who focus their analysis on ASEAN. The trends in international trade studied by the authors are

> dominated by major shifts in the distribution of factor endowments (particularly physical and human capital) between countries in the Pacific Basin and their associated impacts on specialization in exports.

The authors document the shifts in production patterns in the Basin which respond to changing factor availability and prices.

> There has been a striking decline in the relative importance of labour-intensive exports from Japan.... Correspondingly, Japan has developed a significant comparative advantage in technology- and human-capital-intensive goods.... A similar but more subdued pattern is observable for the Asian NICs.... As real wages continue to grow in the Asian NICs, their degree of export specialization in labour-intensive goods can be expected to decline further. Although this trend should see an expansion in the role of labour-intensive manufactures in ASEAN exports, the gap left by the Asian NICs is more likely to be filled by China....
>
> As the capital endowments of the ASEAN countries continue to rise, these countries should specialize increasingly in manufactured exports. Relative to their principal trading partners, the ASEAN countries have a growing comparative advantage in labour-intensive goods. Relative to China, however, their comparative advantage remains in natural-resource-based goods. In the world market for labour-intensive manufactures China may be a formidable competitor. The degree to which ASEAN manufactured exports are labour-

Figure I-1
CLOTHING EXPORTS OF SELECTED PACIFIC RIM COUNTRIES

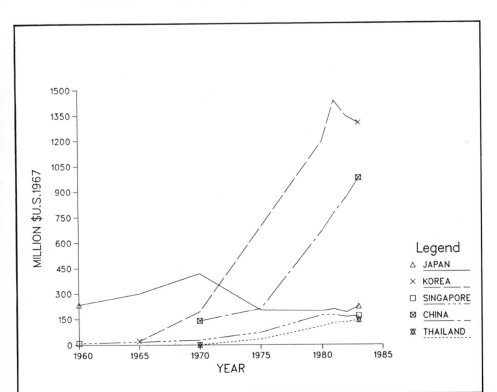

intensive may depend, therefore, on the pattern and growth of China's exports.

This analysis suggests a dynamic and healthy evolutionary pattern where groups of nations are passing through successive stages of industrialization relatively rapidly in response to changing patterns of investment, factor availability and prices. The generally increasing wealth associated with this process is no small reason why many of the other global trading blocs have looked to the Pacific Rim as a strong and continuing source of imports and as a market for exports.

A cogent example of these evolutionary changes in production and trade is provided by Figures I.1–I.5 which focus on a range of important industrial commodities. The first three figures, concerning clothing exports, aluminum production and shipbuilding, illustrate in particular how

Figure I-2
PRIMARY ALUMINUM PRODUCTION OF SELECTED PACIFIC RIM COUNTRIES

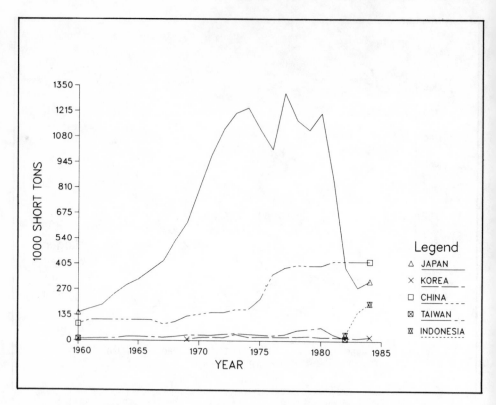

several critical adjustments in Japan's industrial base have been accompanied by compensatory changes in other Pacific Basin nations. The best example is provided by clothing exports, the production of which has been traditionally labour intensive and consequently highly sensitive to wage rates. Figure I.1 demonstrates how Japan's decreasing role in this market has been followed by the successive entry of Korea, China and several of the ASEAN countries. In a somewhat similar manner, Japan's sensitivity to energy costs and environmental concerns has prompted a shift away from aluminum production (Figure I.2)—a change which has been accompanied by increased output in China and Indonesia, although trading patterns have not demonstrated as marked a change as of yet. Finally, Figure I.3, while illustrating Japan's continuing pre-eminence in the shipbuilding industry, also demonstrates the increasing role in this field of a newly industrializing country such as Korea. In moving away

Figure I-3
SHIP AND BOAT EXPORTS OF SELECTED PACIFIC RIM COUNTRIES

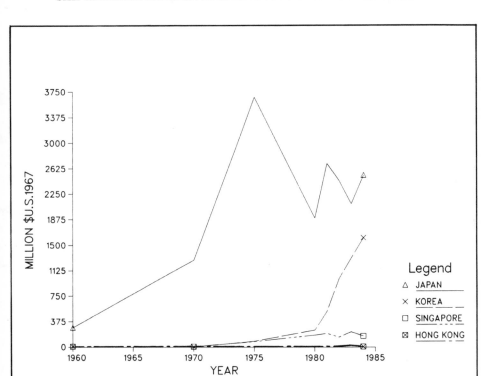

from such basic goods as clothing, aluminum and petro-chemicals, Japan has opted for more capital- and technology-intensive commodities such as road vehicles and electrical machinery including computers. (See, for example, Kodama, 1986.) Some of these shifts are illustrated in Figures I.4 and I.5.

While offering the tempting promise of revitalization for a stagnant world economy, the economic situation in the Western Pacific is more complex and uncertain and indeed unstable than it may first appear. There are several symptoms which suggest this more cautious prognosis: falling prices for commodities such as oil, rubber, tin, palm oil, timber, sugar, copra, rice, and tapioca (see Tables I.6 and I.7); growing protectionist sentiments in such large and crucial markets as the United States concerning critical goods such as textiles and automobiles; and "shakeouts" in specific international industries such as computers and related

Figure I-4
ROAD VEHICLE EXPORTS OF SELECTED PACIFIC RIM COUNTRIES

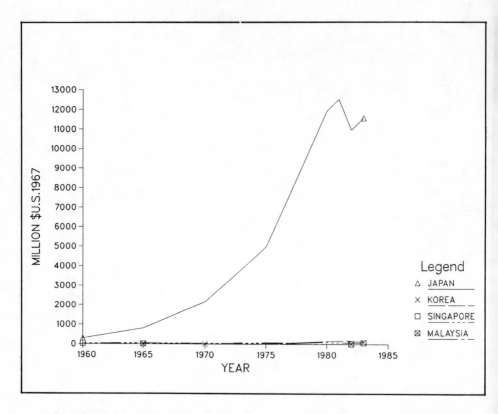

microelectronics. Particularly hard hit have been the ASEAN nations, which in 1985 experienced their lowest growth rates in the last decade. Singapore and the Philippines both registered contractions in total economic activity during this last year.

Underlying the potential difficulties which face Southeast Asia are several political and social factors whose contribution to instability can increase in an adverse economic environment. Included among these are communist insurgency in the Philippines, racial and religious friction in Malaysia and Indonesia, and external military pressure on Thailand.

While Japan has been instrumental in the vitalization of the Pacific Basin, the United States has played an equally important although slightly different role. The U.S. has, in a manner similar to Japan, provided extensive import and export opportunities to the Pacific Rim nations, but the nature of its investment activities has been somewhat

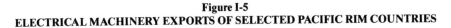

Figure I-5
ELECTRICAL MACHINERY EXPORTS OF SELECTED PACIFIC RIM COUNTRIES

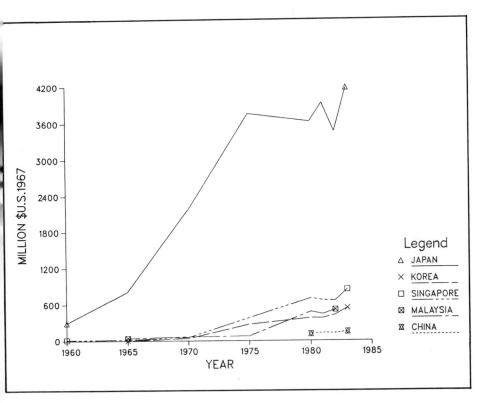

more contentious. The central issue is the purported role of American "deindustrialization." The extent or even existence of this phenomenon is controversial (e.g., Bluestone and Harrison, 1982; Fallows, 1980; Lawrence, 1984; Reich, 1983; U.S. OTA, 1981; Abernathy et al., 1983), but a forceful expression of the case has been presented by Hajime Karatsu of Matsushita Communication Industrial Company in an article which first appeared in Japanese in the September 1985 issue of the journal *Voice*.

To quote:

> "Shooting oneself in the foot" is an American expression for rash, self-destructive actions. It is an apt description of what the United States does when it takes the high-technology industries that it has

Table I.6
Major Commodity Exports by Country in the Asia-Pacific

	Australia	New Zealand	Indonesia	Malaysia	Philippines	Singapore	Thailand	Brunei	S. Korea
Agricultural Products & Foodstuffs									
Bananas									
Beef	X	X							
Butter		X							
Cocoa Beans									
Coffee									
Copra/ Coconut Oil					X				
Corn							X		
Fish & Products									X
Lamb & Mutton		X							
Palm Oil				X					
Rice							X		
Sugar					X		X		
Tapioca							X		
Wheat	X								
Wool	X	X							
Minerals & Ores Basic Metals									
Coal	X								
Copper or Concentrates					X				
Iron Ore	X								
Petroleum & Products			X	X		X		X	
Phosphate									
Tin				X			X		
Wood Products, Logs, Timber			X	X	X				
Footwear									X
Textiles & Clothing									X
Chemicals									
Steel									X
Handicrafts									
Rubber			X	X		X	X		
Plastic Products									
Metallurgical Products									
Light Metal Manufactures									
Misc. Manufactures									
Machinery & Equip.									
Electrical Machinery									X
Electrical Goods									
Automobiles									
Ships									X

Sources: U.S. CIA, 1984; IMF, 1985; World Bank 1983, Vol II

Taiwan	Hong Kong	Japan	China	Fiji	Kiribati	Nauru	Papua New Guinea	Samoa	Solomon Islands	Tonga	Tuvalu	Vanuatu	North Korea	Vietnam
X			X										X	X
										X				
							X	X						
							X					X		
				X	X		X	X	X	X	X	X		
			X						X					
									X					
				X										
X			X										X	X
			X											X
							X							
			X											
					X	X								
X									X					
	X													
X	X	X	X											
		X												
		X												
														X
	X	X												
		X										X		
	X	X												
	X	X										X		
X		X												
X		X												
	X	X												
		X												
		X												

Table I.7

Price Indexes of Major Commodity Exports of the Asia-Pacific (1980 – 100%)

COMMODITY	LOCATION	TIME	INDEX
Food		1985(III)	61
Agricultural Raw Materials		"	
Metals		"	
Bananas	Latin America	"	74.8
Beef	All (New York)	"	70.0
Butter	New Zealand (London)	"	98.1
Coal	Australia	1985(II)	74.7
Cocoa Beans	New York & London	1985(III)	70.5
Coconut Oil	Philippines (New York)	"	86.2
Coffee	All (New York)	"	87.5
Copper	London	"	90.1
Copra	Philippines (Europe)	"	79.6
Hides	Australia	1985(II)	65.0
Iron Ore	Brazil	1985(III)	71.0
Lamb	New Zealand (London)	"	50.7
Logs	Philippines (Tokyo)	"	81.0
Maize	Thailand	1985(II)	67.1
Palm Oil	Malaysia (Europe)	1985(III)	69.2
Pepper, Black	Malaysia (New York)	"	78.4
Petroleum	Saudi Arabia	"	71.8
Phosphate Rock	Morocco	"	202.9
Plywood	Philippines (Tokyo)	"	97.7
Rice	Thailand	"	74.5
Rubber	Malaysia (Singapore)	"	77.2
Sawnwood	Malaysia (France)	"	48.4
Sugar	Australia	1985(II)	53.1
	Philippines	"	73.8
Tin	Malaysia	1985(III)	17.3
	Thailand	1985(II)	88.8
Wheat	Australia (Sydney)	"	75.3
Wool	Australia-New Zealand (United Kingdom)	1985(III)	70.4
			48.3
		71.0/82.2	

Source: IMF, 1985

successfully developed and sends them overseas just to reduce production costs. . . .

Much more serious than U.S.-Japan issues is the effect of allowing American industry to stampede out of the country, thereby destroying the domestic industrial base. . . . Look at the steel industry, for example. Coddled into self-complacency by import quotas, steel has lost any hope of recovery. And other U.S. industries are marching merrily down the same path. Domestic television manufacturing has failed, and such flagships of high technology as semiconductors and personal computers may also be on the verge of fleeing the country. . . .

That the deindustrialization of America now in progress is evident from recent U.S. labor statistics, which show that every month 20,000-30,000 manufacturing-industry workers lose their jobs. This is an alarming figure. . . .

The abnormally strong dollar is doubtless one of the factors that has gutted manufacturing activity of its substance. There is another cause, though, that bears mentioning, namely, the stance taken by American business leaders.

These are strong words, and some critics might suggest that such a harsh analysis is provided at least in part to shield Japanese trade practices from critical commentary. To so dismiss Karatsu's analysis would be a mistake, however, as he has identified a phenomenon which has already generated domestic American debate.

In a recent special issue devoted to the problems facing American manufacturing, *Business Week* (March 3, 1986) focused on what it called the new "hollow corporation." To quote:

A new kind of company is evolving in the U.S.—manufacturing companies that do little manufacturing. Instead, they import components or products from low-wage countries, slap their own names on them, and sell them in America. Unchecked, this trend will ultimately hurt the economy—retarding productivity, innovation, and the standard of living. And even the rise of a strong service economy is not likely to offset the decline in manufacturing.

The misplaced faith in the capacity of the service industries to maintain the strength of the American economy is also criticized by Lester Thurow in his recent book, *The Zero-Sum Solution*:

The current plight of American industry is sometimes dismissed as a sign of the second industrial revolution. The first industrial revolution saw a shift from agriculture to industry; the second industrial revolution represents a shift from industry to services. . . . Between 1977 and 1982 . . . thirty-seven percent of all those new service workers went into health care. Whatever you believe about the desirability of more health care, Americans are not going to generate a high standard of living giving each other heart transplants. . . . Another 33 percent of all those new service workers went into business or legal services. . . . Suing each other is good clean fun and generates a lot of jobs, but it is not productive. . . . One has only to look at Great Britain to see what happens to service industries when manufacturing collapses. . . . While the pattern of industrial activity is indeed changing, as it must, America is not now experiencing a benevolent second industrial revolution but a long-run economic decline. (Thurow, 1985, pp. 56-59.)

What is the import of Karatsu's and Thurow's conclusions for the economic vitality of Pacific Basin economic activity? First, as explicitly stated by Karatsu, through the export of capital and accompanying jobs, the U.S. "boosts the industrial potential of the recipient countries, giving them a weapon that sooner or later will be turned against it." This is clearly not an argument against trade or investment per se in the Pacific Basin. What it does imply is that, *in extremis*, a deindustrialized United States, should it materialize, might lack the purchasing power to sustain this trade and investment. Ultimately, Karatsu argues for a revolutionary change in U.S. management practices which can recreate an American competitive position in world markets. In this sense, Karatsu is far from alone.

Second, while the process of American investment in Southeast Asia, for example, promises increased employment opportunities in the short run, rapidly shifting investment patterns may create an unstable economic environment. An example of this phenomenon is the offshore assembly of semiconductors where several plants established in Southeast Asia have already been closed and/or relocated. The disruptive impact of this type of occurrence on local economic structure and activity cannot be overestimated.

Third, a comparison of Japanese and American investment in the Pacific Rim reveals some important differences. While to some analysts the process of offshore investment and the shifting of manufacturing activity is weakening the American economy, only recently has there been any suggestion that Japanese investment activity may have a similar type of effect, and some concerns have been expressed over future investment patterns (Yamada, 1982; *Globe and Mail,* December 2, 1986).

To return once again to Karatsu's analysis, the answer lies in management attitudes and practices. Inherent in the reformulation of American management should be a realization that North America cannot and should not compete against the less developed countries on the basis of near-starvation wages, but on the basis of higher quality manufactures, our traditional strength. This necessary concern over American industrial policy is not just of relevance to the United States. As Karatsu concludes: "the collapse of [U.S.] manufacturing industry... may lead to the breakup of the free-world community." The devastating impact of such an event on the Pacific Rim requires no elaboration.

In light of the extraordinary and interrelated opportunities and risks which accompany the rapid economic expansion of the Pacific Basin, what are appropriate strategies for the countries in the process of economic development? Professor Theodore Panayotou, in his contribution to this volume, feels that the lessons derived from Thailand "are of relevance... to other developing countries in the region, such as the Philippines, Indonesia and Malaysia which have been following similar development strategies." As Panayotou states the problem:

Agriculture, which receives the lion's share of development assistance, faces absorptive capacity constraints at home and depressed prices abroad. Industrial exports, which enjoy generous promotional privileges, face increasing protectionism from developed countries, at a time when foreign exchange earnings are needed to service a rising foreign debt and to contain a growing balance of trade deficit. Equally disturbing is the growing employment deficit at home. Agriculture is increasingly becoming labor-saving as it shifts from the extensive to the intensive margin, while urban-based industry is increasingly capital-intensive because of factor-price distortions and promotional incentives.

Panayotou makes the case for

investment in the development of labor-intensive rural industry to support and supplement agricultural development which faces absorptive capacity constraints and to compete with the capital intensive urban-based industry which has been overpromoted with little regard to employment, market demand and balanced growth.

There are two areas of concern mentioned by the author which are particularly relevant to the discussion of the continuation and stability of the process of economic growth in Southeast Asia and in many other developing countries. The first is the ecological price frequently associated with population growth and economic development. In Thailand, "rapid expansion into watershed areas and marginal lands has brought about second-generation problems (erosion, floods, droughts, etc.) which pose a threat to the resource base and hence to the sustainability of Thai agriculture" (Panayotou).

Unfortunately, the problem is not confined to Thailand, as illustrated by the selected data on global deforestation rates in Table I.8. The reasons are multifold but, in essence, they are attributable to several basic pressures: (a) a need for greater fuelwood supply for domestic heating and cooking; (b) a requirement for greater land area for agriculture; and (c) a demand for domestic and foreign exchange earnings from tropical wood products. The issue of deforestation has approached the crisis level in the developing world and has prompted several major studies of possible policy reforms (see, for example, World Resources Institute et al., 1985).

The second critical issue touched on by Panayotou is socioeconomic and political stability. The events of the past two decades have begun to offer the prospect of improvement in the living conditions for hundreds of millions of people. The process of economic growth has a profound impact on social and political institutions and can create a momentum of expectations which, should that growth falter, can ultimately lessen the stability of these institutions and their inherent processes.

While the slowing or loss of economic growth may portend social and political dislocation on a national scale, it is frequently smaller population subgroupings which first feel the brunt of these difficulties. An example of such a group are the Nanyang (or Overseas) Chinese who have played a central role in the commercial development of Southeast Asia. The treatment of Nanyang Chinese, and indeed any significant minority, can provide a bellwether of the social, economic and political health of a nation. Past events in Indonesia and current stresses in Malaysia are indicative of this phenomenon.

Professor Michael Goldberg presents an instructive picture of the activities of overseas Chinese through an examination of their real estate investments in Pacific Rim cities. Drawn from extensive interviews in Hong Kong, Singapore, Kuala Lumpur and Bangkok, Professor Goldberg's research focuses on the critical role that Nanyang Chinese can play in the world economy.

Table I.8
Rates of Deforestation in Selected Countries (1981–85)

PACIFIC RIM	ANNUAL PERCENTAGE
Thailand	2.7
Brunei	1.5
Malaysia	1.2
Philippines	1.0
Vietnam	0.7
Indonesia	0.5
Papua New Guinea	0.1
SELECTED OTHER COUNTRIES (for comparative purposes)	
Ivory Coast	6.5
Nigeria	5.0
Paraguay	4.7
Nepal	4.3
Costa Rica	4.0
Haiti	3.8
Sri Lanka	3.5
El Salvador	3.2
Jamaica	3.0

Source: U.S. OTA, 1984, p. 10.

As the world moves toward economies strongly rooted in both information networks and advanced professional skills for generating and analyzing data, Chinese enterprises and families should share disproportionately in this movement in view of their extensive international commercial ties and their past and continued heavy emphasis on education, particularly in the professions. Second, the growing importance of international finance, and its increasing focus on "world cities" again implies an expanded role for overseas Chinese in the development of world cities and the accompanying world financial dealings. Their traditional skills and experience with money and in international and regional banking place the Chinese in an ideal position to take advantage of the kinds of changes that we have been discussing in the world economic and urban order.

Much of the focus of this book, and indeed of global economic attention, centres on Japan, China, Australia, ASEAN, and the Pacific Basin newly industrializing countries (NICs). Of lesser immediate concern because of their dispersion and low levels of population and resource endowments are the multitude of island states and dependencies scattered across Melanesia, Micronesia, and Polynesia. What prospects does the success or failure of the Pacific Rim economy hold for these disparate entities?

The economic fortunes of many of these islands have depended largely on tourism, basic raw materials and foodstuffs, and some onshore mineral deposits. Recent discoveries of undersea minerals may hold the promise for significant increments of wealth in the future. The potential extent and importance of manganese nodules, cobalt-rich manganese crusts and polymetallic sulphide deposits are just now beginning to be assessed under the leadership of research institutes such as Hawaii's East-West Center. Charles Johnson, Allen Clark and James Otto, in their contribution to this book, conclude that while

> no full-scale, private sector financed commercial operation is likely to occur before approximately 2000 . . . the potential economic importance to small island nations is so large, and the present state of knowledge about the extent of crust resources [considered by the authors to offer the greatest promise of development] is so limited, that priority is justified in evaluating the crust potential of the EEZs [Exclusive Economic Zones] of all Pacific countries and territories known to contain seamounts of about twenty-five million years or older.

The critical role of energy in economic development has become a central focus of economic planning since 1973; and it is this subject which provides the principal focus of the second half of this book. As documented in Table I.9, there is a wide disparity in energy resources among the nations of the Western Pacific, with seven countries in particular holding the bulk of the reserves of crude oil, natural gas and coal. An assessment of the long-term importance of these resources to each nation requires additional information, however, such as a comparison of reserves to current production (see Table I.10). While these R/P ratios, or supply/demand surrogates, are a useful first approximation to anticipated reserve life, any detailed utilization of these data in energy policy analysis must incorporate at least four major adjustments for: (i) anticipated growth in final demand associated with increases in population, industrialization and general economic well-being; (ii) projected patterns of interfuel substitution in response to changing prices and the availability of competing fuels; (iii) expected exports of fuel; and (iv) anticipated accretions to reserves through additional exploratory activity. Each one of these forecasts is a complex and subjective undertaking fraught with uncertainty but one which is essential to the design and implementation of an effective national energy policy.[2]

Table I.9

Proved Energy Resources of the Major Asia-Pacific Countries (1984)

COUNTRY	OIL (million bbl)	NATURAL GAS (TCF)	COAL (million metric tons)
Australia	1400-1600	17.8	6,500
New Zealand	200	5.4	290
Indonesia	8700-9100	40.0	1399-2600[b]
Malaysia	3,000	50.0	400-500[b]
Philippines	500[c]	0.2[c]	261[b]
Singapore	-	-	-
Thailand	100[b]	8.5	103[b]
South Korea	-	-	636
Taiwan	7-13	0.5-1.0[a]	205[a]
Hong Kong	-	-	-
Japan	100	0.7	1,006
China	19,100	30.9	97,600
Brunei	1,400	7.3	-

Sources: B.P., 1985a,b; Financial Times, 1985; Sycip et al., 1983; Economist, 1983; Republic of China, 1985; BID, 1983
a. 1980
b. 1982
c. 1983

Table I.10

Reserve to Production (R/P) Ratios of the Major Fuels by Country

COUNTRY	OIL	NATURAL GAS	COAL
Australia	7.6-11	33.5-87	335-340
New Zealand	23.5	58.0	76+
Indonesia	16.8-19	48-62.2	365+
Malaysia	16.3-22	378	d
Philippines	100[c]	n.a.	40
Singapore	-	-	-
Thailand	b	158	36
South Korea	-	-	9-30
Taiwan	10-18[a]	11-23[a]	40
Hong Kong	-	-	-
Japan	18.0	12.8	60
China	22.8-25	40-68.5	156
Brunei	23.8-25	22.5	-

Sources: B.P., 1985a,b; Financial TImes, 1985; BID, 1985; U.N., 1985; Grossling, 1981; New Zealand, 1983
a. 1982
b. virtually all of Thailand's oil needs are met by imports
c. see the caveat in footnote 2 concerning the difference between R/P and R/C ratios
d. current usage is very low so the R/P ratio is unrealistically high

Table I.11
Major Energy Trade in the Pacific Rim

A. NATURAL GAS (1984, billion cubic metres)

	Importer
Exporters	Japan
Alaska	1.4
Brunei	7.2
Indonesia	19.4
Malaysia	4.8

B. OIL (1984 million tonnes)

	Importers				
Exporters	Western Europe	Africa	Southeast Asia	Japan	Australasia
US			3.8	5.2	0.3
Canada			0	0.3	0
Middle East			77.4	140.8	5.4
South Asia	0.9	0.3	0.6	0.7	5.2
Southeast Asia	1.6	0.5	0	43.6	5.2
Japan	0	0	0.5	0	0
Australasia	0	0	0.7	0.3	0

Sources: BP 1985a,b.

C. STEAM COAL (1983, million short tons)

	Importers										
Exporters	Belgium	Denmark	France	West Germany	Netherlands	U.K.	Hong Kong	Japan	South Korea	Malaysia	Taiwan
US	0.2						0.2	2.5	0.4	0	1.2
Australia		0.6	1.3	0.4	1.0	0.6	0.6	6.8	0	0	1.0
South Africa							0.4	3.7	1.5	0	1.4
U.S.S.R.							0	0.6	0	0	
Canada							0	0.4	0.2	0	0.6
UK											
China	0	0	0	0	0	0	1.0	2.4	0.7	0	0
Other							0	0.2	0.3	0.2	0

D. <u>METALLURGICAL COAL</u> (1983, million short tons)

Exporters	Importers Belgium	Egypt	France	Italy	Nether-lands	Spain	U.K.	Japan	South Korea	Taiwan	Eastern Europe
US	0.2	0.8	1.7	1.9	0.7	0.8	2.1	14.7	1.5	0.3	0
Australia								32.6	3.6	2.3	
South Africa								2.8	0	0.1	
U.S.S.R.								1.5	0	0	
Canada	0	0	0	0	0	0	0	11.5	2.6	0	
China	0	0	0	0	0	0	0	1.8	0	0	0.3

<u>Source</u>: U.S. EIA, 1985

The marked discrepancies in energy resource endowments in the Pacific Rim have led, as they have throughout the globe, to a significant international trade in energy commodities, most notably crude oil, natural gas and coal. (See Table I.11.) Parenthetically, it is important to make a distinction between "thermal" or "steaming" coal used by utilities and industry to produce electricity and/or process heat, and "metallurgical" or "coking" coal utilized principally as a reducing agent in the production of steel.

The study of energy use in industrial production and economic development began in earnest after the OPEC price shock of 1973 although pioneering work on this issue had been conducted by such research groups as Resources for the Future prior to that date (e.g., Darmstadter, 1971). One of the earliest analytical devices developed in an attempt to probe the energy-economy linkage was the double logarithmic comparison of energy consumption and gross domestic product, both expressed per capita. An example of this approach for the Pacific Rim is provided in Figure I.6. Canada and the United States have been included for comparative purposes since they are among the highest per capita users of energy in the world.

Initial conclusions from this type of analysis suggested a strong linear relationship between these two variables, leading, in turn, to an equally strong policy conclusion that increasing industrialization and wealth would inevitably entail a comparable increase in the demand for scarce energy resources. In the post-1973 world of rising energy prices and increasing concern over the finite limits to fuel supplies, this early conclusion had serious implications for the process of industrialization in the Third World.

Fortunately, there are several reasons why the early conclusions from this type of analysis have turned out to be overly pessimistic. First, as Corazon Siddayao (1982) has demonstrated, there are numerous and major conceptual problems in the generation of commensurable estimates of cross-national GDP and diverse forms of energy; and second, post-1973 energy price increases have had a dramatic effect on the use of energy.

While some of the decrease in energy use can be explained by the global economic recession, itself a reaction to increasing energy prices, at least two other major phenomena are responsible. First is the increasingly efficient use of energy, particularly within the industrial sector. While this has occurred to some degree in the United States (Marlay, 1984), the most remarkable example is provided by Japan (Nemetz and Vertinsky, 1984; Nemetz et al., 1984-85). The second factor is a shift in the industrial mix away from energy-intensive processes and industries. Again, the foremost illustration of this phenomenon is provided by Japan which has steadily reduced its activities in such energy-intensive industries as aluminum and petrochemicals (see, for example, Samuels, 1983). Some caution should be exercised in the interpretation of this second phenomenon, however. From a global perspective, the transference of energy-intensive manufacturing from one country to another does not, in itself, represent aggregate energy savings. This can only be achieved if new processes are adopted and/or new products emerge which displace older, energy-intensive goods.

Professor Vaclav Smil, a leading expert in the field of energetics, presents, in this volume, a striking comparison of the post-1973 changes in the energy systems of two remarkably different nations, Japan and the People's Republic of China. As Smil observes, "shifts of surprising similarity . . . have demonstrated several essential commonalities guiding the development of energy systems in otherwise very disparate societies." He concludes that

> when prices rise enough, impressive conservation efforts and efficiency increases will follow. . . .The most encouraging finding in this respect is that the slack in the system is large enough even in the world's most energy efficient economy [Japan]. Second, the right prices trigger substantial fuel substitutions. . . .The experience of Chinese and Japanese energetics during the first decade of the new energy era is thus clearly encouraging.

A major transformation has been wrought in the way that modern industrial societies utilize energy and it is now possible to foresee, at least in some countries, the possibility of significantly increased economic activity with lower total energy consumption. These impressive developments in efficient energy utilization do not suggest that major growth in Pacific Rim energy consumption will not materialize. To the contrary; the rapidly industrializing nations of this area will still require significant accretions to their current energy use, and the guaranteeing of the required supply has become, and will continue to be, a central preoccupation of national economic planners.

One of the most urgent questions to be addressed is the form of government participation in, and direction of, the energy sector. Concerns over energy security have become so important that the question of government intervention is no longer an issue—the principal policy focus is on the nature of this activity and its economic efficiency. This is the problem addressed by Professor Corazon Siddayao in her contribution to this volume. In asking the question: "to what lengths can one stretch the security basis for government intervention?", Professor Siddayao concludes:

Figure I-6
ENERGY CONSUMPTION PER CAPITA VERSUS GDP PER CAPITA

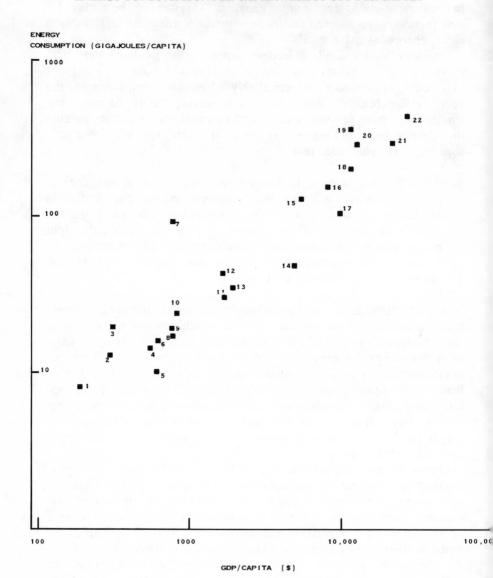

ENERGY
CONSUMPTION (GIGAJOULES/CAPITA)

GDP/CAPITA ($)

NOTES TO FIGURE I.6

A.   COUNTRY CODE   COUNTRY
                1   Vietnam
                2   Samoa
                3   China
                4   Indonesia
                5   Tonga
                6   Solomon Islands
                7   North Korea
                8   Philippines
                9   Thailand
               10   New Guinea
               11   Malaysia
               12   South Korea
               13   Fiji
               14   Hong Kong
               15   Singapore
               16   New Zealand
               17   Japan
               18   Australia
               19   Canada
               20   United States
               21   Nauru
               22   Brunei

B. REGRESSION RESULTS   (1982)
   log energy/capita = -0.91 + 0.79 log GDP/capita
   r^2 = .86
Note: these data have been drawn from Table 4 of U.N. (1985) with
the exception of data for Taiwan. The energy use is based on
``total energy requirements,'' which include commercial energy sources
as well as traditional fuels such as fuelwood, charcoal, bagasse,
animal, vegetable and other non-commercial wastes. Most analyses
of this type focus on commercial energy only because of the difficulty
of obtaining comprehensive and complete information on traditional
fuel use.
   The regression was also run on commercial energy only for the
aforementioned countries and the data were drawn from Table 3 of U.N.
(1985) with the exception of data for Taiwan. The regression results
for commercial energy only are as follows:

   log energy/capita = -1.41 + 0.90 log GDP/capita
   r^2 = .85

Sources: United Nations, 1985; Republic of China, 1985.

Security of petroleum supply is a priority in the agenda of most net-oil-importers. Their responses to the instabilities created by the 1973-74 and 1979-80 threats to petroleum supply... have sometimes appeared to be socially costly, especially where the impacts of errors extend beyond national borders.

Professor Siddayao describes in detail the emergence of new institutions, fiscal regimes and shifts in investment and trading patterns. She concludes that

> Overall, a general assessment suggests that present arrangements are far from optimal. To date this situation has not been aggravated by potential conflicts that could arise from boundary problems in the process of developing these traded resources. There is no guarantee, however, that the present amicable situation, or at least dormant hostility, will prevail and that countries will always see the benefits of settling disputes amicably.

One of the principal short-run concerns among national energy planners over the last decade and a half has been determining the appropriate response to rapidly changing prices of oil and natural gas. These price changes and the resulting cyclical global economic reaction have created major balance-of-payment and budgetary problems for many energy exporters as well as importers. (See Tables I.12 and I.13.)

One of the major strategic responses to these instabilities has been a growing interest in coal development and use. In this volume, Dr. Toufiq Siddiqi of the East-West Center surveys the "Factors Affecting Steam Coal Trade in Asia and the Pacific" and concludes that

> unlike oil, there appears to be no danger of our running out of coal resources even during the 21st century....
> Probably the largest uncertainties affecting the use of coal beyond the next decade are those associated with the effect of carbon dioxide on the world's climate. The general view at present is that increases in carbon dioxide in the atmosphere could lead to a gradual warming of the earth, with possibly severe implications for food production and coastal populations. The largest contribution to a buildup of carbon dioxide is the use of fossil fuels and, during the 21st century, this is likely to be coal.

The subject of both coal and LNG development and trade raises several interesting questions concerning the role of fuel procurement poli-

Table I.12
Foreign Debt of Major Asia-Pacific Debtor Nations*

COUNTRY	YEAR	DEBT OUTSTANDING (DISBURSED) ALL CREDITORS	DEBT OUTSTANDING (INCLUDING UNDISBURSED) ALL CREDITORS	INTEREST PAYMENTS ALL CREDITORS	PROJECTED TOTAL DEBT SERVICE ALL CREDITORS	EXTERNAL PUBLIC DEBT OUTSTANDING AND DISBURSED AS A % OF GNP	DEBT SERVICE AS A % OF GNP	DEBT SERVICE AS A % OF EXPORTS OF GOODS AND SERVICES
Indonesia	1984	22,882.8	36,912.8	1,619.5	3,579.5	30.2%	4.3%	14.7%
South Korea	1984	24,642.0	29,066.5	2,070.5	4,557.0	30.4	5.6	13.5
Malaysia	1984	11,846.0	14,861.9	9,958.7	1,544.9	39.4	4.9	7.7
Philippines	1984	11,175.6	15,726.9	790.0	1,966.1	34.7	3.5	14.1
Thailand	1984	7,567.7	10,570.4	560.3	1,171.5	18.2	3.0	12.0
Singapore	1984	1,679.0	1,991.5	116.6	511.0	10.6	1.8	1.0
Papau New Guinea	1984	905.2	1,189.4	86.3	129.2	39.8	5.7	12.9
Fiji	1984	289.6	324.1	24.4	54.5	n.a.	n.a.	n.a.
Hong Kong	1984	170.3	183.2	16.8	65.8	0.8	0.2	0.2
Western Somoa	1984	61.0	81.9	1.4	5.1	n.a.	n.a.	n.a.
Solomon Islands	1984	25.8	55.4	0.2	0.8	n.a.	n.a.	n.a.
Vanuatu	1984	5.2	11.6	0.1	0.9	n.a.	n.a.	n.a.

*million U.S. $
Sources: I.P.Sharp Associates, 1986

n.a. = not available or not appropriate

Table I.13
Energy Imports as a Percentage of All Imports (CIF) by Value

COUNTRY		
Australia	6.5	1985 II
New Zealand	18.2	1982
Indonesia	n.a.	–
Malaysia	4.3	1984 II
Philippines	29.3	1985 II
Singapore	29.6[a]	1985 II
Thailand	15.6	1985 II
South Korea	18.0	1985 II
Taiwan	21.5	1984
Hong Kong	5.3	1984
Japan	28.9	1985 III
China	n.a.	–
Fiji	23.0	1985 III

Sources: IMF, 1985; Republic of China, 1985; New Zealand, 1983; Hong Kong, 1984
a. Singapore petroleum product exports represent 94 percent of petroleum imports by value.

cies in Japan, the world's foremost energy importer. Also evident are much more difficult questions concerning the uncertainty of energy demand forecasting and the related issue of appropriate resource development policies in energy exporting countries. Several authors such as Siddiqi (this volume), Fesharaki and Schultz (1983), Morse (1984) and Nemetz and Vertinsky (1984), have remarked on the current oversupply of certain fuels such as coal and natural gas which allows Japan to extract significant price concessions from offshore suppliers. There is no indication that this situation will change in the foreseeable future, implying potentially severe financial difficulties for some suppliers.

A similar situation exists with respect to metallurgical coal. The fundamental question remains whether the resource suppliers could have foreseen this development and adopted some form of self-protective measures. In at least one case, there is strong evidence to suggest that foresight was possible but ignored out of ignorance or for short-sighted political reasons. As Harold Halvorson states in his assessment of "The British Columbia Coal Industry," the problem was "overly optimistic forecasts of Japanese crude steel production and hence coking coal imports." A critical piece of evidence is displayed in his Figure 9.1 where

the Canadian/B.C. government forecasts lagged those being made in Japan. For example the Japanese May 1981 forecast was less optimistic than the Victoria/Ottawa forecast made in July 1982, over a year later. Subsequently, when Japanese companies and government agencies were forecasting crude steel production levels in 1983 in the 100 million tpy range, certain Canadian circles were dismissing such low forecasts as an attempt by the Japanese to effect lower coal prices.

It must be remembered when reviewing the forecasts shown in Figure 9.1 that even had the optimistic forecasts made in the 1980-82 period been realized, there was still too much coking coal capacity built. It was possible as early 1980 to foresee a glut of coking coal on world markets.

As a result of these mistakes, Halvorson concludes that "the outlook for the B.C. coal industry is not optimistic. . . . Closure of B.C. capacity is a distinct possibility." Recent events in British Columbia have borne out this assessment (*The Globe and Mail*, January 15, February 3, 1986; Midland Doherty, December 16, 1985).

This unfortunate series of events is just symptomatic of a broader deficiency in the Canadian and indeed North American capacity to understand and formulate an appropriate response to the opportunities and risks inherent in expanded Pacific Basin trade and investment.

Before turning to a discussion of this specific issue, however, it is instructive to produce an overview of energy supply and demand in the Pacific Rim. In characterizing the energy demands and political capacities of East Asian countries to meet their anticipated fuel requirements, it is important that the fundamental diversity of these nations be recognized. From the point of view of energy analysis, this heterogeneity is manifested on at least two dimensions: first, the availability of domestic energy resources; and second, national wealth, or the capability to pay for imported energy if required. This diversity is explicitly addressed in Figure I.7 and Table I.14 by a typology of countries used to structure the analysis of energy supply and demand patterns and opportunities. The typology can be represented in its simplest form by the following matrix.

	energy poor nations	energy rich nations
Developed nations	A	C
Developing nations	B	D

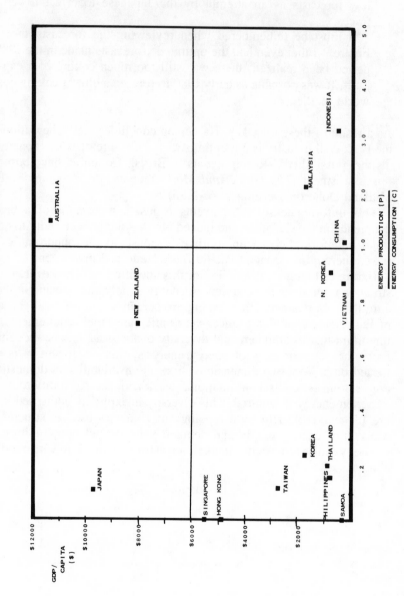

Figure I-7
A TYPOLOGY OF ENERGY AND DEVELOPMENT

NOTES TO FIGURE I.7

Included in the production of commercial primary energy are
hard coal, lignite, peat, oil shale, crude petroleum, natural
gas liquids, natural gas and primary electricity generation
from hydro, nuclear and geothermal sources.
Included in the consumption of commercial energy for solids are
consumption of primary forms of solid fuels, net imports and changes
in stocks of secondary fuels; liquids are comprised of consumption
of energy petroleum products including feedstocks, natural gasoline,
condensate, refinery gas and input of crude petroleum to
thermal power plants; gases include the consumption of natural
gas, net imports and changes in stocks of gas-works and coke-oven
gas; and electricity is comprised of production of primary electricity
and net imports of electricity.
Consumption is defined as: production + imports - exports - changes
in stocks - bunkers.

Source: United Nations, 1985, Table 3.

Additional source: Republic of China, 1985

In a more detailed analysis, it would be necessary to differentiate, for each country, among specific fuels, and between short-term problems of energy supply and demand imbalance and longer-term prospects. The typology does, however, identify characteristics which differentiate among countries with energy surpluses and deficits. These differences play the central role in delimiting the policy options available to each nation in addressing its respective energy problems and/or opportunities. Two general types of conclusions emerge from this preliminary analysis. The first focuses on the relative likelihood and attractiveness of alternative energy development and utilization strategies by both energy rich and energy poor nations within the Pacific Rim.

(1) Group "A" — energy "poor," developed nations

Japan, with an approximately 93 percent reliance on offshore energy supplies, presents an archetypal example of how to cope successfully with an extreme deficiency in a critical natural resource. It has adopted a multifaceted strategy which entails a diversification of fuel types and foreign supply sources while investing heavily in a nuclear option to provide some degree of insulation from external economic and political perturbations. It is noteworthy that while Japan has engaged in research on alternative sources of energy such as geothermal, solar power, wind, ocean thermal, and hydrogen, much less commitment has been demon-

Table I.14
A Typology of Energy and Development
1983 Commercial Energy Only (000 terajoules)

COUNTRY	GDP/CAPITA (US$)	ENERGY PRODUCTION (P)	ENERGY CONSUMPTION (C)	P/C
Brunei	27,000	708	78	9.08
Indonesia	564	3,521	1,121	3.14
Malaysia	1,717	827	390	2.12
Australia	11,362	3,969	2,697	1.47
China	308	20,005	18,438	1.08
North Korea	786	1,401	1,532	0.91
Vietnam	189	182	210	0.87
New Zealand	8,017	245	342	0.72
South Korea	1,668	407	1,694	0.24
Thailand	759	102	511	0.20
Philippines	785	77	478	0.16
Taiwan	2,673	162	1,306	0.12
Japan	9,705	1,284	11,836	0.11
New Guinea	831	1	27	0.04
Singapore	5,502	0	392	0
Hong Kong	4,900	0	298	0
Fiji	1,940	0	9	0
Samoa	300	0	2	0

Source: U.N., 1985a.

strated to the development of these sources than in several other Pacific Rim countries such as New Zealand, the Philippines, and Indonesia (Nemetz and Vertinsky, 1984; Nemetz et al., 1984-85).

New Zealand, also faced with continuing dependence on external supplies of crude oil, has displayed several bold initiatives in the development and use of non-conventional fuels based on extensive domestic natural gas reserves. Foremost among these are the production and use of synthetic gasoline and compressed natural gas in the transportation sector as substitutes for crude oil imports (Kanetkar et al., 1983; Nemetz et al., 1984).

(2) Group "B" — energy "poor," developing nations

In many respects, it is this group of nations which faces the greatest challenge; yet some have already demonstrated a remarkable degree of success in the face of this adversity. Four of the nations within this category are NICs; Hong Kong, Korea, Taiwan and Singapore — a tribute to the strength and resilience of their economic systems.

Singapore is a major entrepôt centre and has one of the largest global concentrations of oil-refining activity. Yet the economic health of this small island state is precariously tied to international financial flows and the increasing preference of some Pacific Basin nations such as Indonesia to assume the refining of their own or imported petroleum (Riek et al., 1985).

The vitality of the Korean and Taiwanese economies has, to this point, enabled them to overcome the potential constraints of offshore energy supply, although it is clear that the post-1973 price increases have presented particularly challenging problems for economic planning (Stewart and Nemetz, 1982a,b).

Of the countries within this category, it is perhaps the Philippines which faces the greatest challenge in meeting her energy requirements. Energy commodities amounted to 31 percent of all imports in 1981 (see Table I.13), and primary energy consumption patterns have been dominated by oil, 80 percent of it imported in 1981. In that same year, domestic oil supplies contributed only 1.6 percent of the energy source mix. The serious economic implications of this dependence are apparent in the national balance of trade figures for the decade following the 1973 oil crisis. The main thrust of Philippine energy policy is to substitute domestic energy sources such as coal, hydropower and geothermal resources for foreign oil. It appears unlikely that the country will be able to meet her domestic coal demand in the next five to ten years, and the success or failure of the large scale developments of geothermal and hydroelectric power will depend mainly on capital availability in foreign markets (Carley et al., 1985). The Philippines is in a unique position, however, in light of its special relationship with the United States. Ultimately, if the U.S. chooses to retain its military bases in this country, it will probably feel compelled to sustain the Philippine economy if such a course of action is required.

Thailand has had, like the other nations within this category, a heavy reliance on imported oil. Not surprisingly, it has placed a large emphasis on energy alternatives by investing in the development of newly discovered natural gas fields, hydroelectricity, lignite, and a range of nonconventional sources such as bagasse, garbage, micro-hydro and biogas. Although the greater utilization of domestic energy resources to back up imported crude and refined products will rely largely on the development of natural gas, the government's success in achieving its policy goals may be constrained by several factors. First, in the short term, the government has a mixed record in its ability to limit the growth in energy demand. Second, because of a poor balance-of-payments position, there is a strong rationale for allowing natural gas exports to proceed, implying a trade-off of domestic energy security for foreign exchange earnings. And third, there has been some continuing ambiguity in government policy toward oil and gas exports and the terms of natural gas refining contracts (Riek et al., 1985).

(3) Group "C" — *energy rich, developed nations*

Australia, the principal Pacific Rim nation in this category, has very large reserves of coal and uranium and significant quantities of natural gas. To a certain extent, Australia has the luxury of choice in determining the timing and scope of energy exports required to help finance continuing oil imports and economic development. She is currently one of the world's largest exporters of coal and has recently initiated development of natural gas reserves off her west coast for shipment in the form of LNG to Japan. Australia has, however, displayed considerable circumspection over the role of uranium as a potential export, citing concern over the issue of nuclear proliferation (Nemetz et al., 1984).

(4) Group "D" — *energy rich, less developed countries*

Although "rich" in energy resources, these nations face problems considerably more complex than industrialized countries such as Australia. This is particularly the case for the People's Republic of China and Indonesia with extraordinarily high "absorptive capacities" (Teece, 1982) based in part on their very large populations at minimal income levels.

China is constrained by, among other variables, inadequate infrastructure, a relatively rigid economic and political system, and the legacy of political and economic disruption. Her future role in international energy trade remains uncertain. China holds the potential for significant exports of oil and coal over the longer term, but issues of domestic demand, capital availability, technology and infrastructure remain unresolved (Ho and Huenemann, 1984; see also U.S. CIA, 1986).

Indonesia, with a population of 150 million, must grapple with the problem of a remarkably skewed population distribution spread over 13,677 islands. While over half the population is concentrated on Java, this island is energy deficient. The nation is highly dependent on oil and is attempting to diversify its domestic energy supplies. Fortunately, it has the natural resources to do so. The challenge facing Indonesia is to establish a pricing policy which reduces its present energy consumption/GNP ratio and yet does not sacrifice economic growth and development (Carley et al., 1985). The country is attempting to capitalize on income from its energy exports to encourage the production of textiles and other manufactures that will provide long-term employment for its plentiful labor resource. It is frequently the irony of oil wealth that the development of a resilient industrial structure designed to ultimately replace depleting energy reserves can be frustrated by an overvalued currency resulting from energy exports.

Malaysia's large natural gas reserves, as well as high quality crude petroleum resources, place her in a favourable position to develop export markets and generate revenue to encourage economic growth. Energy policies have stressed the reduction of domestic consumption of oil to accomplish a threefold objective: to lower the nation's import bill, to increase the availability of domestic resources for export, and to foster increased use of more extensive natural gas reserves (Riek et al., 1985).

The second major conclusion which may be drawn from this typology of national energy supply and demand concerns the role that Canada can play for each category of country:

(i) for energy poor but developed countries such as Japan, Canada can directly fill some of the energy requirements. This energy export may be in raw or embodied form, but clearly the latter would be to Canada's greater benefit. In either case, such exports would help to finance the importation of Japanese goods essential for the Canadian economy;

(ii) for energy poor and less developed countries, Canada can facilitate the development and utilization of "appropriate" energy technology. Some of this work is already being conducted under the auspices of CIDA and IDRC; and

(iii) for energy rich, developing nations, Canada can aid in the development of domestic energy capability through the loan or transfer of advice, expertise and equipment. Both the private and public sectors of the Canadian energy industry have in fact been engaged in just such activity. It is important to note that in all three of these cases, both Canada and the recipient countries stand to reap both economic and political benefits.

In sum, what is the role that Canada can play in the Pacific Rim and what impact can the development of this vast and diverse region have on our country? Canada is facing an historical turning point. While our traditional economic, political and social bonds have been with Europe and the United States, we now have the opportunity to diversify these linkages by participating in the development and integration of the Pacific Basin. At least three factors are responsible for the emergence of this opportunity: (i) the trend toward rapid economic growth in many Asian countries within the past decade and a half; (ii) new patterns in the organization of international economic activities which facilitate the coordination and integration of business ventures; and (iii) recent price instability and supply dislocations in petroleum—the principal energy source for modern industrialized economies. Canada's geographic location, coupled with increasing economic and cultural ties to East Asia, suggest that this nation can have a profound effect upon, and be profoundly affected by, Pacific Rim development in the coming decades.

Canada's overwhelming dependence on the American market has prompted several relatively unsuccessful efforts in the past to seek more diversified markets for our products. (See Langdon, 1983, Ch. 5; and Tables I.15a and I.15b, this volume.) At a time of a potentially unique historical opportunity for Canada in the Pacific Basin, a harsh economic environment has prompted an increased interest in and pressure for a bilateral free trade agreement with the United States. Despite the growing reliance of Canada as a whole on U.S. markets, there has been a strong orientation of exports from Pacific ports towards the Pacific Rim with 41.5 percent of trade in 1984 destined for Asian countries (B.C., 1985). (See Table I.16.)

The conscious effort to seek Asian markets in the face of the almost irresistible imperative of Canadian-American linkage is clearly a strategy which entails risk. Yet, bilateral free trade bears risks of its own. Canada may face increased deindustrialization and an ultimate economic, social and political union with its powerful southern neighbour. The recently completed MacDonald Royal Commission on the Economic Union and Development Prospects for Canada, after extensive and thoughtful consideration, concluded that a bilateral free trade agreement with the United States would be in Canada's best interest. Before such a momentous and potentially irreversible step is taken, it might be wise to consider investing a comparable amount of intellectual resources in re-examining the option of Canada's role in Pacific Rim integration.

Where does one begin in such a daunting inquiry? Professor Edward English, in his essay in this volume, gives us some inkling of what is entailed. It involves a significant commitment of human and material resources to study the unique problems and opportunities afforded by increased Pacific Basin linkages. But much more than that, it requires a fundamental shift in our attitudes toward time and risk in the negotiation of commercial and political ties. While the risks may be high and the payback period long, the return on this investment is potentially very large. To quote Professor English:

One can only hope that stronger financial and policy development will eventually enable a better balance between concern for short-

Table I.15a
Canada's Export Markets (January – December 1984) (millions of CDN $)

COUNTRY	VALUE ($)	PERCENTAGE OF TOTAL
WESTERN EUROPE	7,932	7.2
United Kingdom	2,443	2.2
EASTERN EUROPE	2,480	2.3
MIDDLE EAST	1,664	1.5
OTHER AFRICA	1,125	1.0
OTHER ASIA	9,743	8.9
Hong Kong	215	0.2
Malaysia	188	0.2
Singapore	143	0.1
China	1,272	1.2
Indonesia	290	0.3
Japan	5,629	5.1
North Korea	3	0.003
South Korea	713	0.7
Philippines	57	0.1
Taiwan	401	0.4
Thailand	117	0.1
Vietnam	2	0.002
OCEANIA	816	0.7
Papua New Guinea	2	0.002
Australia	617	0.6
Fiji	2	0.002
New Zealand	189	0.2
British Oceania nes	0.4	0.0004
French Oceania	1	0.001
United States Oceania	3	0.003
SOUTH AMERICA	1,531	1.4
CENTRAL AMERICA & ANTILLES	1,427	1.3
NORTH AMERICA	82,827	75.6
United States	82,796	75.6
ALL COUNTRIES	109,543	100.0

Source: Statistics Canada, 1985

Table I.15b

Canada's Domestic Exports, Excluding Gold (1946–1975) (million CDN $)

YEAR	US	UK	JAPAN	OTHER ECC	OTHER AMERICA	CENTRALLY PLANNED	OTHER COUNTRIES
1975	21,074	1,795	2,130	2,347	1,583	1,049	2,571
1970	10,563	1,481	810	1,226	750	311	1,261
1965	4,840	1,174	316	626	433	418	717
1960	2,932	915	179	439	255	47	488
1955	2,548	768	91	261	216	12	363
1950	2,021	468	20	117	188	7	284
1946	884	594	1	189	202	91	312

Source: Statistics Canada, 1983

Table I.16
Destination of Exports from Canada's Pacific Ports (Percent)

	1984	1979	1974	1969	1964
WESTERN EUROPE	10.0	14.3	14.6	19.1	20.1
EASTERN EUROPE	2.2	2.3	0.2	0.2	5.1
MIDDLE EAST	1.7	0.3	0.7	0.2	0.1
OTHER AFRICA	1.6	1.0	0.6	0.8	1.5
OTHER ASIA	41.5	36.3	41.7	31.0	29.0
China	5.7	4.2	4.8	5.3	8.4
Japan	25.9	26.7	30.6	21.9	16.8
OCEANIA	2.3	2.2	2.4	3.1	2.6
SOUTH AMERICA	2.2	1.6	1.8	1.3	2.6
CENTRAL AMERICA & ANTILLES	0.8	0.6	1.3	0.9	1.0
NORTH AMERICA	37.7	41.5	36.8	43.5	37.9
TOTAL	100.0	100.0	100.0	100.0	100.0
TOTAL VALUE (billion CDN)	$18.25	$12.72	$6.23	$2.29	$1.62

Source: B.C., 1985, 1980, 1975, 1970

term domestic political and commercial concerns and the longer-term foundations for Canadian economic, cultural and political relations with the Western Pacific.

In fact, the issues are even broader, as a preoccupation with short-term domestic political and commercial concerns could have a profound and potentially detrimental impact on Canada's economic, cultural and political future.

NOTES

1. See, for example: Christopher, 1983; Crocker et al., 1984; The Economist, 1983; Kuninori, 1985; Minabe, 1986; Nagato, 1985; Ouchi, 1981; Pascale and Athos, 1981; Peters and Waterman, 1982; Roberts, 1973; Sethi et al., 1984; Taylor, 1983; Uchino, 1978; Vernon, 1983; and Vogel, 1979.
2. A systematic analysis of long-term energy supply security for any nation must also include a comparison of reserves and levels of current consumption (R/C). R/P and R/C ratios can frequently differ by a significant magnitude. For example, a country which is extracting oil, gas or coal at a low rate from a rather limited resource base may have a relatively high R/P ratio because of its principal reliance on energy imports to satisfy domestic demand. Under these circumstances, the R/C ratio would be considerably lower and would provide a more accurate measure of that country's ability to meet future energy demand from domestic reserves.

REFERENCES

Abernathy, William J., Kim Clark, and Alan M. Kantrow, (1983) *Industrial Renaissance: Producing a Competitive Future for America*, New York: Basic Books.

The Aluminum Association Inc., (various years) *Aluminum Statistical Review*, Washington, D.C.

Batsavage, Richard E., and John L. Davie, (1978) "China's International Trade and Finance," in *Chinese Economy Post-Mao*. A Compendium of Papers Submitted to the Joint Economic Committee, Vol. 1, Policy and Performance, U.S. Congress.

B.C. Department of Industrial Development, Trade, and Commerce, (1970) *External Trade Through British Columbia Customs Ports, 1969*, Victoria.

B.C. Department of Economic Development, (1975) *External Trade Report, 1974, Trade Through British Columbia Customs Ports*, Victoria.

B.C. Ministry of Industry and Small Business Development, (1980) *External Trade Report 1979: Trade Through British Columbia Customs Ports*, Victoria.

B.C. Ministry of Industry and Small Business Development, (1985) *British Columbia External Trade Report 1984*, Victoria.

B.P. Gas, (1985) *B.P. Review of World Gas*, London, August.

British Petroleum Co., (1985) *BP Statistical Review of World Energy*, London, June.

Bluestone, Barry, and Bennett Harrison, (1982) *The Deindustrialization of America*, New York: Basic Books.

Brown, Lester R. et al., (1986) *State of the World 1986*, A Worldwatch Institute Report on Progress Towards a Sustainable Society, New York: W.W. Norton & Co.

Bunge, Frederica M. (ed.), (1982a) *South Korea: A Country Study*, Foreign Area Studies, The American University, U.S. Government Printing Office, Washington, D.C.

Bunge, Frederica M. (ed.), (1982b) *Japan: A Country Study*, Area Handbook Series, Foreign Area Studies, The American University, U.S. Government Printing Office, Washington D.C.

Business Information Display Inc. (BID), (1983) *World Energy Industry, 4th Quarter, 1982*, Volume III, Number 1, September.

Business Week, (1986) Special Report: "The Hollow Corporation," March 3.

Carley, J. Scott, Peter N. Nemetz, Ilan Vertinsky, and Vinay Kanetkar, (1985a) "Energy Policy in ASEAN: The Philippines," UBC Institute of Asian Research, Working Paper #25, Vancouver, July.

Carley, J. Scott, Peter N. Nemetz, Ilan Vertinsky, and Alfred Stewart, (1985b) "Energy Policy in ASEAN: Indonesia," UBC Institute of Asian Research, Working Paper #27, Vancouver, July.

Chen, Nai-Ruenn, and Jeffrey Lee, (1984) *China's Economy and Foreign Trade, 1981–85*, U.S. Department of Commerce, International Trade Administration, September.

China, Republic of, (1985) *Statistical Yearbook of the Republic of China*, Directorate General of Budget, Accounting & Statistics, Executive Yuan, Taipei.

China, Republic of, (1986) *Handy Economic Data Kit 1985*, China External Trade Development Council, Taipei.

Christopher, Robert C., (1983) *The Japanese Mind: The Goliath Explained*, New York: Linden Press.

Crocker, Olga, Cyril Charney, and Johnny Sik Leung Chiu, (1984) *Quality Circles: A Guide to Participation and Productivity*, Methuen: New York.

The Economist, (1983) *Japan*, London.

The Economist Intelligence Unit, (various issues) *Quarterly Energy Review, Far East and Australasia*, London.

Fallows, James, (1980) "American Industry, What Ails It, How to Save It," *The Atlantic Monthly*, September, pp. 35-50.

Financial Times, (1985) *Financial Times Energy World*, compiled and edited by Andrew Holmes & Christopher Cragg, Financial Times Business Information, London.

The Globe and Mail, (1986) "Denison writes off Quintette investment," Thursday, January 16, p. B.1.

The Globe and Mail, (1986) "Quintette seeks way to repay debts in wake of price, shipment cuts," February 3.

The Globe and Mail, (1986) "Report urges Japan to revamp economic structure," December 2, p. B20.

Grossling, Bernardo, F., (1981) *World Coal Resources*, 2nd Edition, Financial Times, Business Information Limited, London.

Hitachi, "Internationalization of the Japanese Palate," *Age of Tomorrow*, No. 98, March 1986, pp. 5-9.

Hong Kong, (1984) *Monthly Digest of Statistics*, December.

Ho, Samuel P.S., and Ralph W. Huenemann, (1984) *China's Open Door Policy: the Quest for Foreign Technology & Capital. A study of China's special trade*, Vancouver, B.C.: UBC Press.

I.P. Sharp Associates, (1986) Economic Data Bases.

International Monetary Fund, (1964, 1965) *International Financial Statistics: Supplement*.

International Monetary Fund, (1985) *International Financial Statistics*, December.

Japan External Trade Organization (JETRO), (1982) *White Paper on International Trade*.

Kanetkar, Vinay, Peter N. Nemetz, Sandra Schwartz, Ilan B. Vertinsky, Patricia Vertinsky, and William Ziemba, (1983) "The Energy Future of Australia and New Zealand: A First Round of Modelling," in proceedings of the International AMSE Conference, "Modelling and Simulation," Nice (France), September 12-14, Vol. 5, pp. 265-302.

Karatsu, Hajime, (1985) "The Deindustrialization of America: A Tragedy for the World," *KKC Brief*, Keizai Koho Center, Japan Institute for Social and Economic Affairs, No. 31, October.

Keizai Koho Center (Japan Institute for Social and Economic Affairs), (1985) *Japan 1985—An Industrial Comparison*, Tokyo.

Kodama, Fumio, (1986) "Technological Diversification of Japanese Industry," *Science*, July 18, pp. 291-296.

Kuninori, Morio, (1985) "U.S. Capital Stock Still Older Than Japan's" *Economic Eye*, A Quarterly Digest of Views from Japan, Keizai Koho Center, Japan Institute for Social and Economic Affairs, Vol. 6, No. 1, March, pp. 29-32.

Langdon, Frank, (1983) *The Politics of Canadian-Japanese Economic Relations 1952-1983*, Vancouver, B.C.: UBC Press.

Lawrence, Robert Z., (1984) *Can America Compete?* Washington, D.C.: The Brookings Institution.

Marlay, Robert C., (1984) "Trends in Industrial Use of Energy," *Science*, December 14, pp. 1277-1283.

Midland Doherty, (1985) "Quintette Coal Limited," Institutional Research, G.S. Carter, Toronto, December 16.

Minabe, Shigeo, (1986) "Japanese Competitiveness and Japanese Management," *Science*, July 18, pp. 301-364.

Morgan, John D., (1986) "U.S. and the World Mineral Positions, 1985 to the Year 2000," *Mining Engineering*, April, pp. 245-248.

Morse, Ronald A., (1984) "Japan's Liquefied Natural Gas Dilemma: Oversupply and Lower Demand," Chapter 8 in R. Morse and C. Ebinger (eds.) *U.S.-Japan Energy Cooperation and Competition*, Westview.

Nagato, Kazuhiko, (1985) "The Japan-U.S. Saving-Rate Gap," *Economic Eye*, A Quarterly Digest of Views from Japan, Keizai Koho Center, Japan Institute for Social and Economic Affairs, Vol. 6, No. 2, pp. 18-21.

Nemetz, Peter N., and Ilan B. Vertinsky, (1984) "Japan and The International Market for LNG," *The Columbia Journal of World Business*, Vol. XIX, No. 1, Spring, pp. 70-76.

Nemetz, Peter N., I. Vertinsky, and P. Vertinsky, (1984-85) "Japan's Energy Strategy at the Crossroads," *Pacific Affairs*, Vol. 57, No. 4, Winter, pp. 553-576.

Nemetz, Peter N., Ilan B. Vertinsky, Patricia Vertinsky, and Vinay Kanetkar, (1984) "Threat in Opportunity and Opportunity in Threat: Energy Prospects for Australia and New Zealand," *The Journal of Energy and Development*, Vol. 9, No. 2, Spring, pp. 236-288.

New Zealand Department of Statistics, (1983) *New Zealand Official Yearbook 1983*, 88th Annual Edition, Wellington.

Ouchi, William, (1981) *Theory Z: How American Business Can Meet the Japanese Challenge*, Reading, MA: Addison-Wesley.

Pascale, Richard Tanner and Anthony G. Athos, (1981) *The Art of Japanese Management: Applications for American Executives*, New York: Simon and Schuster.

Peters, Thomas J., and Robert H. Waterman, Jr., (1982) *In Search of Excellence: Lessons from America's Best-Run Companies*, Cambridge: Harper and Row.

Reich, Robert, (1983) *The Next American Frontier*, New York: Times Books.

Riek, Christine, Peter N. Nemetz, Ilan B. Vertinsky, Martin Dresner, Vinay Kanetkar, and A.J. Hesford, (1985a) "Energy Policy in ASEAN: Malaysia and Singapore," UBC Institute of Asian Research, Working Paper #26, Vancouver, July.

Riek, Christine, Peter N. Nemetz, Ilan Vertinsky, Martin Dresner, and Alfred Stewart, (1985b) "Energy Policy in ASEAN: Thailand," UBC Institute of Asian Research, Working Paper #28, Vancouver, July.

Roberts, John G., (1973) *Mitsui: Three Centuries of Japanese Business*, New York: Weatherhill.

Ross, Joel E., and William C. Ross, (1982) *Japanese Quality Circles & Productivity*, Reston, Virginia: Reston Publishing.

Samuels, Richard J., (1983) "The Industrial Destructuring of the Japanese Aluminum Industry," *Pacific Affairs*, Vol. 56, No. 3, Fall, pp. 495-509.

Sethi, S. Prakash, Nobuaki Namiki, and Carl L. Swanson, (1984) *The False Promise of the Japanese Miracle: Illusions and Realities of the Japanese Management System*, Boston: Pitman.

Siddayao, Corazon M., (1982) "Demand for Energy and Economic Growth: Some Measurement and Conceptual Issues," Resource Systems Institute, East-West Center, Working Paper WP-82-13, Honolulu.

Statistics Canada, (1983) *Historical Statistics of Canada*, Second Edition, Ottawa.

Statistics Canada, (1985) *Exports by Countries, January-December 1984*, March, 65-003.

Stewart, Alfred, and Peter N. Nemetz, (1982a) "Patterns of Energy Supply and Demand in Taiwan," UBC Faculty of Commerce Working Paper.

Stewart, Alfred, and Peter N. Nemetz, (1982b) "Patterns of Energy Use in Korea," UBC Faculty of Commerce Working Paper.

Sycip, Gorres, Velayo & Co., (1983) *Energy Balance Forecasts in Developing Countries: The Case of the Philippines*, Institute of Developing Economies, Tokyo, January.

Taylor, Jared, (1983) *Shadows of the Rising Sun: A Critical View of the "Japanese Miracle,"* New York: William Morrow and Co.

Teece, David J., (1982) "A Behavioural Analysis of OPEC: An Economic and Political Synthesis," *Journal of Business Administration*, Vol. 13, Nos. 1 & 2, pp. 127-159.

Thurow, Lester C., (1985) *The Zero-Sum Solution: Building A World-Class American Economy*, New York: Simon and Schuster.

Uchino, Tatruro, (1978) *Japan's Postwar Economy: An Insider's View of Its History and Its Future*, Tokyo: Kodanska International, First English Edition 1983.

United Nations, (various years) *International Trade Statistics*, New York.

United Nations, (various years) *World Trade Statistics*, New York.

United Nations, (1983) *World Statistics in Brief*, New York.

United Nations, (1985a) *Energy Statistics Yearbook 1983*, New York.

United Nations, (1985b) *Statistical Yearbook 1982*, New York.

United States Central Intelligence Agency, (1984) *The World Factbook*,

Nineteen Hundred and Eighty-four, U.S. Government Printing Office, Washington, D.C.

United States Central Intelligence Agency, (1986) "China: Economic Performance in 1985," A Report Presented to the Subcommittee on Economic Resources, Competitiveness, and Security Economics of the Joint Economic Committee, March 17.

United States Department of Commerce, Bureau of the Census, (1983) *Statistical Abstract of the United States*, 104th edition.

United States Department of Commerce, International Trade Administration, (1982) *China's Economy and Foreign Trade, 1979-81*, May.

United States Energy Information Administration, (1985) *Annual Prospects for World Coal Trade 1985, with Projections to 1995*, Department of Energy, Washington, D.C., May.

United States Office of Technology Assessment, (1981) *U.S. Industrial Competitiveness: A Comparison of Steel, Electronics, and Automobiles*, Washington, D.C., July.

United States Office of Technology Assessment, (1984) *Technologies to Sustain Tropical Forest Resources*, Washington, D.C., March.

Vernon, Raymond, (1983) *Two Hungry Giants: The United States and Japan in the Quest for Oil and Gas*, Cambridge, MA: Harvard University Press.

Vogel, Ezra F., (1979) *Japan as Number 1: Lessons for America*, New York: Harper Colophon.

The World Bank, (1983a) *China, Socialist Economic Development*, Volume I, The Economy, Statistical System, and Basic Data, Washington, D.C., August.

The World Bank, (1983b) *China, Socialist Economic Development*, Volume II, The Economic Sectors, Agriculture, Industry, Energy, Transport, and External Trade and Finance, Washington, D.C., August.

The World Bank, (1983c) *World Tables*, The Third Edition, Volume 1, Economic Data, Baltimore: Johns Hopkins University Press.

The World Bank, (1986) *World Development Review 1986,* New York: Oxford University Press, July.

World Resources Institute, The World Bank and the United Nations Development Programme, (1985) *Tropical Forests: A Call for Action*, 3 volumes, October.

Yamada, Mitsuhiko, (1982) "Japan's Direct Overseas Investment and Its Impact on Domestic Industry," *Journal of Japanese Trade & Industry*, Vol. 1, No. 5, September, pp. 18-23.

ACKNOWLEDGEMENTS

I would like to thank both Chris Riek and Sarah Lehman for their assistance in the preparation of this manuscript.

PNN
Vancouver, B.C.
October 1986

1

Japanese Trade in the Pacific Rim: The Relationship between Trade and Investment

YOKO SAZANAMI

INTRODUCTION

The Pacific Rim is the most dynamic region in world trade today.[1] Not only is trade expanding rapidly but also changes in national comparative advantage are occurring. Such changes have altered the commodity composition of both exports and imports in recent years. For example, the large energy price rise in the 1970s induced Japanese firms to adopt energy-saving devices in various stages of production processes and to shift to other production lines when they found their comparative advantage had been eroded. Presently, Japan exports more technology-intensive and fewer energy-intensive goods than she did a decade ago.

Although the changes in relative prices conceal the real changes that took place, the Japanese import market in the 1970s responded quite well to the rise in oil prices, liberalization of trade and appreciation of the yen. When the commodity composition of imports is evaluated in 1970 constant prices, the share of raw materials declined between 1970 and 1983 while the share of manufactured goods increased (see Sazanami, 1983; Bank of Japan, 1984).

Many Asian developing countries also experienced changes in their commodity composition of trade during the 1970s. The Asian NICs succeeded in decreasing the export share of traditional exports such as clothing and other labor-intensive miscellaneous manufactures while increasing the share of more sophisticated exports such as electrical machinery. The exports from ASEAN-4 still consist primarily of raw materials, agriculture and food products, but these nations are trying to diversify their exports to resource-based manufactures, textiles, yarn and clothing and even to some types of electric machinery.

Indeed, the Asian developing countries were able to expand their industrial base in the 1970s. As the economic performance of the Asian developing countries proved better than countries in other regions, they attracted an influx of foreign capital. In addition, the industrialization and export promotion policies pursued by their governments were helpful in sustaining high economic growth and trade expansion.

Japan continued to provide a large outlet for the exports of the Asian developing countries and Oceania. The degree of dependence on the Japanese market increased considerably in the 1970s in the case of ASEAN-4 and Oceania but only moderately in the Asian NICs. The notable difference here was that ASEAN-4 continued to increase exports of raw materials and resource-based manufactures to Japan while the Asian NICs shipped more sophisticated new products to the United States, the European Community and the Middle East, but not much to Japan.

Hiemenz (1983) studied the export performance of Asian NICs and ASEAN countries in the 1970s and found that changes in the commodity composition of their exports clearly followed the standard neo-factor proportions paradigm. In other words, by 1979 Asian NICs exported more engineering products, and ASEAN-4 countries expanded their exports of the traditional trio of textiles, clothing and miscellaneous manufactures while maintaining a comparative advantage in resource-based manufactures and foods. The new exports from Asian NICs penetrated American and European markets in the 1970s. However, they could not erode the Japanese market.

Hamilton and Kreinin (1980) concluded that differences in the trade performance of developing countries in selling manufactured goods to Japan and other industrial nations could be attributed to difficulties in penetrating Japan's domestic distribution system, tariff and non-tariff barriers, and absence of minimum wage legislation, in addition to their own weak bargaining position.

It is quite true that Japan continued to provide the largest market for agricultural, food product and raw material exports from the Asian NICs. And the rapid decline in importance of this commodity group in the exports of Asian NICs as well as the modest market penetration in new products explain the rather small gain in Japanese dependence of Asian NICs in the 1970s. However, it is difficult to attribute the modest market penetration of Asian NICs in the Japanese market to institutional reasons alone.

The penetration into the Japanese market occurred exactly in those fields where Japan lost her comparative advantage in the 1970s because of the oil price rise and wage increases reflecting the appreciation of the yen. These new market opportunities developed in such commodities as textiles, non-ferrous metals, wood and wood products. However, the new product lines in which the Asian NICs gained their comparative advantage, such as electrical machinery and equipment, were fields where the Japanese gain in comparative advantage was the most substantial in the 1970s. Thus, the Asian NICs found it difficult to compete in the Japanese market. In addition, the tendency of Japanese firms to invest in resource development and resource processing in order to cope with the rise in energy prices helped to increase the imports of resource-based manufactures rather than sophisticated new products.

The purpose of this chapter is to assess the overall interdependence of trade and investment between Japan and other Pacific Rim countries in the 1972-82 period; to describe the trade patterns that emerged as a result of industrial development in the Asian NICs and ASEAN-4 in particular; and to point out that Japanese investment in resource development and resource processing after the oil crisis had distorted the application of the standard neo-factor proportions paradigm in the case of trade between Japan and these countries. In other words, the mobility of capital in developing resources and processing resource-based manufactures is making trade relationships between Japan and other Pacific Rim countries look rather different from what the neo-factor proportions paradigm would suggest.

THE GROWING ECONOMIC INTERDEPENDENCE BETWEEN JAPAN AND OTHER PACIFIC RIM COUNTRIES

As indicated in Table 1.1, Japan is the most important market for exports and source of supply for imports of other Pacific Rim countries. The countries that depend most heavily on the Japanese market as the outlet for their total exports are Indonesia (59.7 percent), Australia (34 percent), Malaysia (32.3 percent) and the Philippines (30.2 percent). Those countries endowed with rich natural resources have found the Japanese market particularly important and increased their export dependence on this market in the late 1970s.

In 1981, Singapore and Hong Kong, both leading exporters of manufactured goods among the Asian developing countries, shipped only 9.2 percent and 3 percent of their total exports to Japan respectively. The other major exporter of manufactured goods, Korea, also found the Japanese market less important than before. Sales to Japan declined from 21 percent of all Korean exports in 1977 to 15.9 percent in 1981.

With respect to Pacific Rim imports, Japan continues to be the major source of supply to the countries in the region. There was no observable difference in dependence on imports from Japan between countries like Australia and Indonesia, endowed with rich natural resources, and countries like Hong Kong and Korea that export mainly manufactured goods. Except for Singapore and Malaysia, countries in the region purchased between 20 and 30 percent of their total imports from Japan.

Since the total amount of Japanese trade is substantially larger than that of her trading partners in the region, Japanese trade dependence on these countries is much less than their dependence on Japan. Nevertheless, the Pacific Rim region as a whole supplies about one-quarter of Japanese total imports and provides a market for 20 percent of her exports. As for the sources of supply for Japanese imports, resource-rich Indonesia and Australia are more important than the others.

If we measure trade interdependence by the proportion of bilateral trade in the total trade of all countries listed in Table 1.1, those that increased their trade interdependence with Japan towards the end of the 1970s were Indonesia and Singapore. Korea, which used to have the highest interdependence ratio with Japan, decreased its ratio toward the end of the 1970s. In other words, Korea was increasingly able to diversify her import supply.

The development of Japanese direct investment in Pacific Rim countries between 1973 and 1983 (Table 1.2) generally corresponded to the development of trade interdependence. Indonesia became the largest recipient of direct investment from Japan. The purpose of this investment was to exploit Indonesia's rich natural resources in the first half of the 1970s and to process these resources in the following period. Resource-rich Australia also continued to attract more Japanese direct investment in the late 1970s, but the rate of increase was rather modest compared to the preceding periods. Japanese direct investment in Asian NICs continued to grow, but there was relatively little investment in Korea compared to Singapore and Hong Kong. Hong Kong became the largest host country of Japanese direct investment among Asian NICs in 1983, followed by Singapore.

As of March 1983, the Pacific Rim had received about 32 percent of total accumulated Japanese direct investment. Investment in Indonesia accounted for more than one-third of the total directed to the region. The heavy investment in Indonesia in exploiting her rich natural resources and the subsequent investment in resource processing had promoted close economic interdependence between Indonesia and Japan.

Table 1.1
Japanese Trade Interdependence with Pacific Rim Countries—1977, 1981 (percentage)

	Exports to Japan as % of total Japanese imports		Exports to Japan as % of total exports of exporting nation		Imports from Japan as % of total Japanese exports		Imports from Japan as % of total imports of importing nation	
	1977	1981	1977	1981	1977	1981	1977	1981
ASIANNICs								
Hong Kong	0.49	0.47	3.61	3.05	2.88	3.49	22.17	21.50
Korea	2.99	2.40	21.03	15.90	5.06	3.72	37.72	21.60
Singapore	0.96	1.37	8.33	9.20	2.13	2.91	16.39	16.05
ASEAN-4								
Indonesia	7.08	9.44	46.00	59.70	2.23	2.71	28.84	31.05
Malaysia	2.21	1.86	34.10	32.30	1.07	1.59	18.99	20.92
Philippines	1.27	1.22	28.46	30.20	1.36	1.26	25.73	24.21
Thailand	1.06	0.75	21.48	15.30	1.68	1.48	29.29	22.46
OCEANIA								
Australia	7.49	5.26	39.58	34.08	2.89	3.14	19.03	20.10
New Zealand	0.71	0.62	15.80	15.90	0.55	0.59	13.26	16.02

Source: U.N., Yearbook of International Trade Statistics 1983.

Table 1.2
Japanese Direct Investment in Pacific Rim Countries 1973, 1977, 1983

	AMOUNT IN MILLION US $ᵃ			PERCENTAGE OF JAPANESE TOTAL		
	1973	1977	1983	1973	1977	1983
ASIANNICS						
Hong Kong	100	448	1825	1.47	2.30	3.43
Korea	207	690	1312	3.05	3.55	2.46
Singapore	90	305	1383	1.32	1.57	2.60
Taiwan	108	227	479	1.59	1.16	0.90
ASEAN-4						
Indonesia	473	2703	7268	6.98	13.92	13.67
Malaysia	76	356	764	1.12	1.83	1.43
Philippines	88	354	721	1.29	1.82	1.35
Thailand	129	228	521	1.90	1.17	0.98
OCEANIA						
Australia	307	818	2882	4.53	4.21	5.42
New Zealand	59	109	212	0.87	0.56	0.39
TOTAL	1637	6238	17367	24.12	32.09	32.63

Source: Ministry of Finance, "Zaisei Kinyu Tokei Geppo," various issues.

a. Accumulated total as of March, respective years

JAPANESE DIRECT INVESTMENT IN RESOURCE DEVELOPMENT AND PROCESSING

As the relative size of the Japanese economy in the Pacific Rim is so large, the development of Japanese trade exerts an overwhelming influence on trade flows in the region. Japanese export specialization in heavy industries like iron and steel and chemicals in the 1960s entailed a tremendous import demand for iron ore and petroleum. A huge Japanese import demand for resources and resource-processed manufactures created export opportunities for resource rich countries, particularly those of the Pacific Rim. Their export specialization tended to be formed precisely in those fields where Japanese demand was the strongest.

For a country so poorly endowed with natural resources as Japan, the possibility of attaining high industrial growth by promoting expansion in heavy industries that are also resource-intensive depended on the availability of natural resource imports at low prices. Thus "resource development" has always been the most important motive for Japanese foreign investment. Even in the 1950s when the outflow of capital was under strict government control, foreign investment projects in Alaskan pulp (1953), a steel plant in Brazil (1957), Arabian Oil (1958), and North Sumatra Oil (1960) started with strong government support. The outbreak of the Korean War and the subsequent rise in primary commodity prices was the factor that induced Japan to invest in resource development under government leadership at the time. However, as primary commodity markets became supply-abundant toward the late 1950s, Japan was able to import natural resources necessary for producing such resource-intensive goods as iron and steel or chemicals at relatively low prices during the period of high economic growth. It was not until the late 1960s that Japan again had to emphasize natural resource development projects.

By the end of the 1960s, Japan had become a major world importer of several natural resources, such as iron ore. Japan eventually found that the increase in her imports would affect the world market price. Thus it became increasingly difficult to get a sufficient supply at low prices unless she undertook resource development that would increase world supply.

Several other reasons can be indicated to explain Japan's enthusiasm for investing abroad in the late 1960s. Firstly, the longstanding balance-of-payments deficit in Japan's basic account had turned to a surplus by then and there was a rapid accumulation of foreign currency reserves. It was quite evident that her currency was overvalued at that time, but government and the business community alike had a strong distaste for appreciating the yen. They tried to maintain the 350 yen to a dollar rate by accelerating capital outflow and by trying to keep the basic account in balance. Secondly, neighboring Asian developing countries were turning to foreign capital imports to accelerate their growth. They stressed the importance of direct investment that brought together both capital and management skills necessary for promoting growth, and they welcomed Japanese direct investment in general.

The first boom in Japanese foreign direct investment came in the early 1970s when it grew by 52.7 percent in 1972 and 51.6 percent in 1973. The increase in 1972 reflected the large investment primarily in resource development. At the beginning of the 1970s, one-third of the total accumulated direct investment was in the resource industry. Starting in 1971, the Japanese government provided a tax concession to promote resource development by introducing a system that allowed 30 percent of direct investment in petroleum, non-ferrous metal, iron ore, uranium and coal development to be treated as reserve funds that are tax exempt for five years. In addition, financial support provided from the Export-Import Bank[2] and the Overseas Economic Cooperation Fund helped the resource development projects. (See Sekiguchi, 1982, ch. 2.) Indeed, as much as 42.8 percent of the direct investment undertaken in 1972 was related to resource development.

In 1973, the relative importance of resource development investment decreased and the investment boom shifted to manufacturing. Japanese firms were eager to build foreign subsidiaries to overcome the rise in domestic wage costs after the appreciation of the yen and to avert the various trade barriers in developing countries intended to promote import substitution in manufacturing. The upsurge in Japanese direct investment continued until the end of 1973 when the sudden rise in oil prices caused a rapid deterioration in her balance-of-payments.

In the period that followed the oil crisis, Japanese firms became very cautious about investing abroad. They were busy coping with domestic problems caused by the high energy price and its aftermath. However, the stagnation in Japanese direct investment was more obvious in manufacturing than in resource development. The oil crisis reminded Japan of her poor resource endowment, and there was a growth in investment in petroleum and LNG development projects as in Indonesia. As a result of the sharp rise in domestic energy costs and appreciation of the yen, an energy-intensive resource processing industry, like aluminum smelting, was rapidly losing its competitive strength. To cope with this situation, Japanese firms started to shift energy-intensive resource processing to foreign locations. This trend became more obvious in the late 1970s when Japanese firms adjusted well to the oil crisis and its aftermath and became fully prepared to invest abroad.

Traditionally, Japanese firms prefer to import resources and to undertake the smelting or fabrication process domestically. Such preferences reflect Japan's locational situation, far from the industrial centers of the world. Government policies in the 1960s to promote domestic processing of imported raw materials helped assure employment opportunities at home and saved foreign currencies. At the same time it helped firms to build a self-sufficient production structure within Japan (see Sazanami, 1980, ch. 6). However, these conditions were changing in the early 1970s as liberalization of trade and appreciation of the yen enabled cost savings through production in overseas subsidiaries. Neighboring countries in the Pacific Rim, notably the Asian NICs, were building up an industrial base that could undertake processing for Japanese firms. The sharp rise in energy prices provided another opportunity for Japanese firms to undertake the processing of raw materials, particularly mineral resources, at foreign establishments.

The development of mineral resources requires huge amounts of capital and, as noted earlier, Japanese capital contributed to resource development through investment in petroleum, non-ferrous metals and iron ore from the late 1960s onward. The mineral ores extracted were supplied to Japan in most cases by long-term contracts made at the time of investment. The ore was generally smelted in Japan, but after the oil crisis, the rise in energy costs made smelting in energy-abundant, resource-rich foreign countries more profitable. The rise in energy prices also increased transportation costs, making it more economical to import processed products rather than raw materials in bulk. Another factor that increased Japanese investment in resource processing during this period were the industrialization policies of resource-rich developing countries that favored the construction of fabrication and smelting facilities funded by foreign capital.

JAPANESE DIRECT INVESTMENT IN THE PACIFIC RIM

Japanese direct investment in Pacific Rim countries followed the general trend outlined in the previous section. Since Japanese firms had already built close economic ties through trade with this region, it is not surprising to find that they chose Pacific Rim countries to host their direct investment in the first investment boom in the early 1970s. As of March 1973, Japanese direct investment in the Pacific Rim amounted to (US)$1,788 million, representing 26.3 percent of the total investment in these nations. Pacific Rim countries were the recipients of 31 percent of total Japanese overseas investment for resource development and 46.7 percent of total investment for manufacturing in the same year. In other words, Pacific Rim countries were receiving relatively more Japanese investment in manufacturing than resource development in the early 1970s.

Ten years later, as of March 1983, Japanese direct investment in Pacific Rim countries reached (US)$17,713 million, representing 33 percent of the total. Direct investment in resource development amounted to (US)$7079 million which accounts for over one-third of the direct investment in these countries and 62 percent of Japanese total resource development investment. In other words, not only did the importance of Pacific Rim countries as hosts for Japanese direct investment increase during these years, but so also did the importance of resource development. Japanese investment in manufacturing industries remained important, but its share declined to 39.8 percent of Japan's total world investment in March 1983.

There was an evident shift in the field of Japanese direct investment from manufacturing in the first investment boom in the early 1970s to resource development and processing after the oil crisis. In the former period, the major purpose of investing in Asian developing countries was to mobilize their abundant labor supply and avoid trade barriers intended to promote import substitution. But the prime motive of Japanese investment after the oil crisis was to assure resource supply and to overcome high energy prices by shifting their energy-intensive processes to foreign locations. The resource-rich Asian developing countries tried to attain resource-based industrialization by accommodating Japanese investment.

Differences in investment motives between the first direct investment boom in 1971-72 and after the 1973 oil crisis were well reflected in the regional distribution as well as the industrial composition of Japanese investment in the 1973-83 period. As shown in Table 1.3, the largest amount of Japanese direct investment went into resource-rich ASEAN-4, accounting for 54.3 percent of total Japanese investment in the Pacific Rim between 1973 and 1983. And 58.9 percent of the total direct investment to ASEAN-4 was in resource industries, Indonesia being the largest host country. Major projects in mineral resource development during this period included copper mines in Indonesia and Malaysia, iron ore in the Philippines, and petroleum and LNG in Indonesia.

The importance of investment in forestry and fisheries must not be overlooked since they serve an important role in providing employment opportunities for the host country. The employment effects will be even greater if investments are also made in subsequent stages of resource processing. Some of the Japanese firms that invested in the marine industry also engaged in processing and cold storage. The investments in forestry are also related to production of pulp and paper, sawnwood, and plywood. But the largest amount of investment in resource processing in ASEAN-4 was directed to iron and non-ferrous metal processing during 1973-83 period (see Table 1.3.)

The tendency of Japanese investment in ASEAN-4 to focus more on iron and non-ferrous metal processing than light manufacturing became more pronounced towards the end of the 1970s. As shown in Table 1.3, more than one-third of Japanese investment in manufacturing industries in ASEAN-4 went into the textile industry during the period 1973-77. But in the 1977-81 period, textiles attracted only 11 percent of the investment in manufacturing and, in the 1981-83 period, that proportion declined to 8.1 percent. In contrast to this investment decline in textiles, the iron and non-ferrous metal industry became the major recipient of Japanese investment by the mid-1970s, accounting for more than half of the direct investment in the manufacturing industry between 1977 and 1983. The purpose of the Japanese investment in resource processing was to shift the location of energy-intensive processes to resource-rich countries to meet the domestic demand of the host countries, and to provide an export base. Increases in imports to Japan are causing serious domestic adjustment problems in areas such as wood and wood products. But this process is gradually changing the trade flows between Japan and ASEAN-4 as will be discussed in the following section.

The stagnant demand for textiles in Japan and the world was the primary cause for the small increase in Japanese direct investment in this sector in the Asian NICs after the oil crisis. Because the Japanese direct investment boom in manufacturing in the period prior to 1973 was caused partly by the rise in domestic wages reflecting the tight labor market situation, the firms lost their interest in investing in offshore labor-intensive manufactures when they found a more ample supply of domestic labor during the post-1973 business recession. The policy of the Asian NICs to diversify their industrial structure from labor intensive to more sophisticated lines of products attracted more Japanese investment in the chemical and machinery industries than textiles. In addition, during the 1981-83 period, the relative importance of investment in manufacturing fell, and more investment was directed to service industries and construction in Asian NICs.

Japanese direct investment in resource-rich Oceania generally followed the pattern of ASEAN-4. Investment in the resource industry as a proportion of 'total investment increased, reflecting heavy mineral resource development of such commodities as uranium, coal and aluminum. Following these general trends in resource development, investments in iron and non-ferrous metal processing attracted more capital from Japan.

Table 1.3
Japanese Direct Investment in Manufacturing and Resource Industries in Pacific Rim Countries (in US $ million)

				MANUFACTURING INDUSTRY					
	FOOD	TEXTILES	WOOD & PULP	CHEMICALS	IRON & NON-FERROUS METAL	MACHINERY	ELECTRIC MACHINERY	TRANSPORT MACHINERY	OTHERS
DIRECT INVESTMENT: 1973-1977									
Asian NICs^a mill.$	7	109	14	65	43	44	106	70	45
(%)	(1.4)	(21.7)	(2.8)	(12.9)	(8.5)	(8.7)	(21.1)	(13.9)	(8.9)
ASEAN-4^d mill.$	53	306	64	85	135	9	33	24	139
(%)	(6.2)	(36.1)	(7.5)	(10.0)	(15.9)	(1.1)	(3.9)	(2.8)	(16.4)
Oceania mill.$	14	2	43	90	33	6	9	42	3
(%)	(5.8)	(0.8)	(17.8)	(37.3)	(13.7)	(2.5)	(3.7)	(17.4)	(1.2)
DIRECT INVESTMENT: 1977-1981									
Asian NICs mill.$	20	49	3	265	42	121	150	35	167
(%)	(2.3)	(5.7)	(0.3)	(31.0)	(4.9)	(14.1)	(17.5)	(4.0)	(19.5)
ASEAN-4 mill.$	24	149	27	235	706	26	53	90	47
(%)	(1.8)	(11.0)	(2.0)	(17.3)	(51.9)	(2.0)	(3.9)	(6.6)	(3.5)
Oceania mill.$	8	1	14	2	184	15	9	172	26
(%)	(1.9)	(0.2)	(3.2)	(0.5)	(42.8)	(3.5)	(2.1)	(39.9)	(6.0)
DIRECT INVESTMENT: 1981-1983									
Asian NICs mill.$	13	14	2	205	16	68	54	10	28
(%)	(3.2)	(3.5)	–	(52.0)	(4.0)	(17.2)	(13.7)	(2.5)	(7.1)
ASEAN-4 mill.$	9	57	19	41	473	15	18	64	61
(%)	(1.3)	(8.1)	(2.7)	(5.8)	(67.3)	(2.1)	(2.6)	(9.1)	(8.7)
Oceania mill.$	13	1	28	0	84	8	0	21	40
(%)	(6.6)	(0.5)	(14.3)	(0)	(42.9)	(4.1)	(0)	(10.7)	(20.4)
ACCUMULATED TOTAL: MARCH 1983									
Asian NICs mill.$	45	297	20	548	130	247	354	143	279
(%)	(2.1)	(14.3)	(0.9)	(26.5)	(6.3)	(11.9)	(17.1)	(6.9)	(13.5)
ASEAN-4 mill.$	115	653	133	375	1350	54	123	190	272
(%)	(3.5)	(20.1)	(4.1)	(11.6)	(42.0)	(1.6)	(3.8)	(5.9)	(8.4)
Oceania mill.$	57	6	122	99	338	30	21	242	70
(%)	(5.7)	(0.6)	(12.3)	(10.0)	(34.3)	(3.0)	(2.1)	(24.5)	(7.1)

Table 1.3 (continued)
Japanese Direct Investment in Manufacturing and Resource Industries in Pacific Rim Countries (in US $ million)

	TOTAL MANUFACTURING INDUSTRY	TOTAL RESOURCE INDUSTRY[a]	TOTAL ALL DIRECT INVESTMENT	MFG. AS % OF ALL D.I.[b]	RESOURCE AS % OF ALL D.I.
DIRECT INVESTMENT:					
Asian NICs					
mill.$	503	7	1046	48.1	0.7
(%)	(100)				
ASEAN-4[d]					
mill.$	848	1853	2875	29.5	64.4
(%)	(100)				
Oceania					
mill.$	241	209	660	26.5	23.9
(%)	(100)				
DIRECT INVESTMENT:					
Asian NICs					
mill.$	854	52	1821	46.8	2.7
(%)	(100)				
ASEAN-4					
mill.$	1360	947	2444	55.6	38.7
(%)	(100)				
Oceania					
mill.$	431	549	1433	30.1	38.3
(%)	(100)				
DIRECT INVESTMENT:					
Asian NICs					
mill.$	394	-6*	1256	31.3	0.4
(%)	(100)				
ASEAN-4					
mill.$	703	2373	3189	22.0	74.4
(%)	(100)				
Oceania					
mill.$	196	381	845	23.2	45.0
(%)	(100)				
ACCUMULATED TOTAL:					
Asian NICs					
mill.$	2063	53	4520	45.6	1.1
(%)	(100)				
ASEAN-4					
mill.$	3214	5526	9374	34.2	58.9
(%)	(100)				
Oceania					
mill.$	985	1404	3370	29.2	41.6
(%)	(100)				

Source: Ministry of Finance, ``Zaisei Kinyu Tokei Geppo,'' various issues.

a. Resource Industries include Agriculture, Forestry, Fisheries and Mining.
b. D.I.=Direct Investment
c. Asian NICs: Hong Kong, Singapore, and Korea
d. ASEAN-4: Indonesia, Malaysia, Philippines and Thailand.

The importance of resource development and processing in Japanese investment after the oil crisis affected the Japanese trade relationship with other Pacific Rim countries in various ways. Japan tended to promote a trade relationship with resource-rich countries and also to increase the imports of resource-based products. Thus, resource-rich ASEAN-4 was not following the simple neo-factor proportions paradigm in exporting products to Japan.

JAPANESE MANUFACTURED IMPORTS FROM ASIAN NICs, ASEAN-4, AND OCEANIA—ARE THEY FOLLOWING THE STANDARD NEO-FACTOR PROPORTIONS PARADIGM?

The commodity composition of Japanese imports from Asian developing countries remained almost unchanged in the 1970s and early 1980s. Raw materials plus agricultural and food products still account for over 90 percent of imports from ASEAN-4. This proportion exceeds the comparable ratio for total Japanese-world trade which was about 75 percent in 1981. Although ASEAN-4 increased their share of manufactured goods imported into Japan from 0.8 percent in 1972 to 2.1 percent in 1981, their share of textiles, yarn, fabrics, and clothing was still 3.7 percent and 1.5 percent respectively. The Japanese imports in which ASEAN-4 had the largest share were raw materials (16.3 percent), agriculture and food products (7.2 percent), and resource-based manufactures (4.4 percent).

Considering the decline in the proportion of manufactured goods in total Japanese imports during this period, Asian NICs did quite well in competing with imports from the other regions. In 1981, 45 percent of Japan's imports from Asian NICs were manufactured goods. But the major manufactured imports from Asian NICs continued to be clothing, textiles, yarn and fabrics, and resource-based manufactures. These three groups accounted for 89.8 percent of total imports (see Table 1.4). Indeed, Asian NICs continue to hold a predominant share in Japanese imports of textiles, yarn and fabrics (26.1 percent), and clothing (46.1 percent).

One can see from Table 1.5 that there is a wide difference between the levels of market penetration reached by Asian NICs and ASEAN-4 in Japan. There is no clear indication that ASEAN-4 is expanding import shares in textiles, yarn and fabrics or clothing more rapidly than other manufactures. In the case of ASEAN-4, resource-based manufactures and electrical machinery hold larger import shares in Japan than textiles, yarn and fabrics, or clothing. The commodities for which imports from

ASEAN-4 exceeded those from Asian NICs in 1981 included agriculture and food products as well as raw materials.

Although it is generally difficult to make a precise evaluation of the influence of direct investment on trade flows, the shift in Japanese investment in ASEAN-4 from resource development to processing will eventually change Japanese imports from these countries. There is already a clear indication that technological changes are raising import coefficients (defined as imports used to produce one unit of output) of intermediate products in Japan. This implies that Japanese firms are using more imported intermediate products instead of domestic intermediate products fabricated from imported raw materials (see Sazanami, 1985, pp. 48-50). If direct Japanese investment in resource development can increase the supply of resource-based products in ASEAN-4, this investment can, in turn, accelerate the process of manufactured goods imported into Japan.

Presently, ASEAN-4 is trying to develop resource processing industries in such fields as aluminum (Indonesia), iron ore (Malaysia) and zinc and nickel (Indonesia). The increase in Japanese direct investment in the late 1970s went into these specific fields as indicated in Table 1.3. If the attempt to establish resource processing industries is successful, a shift from raw material to processed intermediate imports may lead to a substantial expansion in imports of manufactured goods. Currently, raw materials still account for over 80 percent of total imports to Japan from these countries.

The lack of corporate data limits the assessment of how Japanese direct investment in resource processing is related to the shift in imports from raw materials to resource-based manufactures. In Table 1.6, we chose three industries to examine whether the shift in imports from raw materials to processed products is taking place: (a) textiles, which received the largest amount of direct investment between 1973 and 1977 in Asian NICs; (b) iron and steel; and (c) non-ferrous metals, which received over 40 percent of direct investment between 1977 and 1983 in ASEAN-4 and Oceania.

In the case of textiles, a large increase in textile imports from Asian NICs proceeded *pari passu* with the shift from textile raw materials to textile products between 1973 and 1982. Now 98.5 percent of Japan's total textile imports from Asian NICs are textile products. Textile imports from ASEAN-4 also increased during this period, but the amount in 1982 was less than one-tenth of Asian NICs, and the share of textile products remained almost unchanged. Oceania countries continued to be a major supplier of textile raw materials to Japan.

A shift in Japanese imports from iron ore and scrap to iron and steel products started in the mid 1970s in the case of Asian NICs. Now 96.5

Table 1.4
Commodity Composition of Japanese Imports 1972, 1975, 1981 (in percentages)

COMMODITIES	FROM ASIAN NICs			FROM ASEAN-4			FROM WORLD		
	1972	1975	1981	1972	1975	1981	1972	1975	1981
1. Total	100.0%	100.0%	100.0%	100.0%	100.0%	100.0%	100.0%	100.0%	100.0%
2. Raw Materials	34.6	23.7	31.0	76.7	70.5	86.2	51.8	61.5	63.0
3. Agriculture & Food Products	17.5	20.0	13.0	14.1	23.8	7.6	18.5	17.9	12.7
4. Chemicals	5.0	3.6	5.0	0.4	0.5	0.6	4.9	3.6	4.3
5. Textile, Yarn & Fabrics	13.3	12.0	7.4	0.3	0.5	0.4	1.7	1.3	1.2
6. Clothing	8.4	13.5	13.9	0.0	0.1	0.2	2.9	0.9	1.3
7. Resource-based Manufactures	6.8	6.2	9.3	1.2	0.8	0.8	2.0	2.7	2.2
8. Electric Machinery	4.8	7.6	2.3	0.0	0.2	0.6	5.6	1.7	1.6
9. Non-electric Machinery	0.4	1.9	2.0	0.0	0.3	0.0	2.5	3.6	2.6
10. Transport Machinery	0.3	0.3	2.4	0.0	0.0	0.0	2.9	1.3	1.9
11. Miscellaneous Manufactures	6.4	5.1	3.7	0.1	0.2	0.2	0.6	1.3	1.2
12. Subtotal (4)-(11)	45.2	50.2	45.1	2.1	2.7	2.9	23.1	16.5	16.3

Source: U.N. Commodity Trade Statistics, Various issues, Statistical paper
Series D.
a. Asian NICs are Korea, Hong Kong and Singapore; ASEAN-4 are Indonesia,
Malaysia, Philippines and Thailand
b. Raw Materials, SITC (2-22)+3; Agriculture & Food products, SITC 0+1+22+4; Chemicals, SITC 5; Textiles, SITC 65; Clothing SITC 84;
Resource-based manufactures, SITC 61+62+63+64+66+67+68; Electric machinery, SITC 76+77; Non-electric machinery, SITC 71+72+73+74+75;
Transport machinery, SITC 76+78; Miscellaneous manufactures, SITC 812+831+89

Table 1.5

Asian NICs and ASEAN-4 Share of Japanese Imports[a] 1972, 1975, 1981

COMMODITIES	PERCENTAGE FROM ASIAN NICs			PERCENTAGE FROM ASEAN-4		
	1972	1975	1981	1972	1975	1981
1. Total	2.8	3.4	4.1	8.9	9.5	12.0
2. Raw Materials	1.9	1.3	2.0	13.2	10.8	16.3
3. Agriculture & Food Products	2.6	3.8	4.3	6.7	12.6	7.2
4. Chemicals	2.9	3.4	4.8	0.6	1.5	1.8
5. Textile, Yarn & Fabrics	22.8	30.3	26.1	0.5	3.2	3.7
6. Clothing	35.5	48.7	46.1	0.6	1.5	1.5
7. Resource-based Manufactures	6.5	7.7	17.6	3.5	2.9	4.4
8. Electric Machinery	6.6	14.7	6.0	0.0	1.3	4.6
9. Non-electrical Machinery	0.2	1.9	3.1	0.0	0.8	0.2
10. Transport Machinery	0.3	0.6	3.1	0.0	0.0	0.3
11. Miscellaneous Manufactures	6.2	13.0	12.9	0.4	1.3	1.7
12. Manufactures Subtotal(4)-(11)	5.5	10.2	11.5	0.8	1.6	2.1

a. See Table 1.4 for source and notes.
Imports from World total to 100

Table 1.6
Japanese Imports of Raw Materials vs. Processed Products, 1973–1982

	Total in million US$			TEXTILE RAW MATERIALS (Total = 100%)			TEXTILE PRODUCTS		
YEAR	ASIAN NICs	ASEAN-4	OCEANIA	ASIAN NICs	ASEAN-4	OCEANIA	ASIAN NICs	ASEAN-4	OCEANIA
1973	$648.3	$67.8	$902.51	3.0%	20.6%	99.3%	87.0%	79.4%	0.7%
1974	718.2	73.3	461.7	11.6	20.2	99.2	88.4	79.8	0.8
1975	533.2	39.6	466.5	6.7	16.7	99.5	93.3	83.3	0.5
1976	824.1	57.3	606.7	3.2	35.1	99.6	96.8	64.9	0.4
1977	811.3	56.1	537.9	6.4	38.7	99.4	93.6	61.3	0.6
1978	1,273.1	75.0	562.8	6.6	26.7	99.4	93.4	73.3	0.8
1979	1,541.8	127.0	680.3	3.3	22.3	99.1	96.7	77.7	0.9
1980	1,099.8	109.4	698.9	3.1	23.1	99.3	96.9	76.9	0.7
1981	1,282.7	102.1	709.3	0.7	24.6	99.4	99.3	75.4	0.6
1982	1,256.8	115.9	720.6	1.5	24.4	99.4	98.5	75.6	0.6

6b. IRON AND STEEL IMPORTS

	Total in million US$			IRON ORE AND SCRAP (Total = 100%)			IRON AND STEEL PRODUCTS		
YEAR	ASIAN NICs	ASEAN-4	OCEANIA	ASIAN NICs	ASEAN-4	OCEANIA	ASIAN NICs	ASEAN-4	OCEANIA
1973	16.9	32.9	874.9	47.6%	100.0%	96.3%	52.4%	0%	4.7%
1974	36.2	31.5	1162.4	58.5	95.3	93.0	41.5	4.7	7.0
1975	22.4	26.7	1117.8	41.4	98.3	98.0	58.6	1.7	2.0
1976	32.9	24.2	1177.0	37.9	70.5	96.6	62.1	29.5	3.4
1977	29.4	84.1	1237.4	26.9	88.0	96.9	73.1	12.0	3.1
1978	51.0	145.5	1145.8	22.4	90.1	98.7	77.6	9.9	1.3
1979	184.0	176.4	1327.0	8.1	88.6	95.8	91.9	11.4	4.2
1980	304.8	198.0	1501.1	6.0	82.6	97.5	94.0	17.4	2.5
1981	406.0	205.3	1503.7	4.0	82.4	97.9	96.0	17.6	2.1
1982	460.5	210.0	1604.3	3.5	81.7	97.2	96.5	18.3	2.8

Table 1.6 (continued)

Japanese Imports of Raw Materials vs. Processed Products, 1973–1982

6c. NON-FERROUS METALS IMPORTS

	Total in million US$			METAL ORE (Total = 100%)			NON-FERROUS METAL PRODUCTS		
YEAR	ASIAN NICs	ASEAN-4	OCEANIA	ASIAN NICs	ASEAN-4	OCEANIA	ASIAN NICs	ASEAN-4	OCEANIA
1973	26.3	509.1	391.1	57.0%	68.0%	70.9%	43.0%	32.0%	29.1%
1974	32.0	847.7	567.7	64.7	71.9	73.1	35.3	28.1	26.9
1975	25.0	523.9	487.4	79.6	71.8	66.4	30.4	28.2	33.6
1976	32.1	654.3	599.2	65.5	64.4	71.7	34.5	35.6	28.3
1977	37.2	726.2	622.8	67.8	59.0	65.5	32.2	41.0	28.5
1978	32.2	846.4	519.7	53.8	57.3	55.4	46.2	42.7	54.5
1979	48.6	1191.0	653.9	38.9	61.9	64.3	61.1	38.1	44.6
1980	56.5	1679.2	770.1	38.1	67.9	70.3	61.9	33.1	35.7
1981	32.4	1284.7	789.1	33.2	65.9	53.7	66.8	34.1	29.7
1982	33.1	1088.6	803.0	13.0	66.3	52.7	87.0	33.7	48.3

Source: Kanzei Kyokai ''Gaikoku Boeki Gaikyo,'' various issues.

a. ASIAN NICs: Hong Kong, Korea and Singapore
   ASEAN-4: Indonesia, Malaysia, Phillipines, and Thailand.
b. Textile raw materials include silk, wool, animal hair, raw cotton, jute and waste materials from textile fabrics. Textile products include thread of synthetic fibres, cotton, woolen and synthetic fabrics, tulle, lace, made up articles of textile materials, floor coverings, undergarments, and knitted articles. Iron and steel includes pig iron, iron and steel bars, rods, universal plates and sheets, tubes and pipes. Non-ferrous metal ores include copper, nickel, zinc, lead, bauxite, chrome, manganese, tungsten and molybdenum ores. Non-ferrous metal products include silver and platinum, and the following and their alloys: copper, nickel, aluminum, zinc, lead, tin and cobalt.

percent of iron and steel are in the form of products. Although ASEAN-4 still supplied a major portion of iron and steel imports to Japan in the form of iron ore and scrap, a gradual increase in the proportion of iron and steel products took place towards the end of the 1970s.

ASEAN-4 was the largest non-ferrous metal supplier to Japan in the Pacific Rim. In 1982, 66 percent of these imports still consisted of metal ore. Asian NICs and Oceania supplied 13 percent and 53 percent respectively of their products in the form of metal ore.

In all three industries, Asian NICs experienced a shift in the exports of raw materials to processed products. Now almost 90 percent of Japanese imports from Asian NICs are processed products. ASEAN-4 is following the pattern of imports from Asian NICs where the proportion of processed products is increasing in the case of iron and steel and non-ferrous metals but not in textiles. For Oceania, non-ferrous metals was the only industry where a shift from imports of ore to products was observed.

From the experience of these three industries, one may conclude that ASEAN-4 is following the general industrialization paradigm in shifting their supplies from raw materials to processed products in the Japanese market, as did the Asian NICs. But ASEAN-4 is not following the Asian NICs in exporting to Japan the traditional trio of products suggested by the standard neo-factor proportions paradigm, namely textiles, clothing and miscellaneous manufactures.

Part of the reasons for ASEAN-4 not following Asian NICs in their trade relationship with Japan can be ascribed to the resource abundance of ASEAN-4 and to the role of resource development and processing investment from Japan. If Japanese investments in resource processing in iron and steel and non-ferrous metals in ASEAN-4 continue to expand as they did in the late 1970s, imports from ASEAN-4 are expected to grow exactly in those fields where investments increased, namely resource-based manufactures rather than textiles.

NOTES

1. In this chapter, Pacific Rim countries are defined as Japan, ASEAN-4 (Indonesia, Malaysia, Philippines, and Thailand), Asian NICs (Hong Kong, Korea, Singapore, and Taiwan), and Oceania (Australia and New Zealand).

Singapore is included in Asian NICs instead of ASEAN because its exports are mainly manufactured goods like other NICs.

2. See the Export-Import Bank of Japan (1984) for details of the export promotion policies of Asian Developing Countries.

REFERENCES

Bank of Japan, (1984) *Recent Trends in Imports, Chosa Geppo*, April.

Crawford, J., and Saburo Okita (ed.), (1978) *Raw Materials and Pacific Economic Integration*, Croom Helm, London.

The Export Import Bank of Japan, (1984) "Report on Research Institute of Overseas Investment," June, Vol. 10, No. 6.

Hamilton, C., and Mordechai E. Kreinin, (1980) "The Structural Pattern of LDCs' Trade in Manufactures with Individual and Groups of DCs," Weltwirtshaftlich Archive.

Hiemenz, U., (1983) "Export Growth in Developing Asian Countries: Past Trends and Policy Issues," Weltwirtshaftlich Archive, Haft 4, Band 119.

Sazanami, Y. (1980) *International Trade and the Japanese Economy* (in Japanese), Toyokeizai Shinposha, Tokyo.

Sazanami, Y., (1983) "Japanese Trade After the Oil Crisis — A structural Approach," *Journal of Japanese Trade and Industry*, May/June.

Sazanami, Y., (1985) "Japanese Trade Liberalization; An Assessment of Implications for Southeast Asian Countries," in W.F. Gossling (ed.), *Western Pacific Trade*, Input-Output Publishing Co.

Sekiguchi, S., (1979) *Japanese Direct Foreign Investment*, Macmillan.

Sekiguchi, S. (ed.), (1982) *Pacific Rim and Japanese Direct Investment* (in Japanese), Nihon Keizai Shimbun-sha Tokyo.

2

ASEAN In Pacific Basin Trade: Export Composition and Performance

RODNEY TYERS and PRUE PHILLIPS *

ASEAN MERCHANDISE TRADE WITH THE PACIFIC BASIN: FACTOR COMPOSITION AND PERFORMANCE

The ASEAN countries are important members of the rapidly growing and increasingly interdependent Pacific Basin economy. Economists have given much attention to the potential for mutual gains through trade liberalization within this region, gains that are seen as feasible because of the geographic proximity of many members, especially in the Western Pacific, the present discriminatory pattern of their trade barriers, and the wide diversity of their resource endowments (Hickman et al., 1977; Crawford, 1981; Anderson, 1983; Ojala and Rae, 1983). The principal trading partners of the ASEAN countries are in the Pacific Basin, and the potential for expansion of their economies is dependent upon changes in the patterns of trade and comparative advantage that are taking place there at present.

The first objective of this chapter is to examine the changes in the patterns of trade and comparative advantage between the ASEAN countries and their major trading partners during the 1970s; the second is to evaluate critically, in this context, both the performance of ASEAN and its competitors in exporting to other Pacific Basin countries and the performance of Pacific Basin country groups in exporting to ASEAN.

Aggregate income in the ASEAN economies is of comparable magnitude to that in Australia and Canada (US$173 billion in ASEAN in 1980, compared with US$148 billion in Australia and US$253 billion in Canada), despite the great discrepancy in their populations (260 million, compared with 15 million and 24 million respectively). The value of merchandise trade is relatively more important to the ASEAN economies, however—almost a third of aggregate GNP, compared with less than a sixth in Australia and about a quarter in Canada.[1] In addition, the rates of growth of real income and total merchandise trade in ASEAN have been very much higher. Average real ASEAN GNP growth exceeded 6 percent a year during the 1970s, while in Australia annual real economic growth averaged less than 3 percent. The average rate of growth of ASEAN merchandise exports exceeded 9 percent a year in real terms, while the corresponding rates for Australia and Canada were about 4 percent (World Bank, 1982, Appendix Tables 2 and 8).

The trends analysed in the paper are dominated by major shifts in the distribution of factor endowments (particularly physical and human capital) between countries in the Pacific Basin and their associated impacts on specialization in exports. Most prominently, Japan's export composition has moved away from labour-intensive goods to goods intensive in technology and human capital. Following Japan are the Asian NICs, whose comparative advantage in labour-intensive goods remains strong despite a significant shift into exports intensive in human capital.[2] For ASEAN as a whole, the shift is away from agricultural resource-based goods toward labour-intensive goods. We expect this transformation to be relatively gradual in the case of ASEAN, however, considering their relatively large endowments of natural resources per capita and the potential for competition with the newly export-oriented manufacturing sector of China.

In the following section, the directions and intensities of the merchandise trade of the ASEAN countries with their major trading partners are examined. Section II then reviews some relevant developments in the theory of comparative advantage and discusses the observed changes in the directions and composition of ASEAN and Pacific Basin trade in this context. The performance of Pacific Basin country groups and the European Economic Community (EEC) in exporting to ASEAN is discussed in Section III, and the corresponding export performance of ASEAN is discussed in Section IV.

I. CHANGES IN THE GENERAL PATTERN OF ASEAN AND PACIFIC BASIN TRADE

Throughout the 1970s the economies of the Asian newly industrializing countries (the Republic of Korea, Taiwan, and Hong Kong, hereafter referred to as NICs) and some other middle-income less developed countries (LDCs), including the members of ASEAN, grew more rapidly than those of the industrialized countries of the OECD. It is not surprising, therefore, that these countries' world trade shares expanded during the decade. The commodity boom of the mid-1970s was a watershed, particularly for the OECD countries and the petroleum-importing LDCs, whose terms of trade deteriorated after 1973. In the first three years of the decade, world trade grew at 24 percent a year in nominal terms; later, it slowed to 18 percent a year.

The slowdown in ASEAN export growth after 1973 was much less marked than that for the world as a whole, in part because the petroleum price increases during the decade were favourable to Indonesia and Malaysia and the ASEAN group is a small net exporter of petroleum.[3] Over the decade, ASEAN exports rose from 2 percent to 4 percent of world trade. The corresponding decline in Australia's export growth after 1973 was considerably greater, however, and Australia's share in world exports declined from 1.7 percent to 1.4 percent (Tyers and Phillips, 1982, Table 1).

The 1970s commodity boom had an adverse effect on the average terms of trade throughout the Pacific Basin, and the share of Pacific Basin countries in world trade (both imports and exports) fell from about a quarter to about a fifth.[4] In nominal terms, the total trade of the Pacific Basin countries increased tenfold between 1965 and 1980. Meanwhile, the share of exports directed to other Pacific Basin countries increased from 54 percent to 60 percent. The corresponding share of imports held steady at about 60 percent.[5] A more detailed picture of ASEAN trade with Pacific and non-Pacific trading partners is provided by Table 2.1. Adding across columns shows that ASEAN increased its intra-Pacific share of total trade during the 1970s — exports grew from 63 percent to 72 percent and imports from 55 percent to 62 percent. Furthermore, there has been a significant increase in intra-ASEAN trade. On the import side, this has been largely at the expense of Japan and the EEC, while on the export side it is primarily a result of a decline in the share destined for non-Pacific countries.[6]

The natural-resource-rich Pacific Basin countries (Australia, New Zealand and Canada) have also increased the share of their imports from other Pacific Basin countries, from 69 percent to 73 percent; the corresponding export share held steady at about 69 percent. From Table 2.1 it is also clear that the imports of the natural-resource-rich countries, particularly those of Australia and New Zealand, have become "Asianized," primarily at the expense of the EEC and the United States. Their exports have been directed increasingly toward the developing countries of East Asia and ASEAN (as well as outside the Pacific Basin, principally to the Middle East) and away from the United States and the EEC.

Table 2.1
Changes in Trade Shares in the 1970s[a] (Percentage)

Share of → in the trade of ↓	X/M	ASEAN 1970	ASEAN 1980	A.NZ[b] 1970	A.NZ[b] 1980	CANADA 1970	CANADA 1980	K.T.HK[c] 1970	K.T.HK[c] 1980	CHINA 1970	CHINA 1980	JAPAN 1970	JAPAN 1980	USA 1970	USA 1980	EEC-9 1970	EEC-9 1980	REST OF WORLD 1970	REST OF WORLD 1980
ASEAN	X	13	17	2	3	1	3	6	7	1	1	23	27	18	17	16	13	21	15
	M	6	13	5	4	1	4	4	6	3	3	25	22	15	16	19	12	23	24
A.NZ[b]	X	5	7	6	6	2	6	2	5	2	4	23	21	12	9	26	8	20	38
	M	2	7	6	6	4	6	2	5	1	1	12	16	23	20	35	12	15	29
CANADA	X	0.5	1	1	1	–	1	0.4	1	1	1	5	6	65	63	16	8	11	18
	M	0.4	1	1	1	–	1	1	2	0.1	0.2	4	4	71	70	11	5	10	17
K.T.HK[c]	X	5	7	2	3	3	2	5	6	0.1	1	12	11	42	31	16	18	13	21
	M	6	8	2	3	1	1	4	5	7	7	34	26	21	19	13	9	12	23
CHINA	X	12	10	2	2	3	2	28	26	–	–	15	25	0	7	20	15	22	14
	M	3	4	8	6	5	3	0.3	2	–	–	35	32	0	24	28	15	17	13
JAPAN	X	9	8	4	8	3	2	11	12	3	4	–	–	31	24	10	13	30	34
	M	8	13	9	13	5	3	3	4	1	3	–	–	29	17	8	5	37	48
USA	X	3	4	2	2	21	15	4	5	0	2	11	10	–	–	26	24	34	38
	M	3	5	2	1	28	16	5	7	0	0.5	15	13	–	–	23	15	25	42
EEC-9	X	0.9	1	2	0.5	1	1	0.7	1	0.4	0.4	1	1	8	6	50	53	35	37
	M	0.7	1	2	0.5	2	1	0.7	1.5	0.3	0.4	1	2	11	8	49	48	33	36
REST OF WORLD	X	0.7	2	1	1	1	1	2	2	0.3	0.3	3	5	10	8	29	23	54	59
	M	0.4	0.6	1	1	1	1	0.5	1	0.4	0.4	3	4	12	8	32	24	49	61

Source: ANU International Economic data bank, based on United Nations Trade Statistics.
a. X and M refer, respectively, to shares of total exports and imports.
b. Australia and New Zealand.
c. Republic of Korea, Taiwan and Hong Kong.

The Asian NICs, on the other hand, have increased their trade shares with non-Pacific countries and reduced their shares with Japan and the United States. A similar pattern is evident for Japan. In both these cases, however, the very large increases in petroleum prices are significant factors in explaining the observed trends, at least on the import side. The share of United States exports destined for Asia increased slightly, but a more significant change appears to be away from Canada and toward non-Pacific countries. United States imports have come increasingly from the developing countries of East and Southeast Asia and decreasingly from Canada, Australia and the EEC.

The ASEAN shares of the imports of other ASEAN countries, the Asian NICs, the natural-resource-rich countries, Japan and the United States have all increased (see the first two columns of Table 2.1). The largest proportional gain is in the share of the imports of the natural-resource-rich countries, particularly those of Australia, where the gain was from 2 percent to 7 percent (Tyers and Phillips, 1984a). Not surprisingly, the shares of the Asian NICs in the imports of their trading partners have also expanded, as have those of China, albeit from a low base at the beginning of the decade. The slower growing natural-resource-rich countries, on the other hand, have lost share in the total imports of all the country groups listed in the table. This trend is most striking in the imports of Japan and the United States, which were strongly affected by the petroleum price increases of the 1970s, and in China's imports, which changed in composition away from natural-resource-based goods towards technology-intensive and human-capital-intensive goods as China's trade expanded in the late 1970s (see Findlay et al., 1985).

Changes in Trade Intensities

The relative importance of a particular bilateral trading relationship can be gauged using the intensity-of-trade index.[7] This is defined as the share of one country's trade with another country (or region) divided by the other country's (or region's) share of world trade. This index has been applied to Pacific Basin trade (for 1979) in a paper by Anderson (1983). By taking a trade-weighted average over all intra-Pacific trading partnerships, Anderson derived a value of 1.84 for the average intensity for all the Pacific Basin market economies (excluding Latin America). Thus, on average, trading partners in the Pacific Basin are roughly twice as important to Pacific Basin exporters as are their counterparts in the rest of the world.

In Table 2.2 the changes that occurred in Pacific Basin trade intensities during the 1970s are highlighted. The importance of exports to the

Table 2.2
Changes in Intensities of Trade in the 1970s[a]

To From	ASEAN 1970	ASEAN 1980	A.NZ[b] 1970	A.NZ[b] 1980	CANADA 1970	CANADA 1980	K.T.HK[c] 1970	K.T.HK[c] 1980	CHINA 1970	CHINA 1980	JAPAN 1970	JAPAN 1980	USA 1970	USA 1980	EEC-9 1970	EEC-9 1980	REST OF WORLD 1970	REST OF WORLD 1980
ASEAN	6.13	5.20	1.28	2.26	0.20	0.16	2.74	2.13	1.38	1.30	3.66	3.79	1.35	1.34	0.41	0.35	0.66	0.46
A.NZ[b]	2.42	2.27	2.98	4.58	0.53	0.63	1.05	1.52	4.36	4.38	3.61	2.97	0.93	0.70	0.68	0.26	0.64	0.97
CANADA	0.23	0.32	0.77	0.82	-	-	0.16	0.38	1.59	1.49	0.76	0.84	4.96	4.99	0.42	0.27	0.34	0.48
K.T.HK[c]	2.46	2.11	1.28	1.89	0.70	0.76	2.49	1.86	0.22	0.78	1.97	1.57	3.21	2.47	0.43	0.50	0.41	0.64
CHINA	5.64	3.11	1.30	1.30	0.25	0.27	13.02	7.90	-	-	2.41	3.55	.0	0.53	0.52	0.42	0.68	0.43
JAPAN	3.80	2.45	1.93	2.45	0.66	0.65	5.09	3.38	5.19	4.52	-	-	2.22	1.79	0.24	0.33	0.88	0.93
USA	1.06	1.11	1.29	1.70	4.69	5.25	1.51	1.41	.0	1.91	1.51	1.19	-	-	0.59	0.58	0.91	1.00
EEC-9	0.52	0:35	0.51	0.27	0.18	0.13	0.33	0.26	0.76	0.45	0.20	0.14	0.62	0.44	1.31	1.46	1.11	1.10
REST OF WORLD	0.31	0.58	0.21	0.34	0.18	0.20	0.94	0.49	0.58	0.35	0.44	0.66	0.73	0.67	0.76	0.64	1.70	1.76

Source: ANU International Economic data bank, based on United Nations Trade Statistics.
a. The intensity of trade index is the share of one country group's exports going to another country group divided by the latter's share of world imports (net of the first group's imports).
b. Australia and New Zealand.
c. Republic of Korea, Taiwan and Hong Kong.

natural-resource-rich countries from all the Asian countries and country groups, including ASEAN, increased. This trend is primarily the result of significant increases in the intensities of the trade flows from all Pacific Basin country groups, including the United States, to Australia (Tyers and Phillips 1984a).[8] The corresponding indexes for exports to ASEAN from the Pacific Basin are also high, but they have not shown significant increases. In fact, while the importance of Japan's exports to ASEAN in relation to all ASEAN imports remains high, it is the increased importance of China as a destination for Japanese exports that is most striking.

As Anderson (1983) indicates, the high levels of trade intensity shown in Table 2.2 are the result not so much of complementarity of the commodity mixes of imports and exports in each bilateral relationship as of "special country bias." That is, these high intensities are explained by low resistances to trade in these particular bilateral relationships (low costs of transportation, communication and other factors associated with trade), relative to those obtaining for trading relationships with the rest of the world (Drysdale and Garnaut, 1982). This is particularly evident from a comparison between the respective trade intensities of Australia and Canada with Western Pacific countries. Their similar factor endowment patterns, and hence their similar potential complementarity with the natural-resource-poor countries of East Asia, are not reflected in the distribution of their exports and imports. Clearly, resistances to trade between Canada and the Western Pacific are substantially higher than they are for Western Pacific trade with Australasia.[9]

That the realized complementarity of import and export commodity mixes in Pacific Basin trade should be low, despite considerable diversity in the factor endowments of Pacific Basin countries, is explained by Anderson as stemming from barriers to trade. Over time, however, these barriers can be expected only to reduce the pace at which the commodity composition of imports adjusts to shifts in comparative advantage (Garnaut and Anderson, 1980). Thus commodity mix complementarity has probably been a contributing factor in the increases in intensity of ASEAN and other Pacific Basin exports to Australia and of Japan's exports to China that occurred in the 1970s. That this is expected can be seen from the analysis of factor composition in the following section.

II. CHANGES IN COMPARATIVE ADVANTAGE

Theoretical Developments and Empirical Studies

Since the 1960s the theory of comparative cost as a means of explaining the location of production has developed considerably. The shortcomings of the Heckscher-Ohlin model (the Leontief paradox, for example, asserts that the model does not accurately predict the pattern of exports of the United States) have long been recognized as stemming in part from the aggregation of factors of production to the levels of "capital" and "labour."[10] Extensions to separate out human (as distinct from physical) capital were made in the 1960s in attempts to explain the Leontief paradox; papers by Kenen (1965) and Keesing (1966) are representative of a considerable body of literature on the independent significance of human capital in the United States, including the relatively recent work of Branson and Monoyios (1977) and Stern and Maskus (1981). This literature has been further extended to cover developing countries in an empirical study by Balassa (1977), in which he regressed the pattern of export specialization against measures of both physical and human capital endowment and found that human capital was a significant explanator in more than half of a sample of thirty-six countries.

Another series of developments in the theory, again primarily in the United States literature, supports the further disaggregation of capital to separate out technology. Contributors to this literature have emphasized the research and development component of value added as a measure of technology intensity; they include Gruber, Mehta and Vernon (1967), Hufbauer (1970), Branson and Junz (1971), Morall (1972), and Goodman and Ceyhun (1976). The incorporation of technology as a factor of production has contributed to dynamic extensions based on product life-cycle theory (Vernon, 1966; Wells, 1968).

A further stream of theoretical developments has emphasized the role of natural resources as a factor of production. Jones (1971) was the first to extend the Heckscher-Ohlin model to incorporate natural resources, and his model was subsequently generalized by Krueger (1977) and applied in explaining the pattern of ASEAN and Western Pacific trade by Garnaut and Anderson (1980) and Anderson and Smith (1981). This branch of the theory defines three factors (capital, labour and natural resources) and two classes of goods (natural-resource-based goods and manufactures). The work of Garnaut, Anderson and Smith has found that this extension to the theory explains well the changes in the patterns of export specialization in the natural-resource-rich Pacific countries, such as Australia and Canada, relative to those in the natural-resource-poor countries, which include Japan and the Asian NICs.

The disaggregation of factors of production to include natural resources, human capital and technology considerably weakens the most general form of the Heckscher-Ohlin theorem—it can only be said that "on average" countries will have lower autarky prices for goods intensive in the factors with which they are well endowed and that lower autarky prices will lead to exports under free trade (Dixit, 1981). The generalizations that remain possible still justify empirical testing, however. Furthermore, the empirical studies based on the disaggregated models mentioned above have had important implications for policy (Krueger, 1978).

A recent study by Krause (1982) goes even further in disaggregating the factors of production that are important in United States exports to ASEAN. Krause's factors are natural resources, labour, technology, and human capital. The present analysis follows that of Krause in that all merchandise is considered to be the result of production processes involving multiple factors and that each item can be classified according to its dominant factor—that used most intensively and/or that which determines the location of production.

The Approach Adopted

To allow a more detailed examination of the structure of ASEAN exports and those of the natural-resource-rich countries, both of which are dominated by natural-resource-based goods, the factors of production are further disaggregated to separate out agricultural from mineral resources. Note that physical capital is excluded. It is assumed to be relatively mobile and therefore not so important in determining the location of production. As Krause asserts, its exclusion, combined with the inclusion of natural resources, helps to remove some problems with factor intensity reversals—mining and crop production, for example, can both be either labour-intensive or capital-intensive, but their location of production is determined by access to natural resources.

The 189 commodities of the three-digit level of the Standard International Trade Classification (SITC) have therefore been divided into five groups, according to their intensities in the five factors—agricultural resources, mineral resources, labour, technology, and human capital. First, agricultural resource-based goods were identified as those for which the location of production depends primarily upon cultivable land. From the remainder, mineral-based goods were similarly identified as those produced in close proximity to mineral and energy-bearing deposits. To identify the labour-intensive goods among the manufactures which remained, we drew upon the work of Garnaut and Anderson (1980), who ranked manufactures at the three-digit level of the SITC in order of increasing value added per worker. Those with particularly low value added per worker were classified as labour intensive. Finally, to separate the technology and human-capital-intensive categories we drew from the results of Krause (1982), who examined research and development expenditures in the United States, classifying goods with high research and development content as technology intensive. The resulting classification is listed in Table 2.3.

In the following analysis, the trade of the ASEAN countries with their principal trading partners is divided into these five factor groups. First, the shares of their total trade in each group are examined and trends in export specialization analysed. In subsequent sections, bilateral trade in each commodity group is examined in more detail. The measure of export specialization adopted is the "revealed" comparative advantage index introduced by Balassa (1965) — the share of each commodity group in an economy's total exports divided by that commodity group's share of world exports. Provided that the economy's export specialization has not been distorted by government policies (which generally distort a country's import mix more than its export mix), index values greater than unity indicate a comparative advantage over the rest of the world.[11]

Results

For the ASEAN countries and their principal trading partners, Table 2.4 lists some rough measures of factor endowments and breaks down their total imports and exports into the five commodity groups according to factor intensity. The petroleum price increases of the 1970s significantly increased the share of ASEAN exports in the mineral-resource-intensive category. As would be expected from their large endowments of natural resources (relative to their East Asian neighbours), they sustained high levels of revealed comparative advantage in natural-resource-based goods. At the same time, their comparative advantage in agricultural-resource-intensive goods declined and that in labour- and skill-intensive goods increased over the decade. This is predicted by the theory, considering that the ASEAN countries sustained high economic growth rates (rates of growth of physical and human capital per worker) during the decade relative to the rest of the world. The increased significance of labour-intensive exports also follows the product life-cycle theories. ASEAN comparative advantage in labour-intensive manufactures would be expected to increase with accelerating wage growth in the countries with which its exports of labour-intensive goods compete, such as Japan and the Asian NICs.[12]

The very low population densities of Australia, Canada, and New Zealand would be expected to lead to specialization by these natural-resource-rich countries in the export of agricultural- and mineral-resource-intensive goods, which would persist despite their relatively high average per capita incomes (proxy for their endowments of capital per worker). As Garnaut and Anderson (1980) indicate, the degree of

Table 2.3

The Classification of Merchandise Into Factor Groups[a]

COMMODITY	SITC, REVISED	COMMODITY	SITC, REVISED
AGRICULTURAL-RESOURCE-INTENSIVE GOODS		TECHNOLOGY-INTENSIVE GOODS	
Food and live animals	0	Chemical elements, compounds	51
Beverage and tobacco	1	Coal, petroleum, etc., chemicals	52
Hides, skins, furs undressed	21	Medicinal etc. products	54
Oil seeds, nuts, kernels	22	Fertilisers, manufactured	56
Crude and synthetic rubber	23	Explosives, pyrotechnical products	57
Wood lumber and cork	24	Plastic materials, etc.	58
Pulp and waste paper	25	Chemicals nes	59
Textile fibres	26	Machinery, non-electric	71
Crude animal and vegetable matter nes	29	Electric power machinery switchgear	722
Animal, vegetable oil, fat	4	Electric distributing machinery	723
Leather, dressed fur, etc.	61	Electro-medical, X-ray equipment	726
Wood, cork manufactures nes	63	Electrical machinery nes	729
MINERAL-RESOURCE-INTENSIVE GOODS		Aircraft	734
Crude fertiliser, minerals nes	27	Instruments, apparatus	861
Metalliferrous ores, scrap	28	Photo, cinema supplies	862
Minerals, fuels, etc.	3	Developed cinema film	863
Non-metal mineral manufactures	661-663	HUMAN-CAPITAL-INTENSIVE GOODS	
Pearls, precious and semi-precious stone	667	Dyes, tanning, colour products	53
Pig iron, etc.	671	Perfume, cleaning etc. products	55
Non-ferrous metals	68	Rubber manufactures nes	62
		Paper, paperboard manufactures	64
		Steel	672-679
		Metal manufactures nes	69

UNSKILLED-LABOUR-INTENSIVE GOODS

Textile yarn, fabric, etc.	65	Telecommunications equipment	724
Glass	664-666	Domestic electric equipment	725
Ships and boats	735	Railway vehicles	731
Plumbing, heating,		Road motor vehicles	732
lighting equipment	81	Road vehicles – non-motor	733
Furniture	82	Watches and clocks	864
Travel goods, handbags	83	Sound recorders, producers	891
Clothing	84	Printed matter	892
Footwear	85	Works of art, etc.	896
Articles of plastic nes	893	Gold, silverware, jewellery	897
Toys, sporting goods, etc.	894		
Office supplies nes	895		
Other manufactured goods	899		
War, firearms, ammunition	951		

a. This classification is based on the work of Krause (1981) and Garnaut and Anderson (1980). Further explanation is provided in the appendix to Tyers and Phillips (1984a).

specialization would be expected to increase with the relatively rapid economic growth of the neighbouring natural-resource-poor East Asian countries. These expectations are borne out by Table 2.4.

The shares of agricultural- and mineral-resource-intensive goods in the exports of the natural-resource-rich countries remained high throughout the 1970s. Their "revealed" comparative advantage in agricultural-resource-intensive goods began high and increased. Although both Australia and Canada were strong exporters of mineral-resource-intensive goods, neither was a large net exporter of petroleum. Thus, while mineral exports grew as a share of their total exports, their revealed comparative advantage declined. Although only very small shares of Australia's exports are in the labour- or skill-intensive commodity groups, human-capital-intensive goods make up about a third of the exports of the natural-resource-rich country group (mostly intra-industry trade across the long Canadian border with the United States). This accords with the fact that the rate of participation in tertiary education in Canada is high compared with that in Australasia.[13]

It is clear also from Table 2.4 that there has been a striking decline in the relative importance of labour-intensive exports from Japan. This is to be expected in view of Japan's very high levels of physical and human capital per worker and their relatively rapid growth through the decade. Correspondingly, Japan has developed a significant comparative advantage in technology- and human-capital-intensive goods, with the latter having been strong and increasing throughout the decade. A similar but more subdued pattern is observable for the Asian NICs. Although they sustained a very strong comparative advantage in labour-intensive manufactures, these fell by 10 percent as a share of their exports, while the share of human-capital-intensive goods in their exports more than doubled (to a level exceeding that for the United States). They finished the decade with a clear comparative advantage in human-capital-intensive goods.

As real wages continue to grow in the Asian NICs, their degree of export specialization in labour-intensive goods can be expected to decline further. Although this trend should see an expansion in the role of labour-intensive manufactures in ASEAN exports, the gap left by the Asian NICs is more likely to be filled by China. Labour-intensive manufactures have had an increasing share of China's rapidly growing merchandise exports. According to Findlay et al. (1985), there is considerable potential for further expansion of China's exports, particularly textiles, clothing and footwear.

The pattern of United States exports remained relatively stable during the 1970s. Most notably, the United States sustained a very strong com-

Table 2.4
Resource Endowment Proxies, Factor Group Shares of Total Trade and "Revealed" Comparative Advantage: ASEAN and Principal Trading Partners[a]

	ASEAN 1970	ASEAN 1980	ANZ,C[b] 1970	ANZ,C[b] 1980	K,T,HK[c] 1970	K,T,HK[c] 1980	CHINA 1970	CHINA 1980	JAPAN 1970	JAPAN 1980	USA 1970	USA 1980	EEC-9 1970	EEC-9 1980	REST OF WORLD 1970	REST OF WORLD 1980
Population density (per km²)	85		24		453		104		314		24		163			
GNP per capita ($US)	716		11000		1941		300		9890		11360		8340			
Tertiary students[e] (percentage of population)	0.73		3.1		1.9		0.13		2.1		5.1		1.9			

FACTOR GROUP[d] SHARES OF TOTAL TRADE (PERCENTAGE)

		ASEAN 1970	ASEAN 1980	ANZ,C 1970	ANZ,C 1980	K,T,HK 1970	K,T,HK 1980	CHINA 1970	CHINA 1980	JAPAN 1970	JAPAN 1980	USA 1970	USA 1980	EEC-9 1970	EEC-9 1980	REST OF WORLD 1970	REST OF WORLD 1980
Agricultural resources	X	62	33	33	33	17	10	52	27	6	3	22	24	14	14	32	15
	M	21	14	12	10	29	20	28	35	34	22	23	12	26	18	19	17
Mineral resources	X	29	45	26	28	11	3	6	28	3	3	10	10	10	15	38	58
	M	16	29	10	19	11	27	14	4	44	61	18	40	23	31	15	23
Unskilled labour	X	3	6	2	2	60	49	28	30	24	11	6	6	14	12	9	7
	M	11	6	10	9	16	11	3	7	3	4	13	8	10	11	12	9
Technology	X	3	11	13	15	8	12	7	8	24	31	43	44	33	34	12	12
	M	28	32	35	34	25	26	25	32	16	10	16	16	23	23	31	29
Human Capital	X	3	5	26	22	13	26	7	7	43	54	20	17	29	26	11	9
	M	24	20	33	29	19	16	30	22	3	3	31	24	18	18	23	22

"REVEALED" COMPARATIVE ADVANTAGE -- GOODS INTENSIVE IN

	ASEAN 1970	ASEAN 1980	ANZ,C 1970	ANZ,C 1980	K,T,HK 1970	K,T,HK 1980	CHINA 1970	CHINA 1980	JAPAN 1970	JAPAN 1980	USA 1970	USA 1980	EEC-9 1970	EEC-9 1980	REST OF WORLD 1970	REST OF WORLD 1980
Agricultural resources	2.78	2.09	1.48	2.08	0.74	0.63	2.34	1.67	0.27	0.16	0.98	1.52	0.63	0.85	1.41	0.92
Mineral resources	1.50	1.47	1.35	0.90	0.18	0.06	0.31	0.90	0.13	0.09	0.52	0.31	0.53	0.49	1.95	1.87
Unskilled labour	0.25	0.60	0.18	0.24	5.31	5.28	2.45	3.23	2.15	1.13	0.51	0.61	1.21	1.23	0.76	0.70
Technology	0.13	0.43	0.51	0.62	0.31	0.51	0.27	0.34	0.96	1.27	1.72	1.82	1.32	1.40	0.47	0.48
Human Capital	0.14	0.27	1.17	1.10	0.57	1.31	0.33	0.37	1.96	2.72	0.89	0.84	1.31	1.33	0.48	0.47

a This table is derived following the earlier work of Anderson (1983). 'Revealed' comparative advantage is defined as the ratio of the share of a commodity group in total exports for a country or group of countries to that commodity group's share of world exports.
b Australia, New Zealand and Canada.
c Republic of Korea, Taiwan and Hong Kong.
d The commodity classification on which the factor groups are based is derived from that used by Krause (1982).
e Figures are for 1978.
Sources: ANU International Economic data bank, based on United Nations Trade Statistics, and World Bank, 1982: The World Development Report, Washington, D.C.

parative advantage in technology-intensive goods throughout the decade. This is consistent with the results of Gruber, Mehta and Vernon (1967) and subsequent authors, who found that research and development expenditures in the United States were greater than those in other countries.

Returning briefly to the measures of comparative advantage for ASEAN and the natural-resource-rich countries of the Pacific Basin, another striking result is the similarity between them. Considering this, it is not surprising that only a small share of the total exports of the natural-resource-rich countries are currently directed to ASEAN and vice versa. The changes over the decade that are of interest in this regard are, first, the decline in the revealed comparative advantage of ASEAN countries in agriculture-based goods—matched by a corresponding increase, particularly in Australia; and, second, the decline in ASEAN's comparative disadvantage in labour-intensive goods relative to the world as a whole—an increase in ASEAN's comparative advantage over Australasia and Canada.

III. PERFORMANCE IN EXPORTING TO ASEAN

Factor composition and country shares

Both the commodity composition of ASEAN imports and the shares in these imports of each of their principal trading partners can be seen from Table 2.5. Consider first the commodity composition rows of the table. These are marked by a significant increase in the share of mineral-resource-based goods. This is, at least in part, a consequence of the inclusion of intra-ASEAN trade. ASEAN is a net petroleum exporter, but the value of petroleum imports by the Philippines, Singapore and Thailand grew significantly during the decade. Despite this, it should be noted that the share of technology-intensive goods expanded to almost a third of all imports and that the share of agriculture-based imports declined by a third.

Consistent with the trends in comparative advantage discussed earlier, the exports to ASEAN of its largest trading partner, Japan, increasingly comprised technology- and human-capital-intensive goods and decreasingly labour-intensive goods. A different pattern is observable in ASEAN's imports from its second-largest trading partner, the United States. These are dominated by technology-intensive goods, the share of which expanded during the decade from about half to about two-thirds. The share of human-capital-intensive exports fell by half over the same period.

Table 2.5 also shows that the United States expanded its share of ASEAN technology-intensive imports at the expense of the EEC, while it lost share in its exports to ASEAN of human-capital-intensive goods, primarily to Japan. Japan increased its share of human-capital-intensive imports, displacing the United States but primarily at the expense of the EEC. In fact, the share of the EEC in ASEAN imports declined by a third during the decade, and the bulk of this substantial decline was in technology- and human-capital-intensive goods. By the end of the decade, EEC exports to ASEAN comprised primarily technology-intensive goods. It therefore came into competition more with the United States than with Japan. The decline in the significance of the EEC as a source of ASEAN imports is not surprising, considering the lower trade resistances that accompany the relative proximity of the United States and Japan to the ASEAN countries.

Australasian and Canadian exports to ASEAN became more intensive in mineral resources and less intensive in labour and human capital (those of Canada became more intensive in technology, while those of Australia became less so). At the same time, these countries' already small shares of ASEAN imports fell slightly, the greatest proportional loss being in the human-capital-intensive group. Table 2.5 shows that the doubling of intra-ASEAN trade over the decade was primarily owing to a fourfold increase in the share of intra-ASEAN trade in ASEAN imports of agriculture-based goods, especially food. Intra-ASEAN trade in manufactures has also expanded, relative to total manufactured imports, increasing its share threefold over the decade. These gains were at the expense of the EEC and other non-Pacific Basin exporters rather than of the Pacific Basin food exporters, Australia, Canada and the United States.

The Asian NICs and China retained relatively small shares of ASEAN imports throughout the decade. Although the Asian NICs did expand their share of ASEAN imports of labour-intensive goods, the share of these goods in total ASEAN imports declined.

Constant market share analysis of exports to ASEAN

Constant market share (CMS) analysis has been a popular method of analysing a country's export performance over time. It takes a base-year set of export shares (across commodities and country destinations) and evaluates the country's export growth over some subsequent interval in terms of these shares and a residual "competitiveness" effect. If the commodity shares are distributed in favour of commodities in which international trade has grown relatively rapidly, the commodity composition of exports has contributed to overall export growth. Similarly, if the

Table 2.5
ASEAN Imports From the Pacific Basin and the EEC—Commodity Composition and Exporter Shares[a]

	MERCHANDISE INTENSIVE IN[b] (PERCENTAGE)											ALL MERCHANDISE	
	AGRICULTURAL RESOURCES		MINERAL RESOURCES		LABOUR		TECHNOLOGY		HUMAN CAPITAL		ALL MERCHANDISE		
	1970	1980	1970	1980	1970	1980	1970	1980	1970	1980	1970	1980	
FROM ASEAN													
Composition	41.2	37.3	42.2	40.0	4.4	3.6	4.1	13.6	8.1	5.6	100.0	100.0	
Share of total imports	10.8	36.5	14.3	18.5	2.3	8.0	0.8	5.8	1.9	3.9	5.6	13.5	
FROM A,NZ,C[c]													
Composition	45.6	38.9	15.8	25.9	2.8	1.7	15.1	18.7	20.8	14.9	100.0	100.0	
Share of total imports	12.8	12.9	5.7	4.1	1.6	1.3	3.2	2.7	5.2	3.5	5.9	4.6	
FROM K,T,HK[d]													
Composition	17.4	14.3	6.2	6.3	35.7	28.0	18.8	25.4	21.9	26.0	100.0	100.0	
Share of total imports	3.3	6.1	1.5	1.3	13.1	27.2	2.7	4.7	3.7	7.8	4.0	5.8	
FROM CHINA													
Composition	43.9	24.8	1.9	32.4	33.9	16.4	8.0	14.9	12.3	11.6	100.0	100.0	
Share of total imports	6.7	5.0	0.4	3.1	10.0	7.5	0.9	1.3	1.7	1.6	3.2	2.8	
FROM JAPAN													
Composition	4.4	3.1	3.9	3.0	18.5	7.4	31.9	38.8	41.2	46.8	100.0	100.0	
Share of total imports	5.3	5.0	6.0	3.0	42.9	27.1	28.9	27.1	43.4	52.6	25.1	22.0	

FROM USA												
Composition	19.0	14.8	6.1	4.0	3.9	2.6	50.5	66.7	20.5	11.9	100.0	100.0
Share of total imports	13.0	16.0	5.4	2.1	5.2	6.5	26.3	31.5	12.4	9.1	14.4	14.9
FROM EEC-9												
Composition	10.1	7.1	4.4	5.7	6.8	6.1	46.8	56.5	31.9	24.7	100.0	100.0
Share of total imports	8.9	6.1	5.0	2.4	11.7	12.1	31.5	21.5	24.9	15.1	18.6	12.0
FROM THE WORLD												
Composition	21.1	13.8	16.4	29.1	10.9	6.0	27.8	31.5	23.9	19.6	100.0	100.0
Share of total imports	100.0	100.0	100.0	100.0	100.0	100.0	100.0	100.0	100.0	100.0	100.0	100.0

Source: ANU International Economic data bank, based on United Nations Trade statistics.
a. This table gives the composition of ASEAN imports from Pacific country groups, from the EEC and from the world across the five commodity groups used in Table 2.4. The shares in the composition rows of the table add across, summing to 100 except where rounding causes small errors. The shares of each country group in total ASEAN imports are also listed. These sum vertically, over country groups. The "rest of the world" group is omitted, however, so that the given import shares sum to less than the 100 listed on the bottom line.
b. See footnote b to Table 2.4.
c. See footnote c to Table 2.4.
d. See footnote d to Table 2.4.

destinations of the exports are distributed in favour of countries whose total imports have grown relatively, it is said to have contributed positively to overall export growth. When these two effects are removed, the residual is the average extent to which individual commodity exports have expanded or contracted. In its simplest form, the method attributes this residual export growth or contraction to changes in the relative prices of the country's exports. This interpretation encounters a number of difficulties, which are reviewed by Leamer and Stern (1970) and Richardson (1971). In what follows, the analysis is restricted to the decomposition of export growth. A more complete presentation of the methodology used is given by Tyers and Phillips (1984b).

One criticism of CMS analysis is that the market shares on which the decomposition is based tend to change during the interval of analysis and that the choice of which set of shares to use is arbitrary (Richardson, 1971). To minimize this problem, the decade of the 1970s has been divided into three intervals, 1970-73, 1973-76, and 1976-80, and a new CMS analysis is conducted on each interval. A second criticism is that inappropriate standards are chosen against which to evaluate export performance. In this case, the performance of exporters to ASEAN is evaluated by comparing it with changes in ASEAN imports from the world as a whole.

A final criticism of the method is that too commonly it must be based on the value rather than the volume of trade. This is important because, even if it is accepted that market shares are dependent only on relative trading prices, an increase in a country's value share does not necessarily mean that the relative price of the country's exports has declined. This is implied only if the elasticity of substitution at the point of destination between the country's exports and those of its competitors is greater than unity—that is, if the country's exports are not greatly differentiated from those of its competitors. The authors have found no solution to this. Trade values are used, and the results should therefore be interpreted with caution.

The CMS analysis of exports to ASEAN decomposes total export growth into components due to commodity composition and market distribution (the distribution of exports over countries of destination, in this case the five ASEAN countries) and a residual component presumed to be the result of competitiveness. The results are summarized in Table 2.6, which presents only the "competitiveness" residuals.[14] The final column of the table lists the competitiveness residuals across all traded merchandise for each of seven countries and country groups of origin. In the body of the table are listed the results from CMS analysis across only those commodities within each factor group, down to the SITC three-digit level.

Consider first the performance of the natural-resource-rich countries' exports to ASEAN. The competitiveness residuals listed in Table 2.6 indicate the average percentage change by which the growth in the value of these countries' exports to ASEAN has differed from that of the standard country group—in this case the rest of the world—after biases arising from differences in commodity composition and market distribution have been removed. From the top three rows of Table 2.6, it can be seen from the competitiveness residuals that Australasia and Canada outpaced their rivals' export growth to ASEAN by 18 percent until 1973. Since then, however, they have performed poorly, with average export growth falling behind by 20 percent over the period to 1976 and by 53 percent between 1976 and 1980.

Two-thirds of these exports to ASEAN are from Australia, while only a fifth come from Canada. They are dominated by natural-resource-based goods, which make up two-thirds of total trade. Agriculture-based exports appear to have lost ground after 1976 with the expansion of intra-ASEAN trade in these commodities. The commodity composition and market distribution effects are both high for this trade, indicating that Australia and Canada were exporting the right commodities to the right ASEAN countries (principally Malaysia and Singapore). Despite the loss of competitiveness, the loss of market share for the commodity group as a whole was therefore only modest in this period.

Neither Australia, New Zealand nor Canada was a net exporter of petroleum products during most of the decade. After 1976, however, Canada's mineral-based exports to ASEAN expanded fourfold. The most substantial increase occurred in Canada's exports to ASEAN of aluminum (32 percent of these exports in 1980), petroleum products (14 percent) and crude minerals including asbestos (18 percent). The remainder of these countries' mineral-based exports to ASEAN comprised crude minerals, intermediate metal products and coal. Their share of ASEAN mineral-based imports fell after 1973 as petroleum prices rose, but improved again after 1976, partly because of the better commodity composition effect achieved with Canada's mineral exports and partly because of the improved competitiveness of Australian crude mineral and coal exports to Malaysia, the Philippines and Singapore.

Most striking for this group of countries was the decline in the competitiveness after 1973 of manufactured exports to ASEAN. This reflects the loss of Australian manufacturing competitiveness because of exchange-rate appreciation and domestic cost increases during the commodity boom of the mid-1970s and the mining investment boom later in the decade—the "Dutch disease" effect (Gregory, 1976; Corden, 1982; Corden and Neary, 1982). Canada's manufactured exports to ASEAN, though small, fared better in this period. Labour-intensive exports from

Table 2.6

ASEAN Imports From the Pacific Basin and the EEC: "Competitiveness" Residuals From Constant Market Share Analysis[a]

(PERCENT)	MERCHANDISE INTENSIVE IN:[b] (PERCENTAGE)					ALL MERCHANDISE
	AGRICULTURAL RESOURCES	MINERAL RESOURCES	LABOUR	TECHNOLOGY	HUMAN CAPITAL	
FROM A,NZ,C[c]						
1970-73	19	12	5	4	61	18
1973-76	1	-32	-42	-11	-65	-20
1976-80	-121	137	-18	-40	-51	-53
FROM CANADA	(16.2)[e]	(38.2)[e]	(8.5)[e]	(21.4)[e]	(15.6)[e]	(1.1)[f]
1970-73	156	-47	-35	-103	-21	-21
1973-76	-3	-37	80	126	77	49
1976-80	-14	209	3	-84	-45	-6
FROM K,T,HK[d]						
1970-73	85	75	160	145	110	125
1973-76	-318	18	77	16	-13	-11
1976-80	145	-94	18	37	122	44
FROM CHINA						
1970-73	94	140	-1	-9	76	52
1973-76	-37	460	-10	-5	-32	-11
1976-80	-27	282	-25	110	-6	35
FROM JAPAN						
1970-73	18	-9	-88	43	61	24
1973-76	-117	68	-3	-5	14	2
1976-80	-66	-125	-159	-12	-56	-58

FROM USA					
1970-73	-5	-29	49	27	41	29
1973-76	-490	-225	-1	-16	9	-103
1976-80	65	-38	-25	-29	-64	-8
FROM EEC-9						
1970-73	-27	-93	-4	19	-16	-10
1973-76	-17	-94	-85	-10	-27	-60
1976-80	-181	-125	-121	-104	-143	-129

a. This table lists the residual terms from the constant market share analysis. These terms indicate the percentage by which the value of trade expanded in the intervals shown, after the effects of commodity composition and market distribution have been removed. The terms, therefore, indicate the average degree to which trade in individual commodities would have expanded had the commodity composition and the distribution across destination countries conformed to that of imports by ASEAN from the world as a whole.

b. See footnote d to Table 2.4.

c. See footnote b to Table 2.4.

d. See footnote c to Table 2.4.

e. The shares of each commodity group in Canada's exports to ASEAN as of 1980 are given in parentheses. These sum across the row to 100 per cent. The corresponding shares for the other countries are listed in Table 2.5.

f. The share of Canada in total ASEAN imports in 1980.

Canada were competitive late in the decade, but these made up only 2 percent of all ASEAN imports in this category. Technology-intensive and human-capital-intensive manufactures constituted 37 percent of Canada's exports to ASEAN, however. These were strongly competitive during the period 1973-76, but lost ground subsequently.

By contrast with Australasia and Canada, whose share of all ASEAN imports fell during the decade, the Asian NICs expanded their share by almost half. Their strong export performance in the manufacturing sector was the source of this expansion. By 1980 manufactures constituted four-fifths of their total exports and manufactured exports to ASEAN were distributed evenly across the three factor groups. Agriculture-based exports (mainly income-elastic processed foods and leather goods) remained important at 14 percent, however. The food exports were destined mainly for Indonesia, where they lost ground as Indonesia expanded its rice imports in the mid-1970s—a high market distribution effect occurs with the low competitiveness residual for 1973-76. The value of these exports expanded sixfold between 1976 and 1980, however, as national income rose in Indonesia and rice imports declined.

China's share of ASEAN imports held steady during the decade at about 3 percent,[15] but the composition of this trade has changed substantially. Early in the decade it was dominated by agriculture-based goods and labour-intensive manufactures, but after 1973 China's exports of these commodity groups to ASEAN proved uncompetitive. In the case of labour-intensive manufactures this may be the result either of discriminatory commercial policies in ASEAN or of a preference for the higher quality textiles, clothing and footwear that the Asian NICs were able to supply late in the decade. Whatever the reason, this loss of share in no way restrained China's total exports of labour-intensive goods (Findlay et al., 1985). As the share of labour-intensive goods in China's exports to ASEAN declined, their place was taken by mineral-based goods—mostly petroleum exports to the Philippines and Thailand—which the CMS analysis shows as highly competitive throughout the decade. throughout the decade.

Imports from the ASEAN countries' largest trading partner, Japan, consisted mostly of manufactures intensive in technology and human capital. During the decade, Japan's share of ASEAN technology-intensive imports declined slightly. Japan's share of overall ASEAN imports expanded until 1973 but declined thereafter because the trade comprised commodities—especially petroleum products—in which ASEAN imports were relatively slow-growing. After 1976, however, the analysis attributes Japan's declining share to competitiveness rather than to commodity composition or market distribution. On the other hand, Japan's share of ASEAN human-capital-intensive imports increased during the decade. Before 1976 this gain was the result of competitiveness, but the analysis indicates that subsequently Japan's exports to ASEAN were uncompetitive. The aggregate market share continued to expand because Japan was exporting the right human-capital-intensive products to the most rapidly growing ASEAN markets, principally Indonesia and Singapore.

The other Pacific trade giant, the United States, maintained its share of total ASEAN imports throughout the 1970s. The composition of United States exports to ASEAN was characterized throughout by the dominance of the technology-intensive factor group. While the United States' share of ASEAN imports of these commodities increased, its share of ASEAN imports of agriculture-based and human-capital-intensive goods declined. The gains in the technology-intensive group did not come from high competitiveness residuals throughout the decade; although competitiveness was the deciding factor before 1973, the gains made thereafter came as a result of positive commodity composition and market distribution effects. The most important destinations for these exports were Malaysia and Singapore, while the countries in which the United States registered positive competitiveness residuals were the Philippines and Thailand.

After 1976, technology-intensive exports to Indonesia from the United States were greatly outpaced by those from Japan, whose technology-intensive exports to Indonesia tripled in this period, making Indonesia Japan's most important ASEAN market for these goods. This result lends some support to Krause's (1982) argument that United States regulations affecting the non-price aspects of competition, which are important in the marketing of technology-intensive goods with a large unit value, have hindered its competitiveness compared with that of Japan.[16] All groups of United States manufactured exports were uncompetitive after 1976, despite the depreciation of the U.S. dollar against the Japanese yen during this period by 30 percent.[17]

IV. ASEAN EXPORT PERFORMANCE

Factor composition and shares of imports

The commodity composition of exports from the ASEAN countries and the shares of these exports in the imports of each of their principal trading partners are listed in Table 2.7. By 1980 the destination where ASEAN exports had the largest share of total imports was ASEAN itself.

Table 2.7

ASEAN Exports to the Pacific Basin and the EEC — Commodity Composition and Shares of Total Imports by Destination Countries[a]

MERCHANDISE INTENSIVE IN: [b] (PERCENTAGE)

	AGRICULTURAL RESOURCES		MINERAL RESOURCES		LABOUR		TECHNOLOGY		HUMAN CAPITAL		ALL MERCHANDISE	
	1970	1980	1970	1980	1970	1980	1970	1980	1970	1980	1970	1980
TO ASEAN												
Composition	41.2	37.3	42.2	40.0	4.4	3.6	4.1	13.6	8.1	5.6	100.0	100.0
Share of total imports	10.8	36.5	14.3	18.5	2.3	8.0	0.8	5.8	1.9	3.9	5.6	13.5
TO A,NZ,C[c]												
Composition	54.5	24.0	39.0	56.4	4.0	10.3	0.6	4.5	1.9	4.9	100.0	100.0
Share of total imports	4.3	6.5	3.4	8.0	0.4	3.1	.0	0.4	0.1	0.5	0.9	2.7
TO K,T,HK[d]												
Composition	79.2	50.8	12.3	29.1	3.4	4.3	2.6	9.4	2.5	6.4	100.0	100.0
Share of total imports	16.5	19.5	6.6	8.2	1.3	3.0	0.7	2.7	0.8	2.9	6.1	7.6
TO China												
Composition	99.7	70.2	.0	1.8	.0	11.4	0.2	6.6	.0	10.0	100.0	100.0
Share of total imports	9.8	8.5	.0	1.9	.0	7.0	.0	0.9	.0	1.9	2.8	4.3
TO Japan												
Composition	50.1	20.5	48.6	76.5	0.6	0.9	0.5	1.6	0.1	0.5	100.0	100.0
Share of total imports	11.3	11.9	8.5	15.8	1.4	2.8	0.2	2.1	0.3	2.2	7.7	12.7

TO USA												
Composition	65.0	19.4	24.6	49.9	6.5	6.7	3.1	18.3	0.8	5.7	100.0	100.0
Share of total imports	8.1	8.6	3.9	6.4	1.5	4.3	0.6	5.8	0.1	1.2	2.8	5.2
TO EEC-9												
Composition	82.7	56.9	13.0	14.5	1.5	12.0	1.9	9.3	0.9	7.3	100.0	100.0
Share of total imports	2.7	3.9	0.5	0.6	0.1	1.4	0.1	0.5	.0	0.5	0.9	1.2
TO THE WORLD												
Composition	61.9	33.3	29.0	45.4	2.8	5.6	3.2	10.5	3.1	5.2	100.0	100.0

Source: ANU International Economic Databank, based on United Nations Trade statistics.
a. This table gives the composition of ASEAN exports to Pacific Basin country groups and to the EEC across the five commodity groups. The shares in the composition rows sum across the table to 100 per cent, except where rounding causes small errors. The shares of ASEAN exports in the imports of each Pacific Basin country group are also listed. These are shares of each country group's total imports.

b. See footnote b to Table 2.4.
c. See footnote c to Table 2.4.
d. See footnote d to Table 2.4.

As noted in Section III, the commodity composition of intra-ASEAN trade changed little during the decade, but there was an almost fourfold increase in the share of intra-ASEAN trade in total ASEAN imports of agriculture-based goods, principally food. This increase in the significance of intra-ASEAN food trade was at the expense of non-Pacific Basin exporters, not of the major food exporters of the Pacific Basin—Australasia, Canada and the United States (see Table 2.5).

The share of intra-ASEAN trade in ASEAN imports of manufactures remained small but showed substantial growth during the decade. Since February 1977 the ASEAN countries have been implementing Preferential Trading Arrangements. Until recently, the most important components of these arrangements were item-by-item reductions in tariffs, but these appear to have had little impact on intra-ASEAN trade (Tan, 1982). The product-by-product approach was dropped at the twelfth ASEAN Economic Ministers' Meeting in January 1982. Since then, a 20 to 25 percent margin of preference has been given automatically to items with import values of less than US$1 million; more recently this limit has been extended to US$10 million, which should prove to have a greater impact on intra-ASEAN trade in the 1980s. There is a danger in taking the recorded increase in intra-ASEAN trade too seriously, however—it may be the result, for example, of the reporting of trade between the four larger ASEAN countries and the non-ASEAN countries as trade with Singapore, where either the goods are directly trans-shipped or minor value is added before re-exportation. To the extent that gains in intra-ASEAN trade have in fact occurred, they are probably attributable to the formation of ASEAN associations of businessmen, bankers and professionals (Naya, 1980; Hiemenz and Naya, 1983).

The performance of ASEAN in exporting to the natural-resource-rich countries, Australasia and Canada, is dominated by growth in the ASEAN share of Australia's total imports. Even by 1980, only 0.47 percent of ASEAN exports—principally non-food agricultural commodities, such as rubber—were destined for Canada, and these made up only 0.65 percent of Canada's total merchandise imports. On the other hand, the share of ASEAN exports in Australia's imports expanded from 2 percent in 1970 to 7 percent in 1980. The factor composition of Australia's imports changed relatively little during the 1970s. Higher petroleum prices led to an expansion in the share of mineral-based goods in the total value of Australia's imports, accompanied by small declines in the shares of agriculture-based and technology-intensive goods.

ASEAN exports to Australia are principally petroleum, petroleum products and agriculture-based goods. This high petroleum content, combined with low trade resistances between the ASEAN countries and Australia, has led the way in a significant expansion in ASEAN's share of Australia's total imports. It does not fully explain the expansion, however, since the ASEAN share of Australia's imports in all five commodity groups increased. The largest proportional increase in the ASEAN share was in labour-intensive manufactures (from 0.4 percent to 6 percent). This accords with the findings from the market penetration analysis of Hamilton (1983): that the Australian producers' domestic trade share of the labour-intensive product group of textiles, clothing and footwear fell over the decade by more than it did in Japan, Canada and the United States; and that, of all the countries studied, Australia showed the largest increase during the decade in the share of ASEAN in total home demand for these goods.

The commodity compositions of exports to Australasia and Canada by their other principal trading partners show similar patterns to their total exports (see Table 2.4). Again, the changes in the pattern of Australia's imports are similar in direction but greater in magnitude than those for the groups as a whole. The most striking changes in the share composition of Australia's total imports during the decade were the rising share of Japan, the Asian NICs and the ASEAN countries and the falling shares of the EEC and the United States. The rise in Japan's share was led by a virtual doubling of its share of Australia's human-capital-intensive imports, while that of the Asian NICs is the result of a doubling of their share of Australia's imports of labour-intensive manufactures. The battle for shares in Australia's imports of technology- and human-capital-intensive goods is still between the United States, Japan and the EEC, with the United States remaining strongest in technology-intensive goods and the EEC losing share to Japan in human-capital-intensive goods.

There was a small increase in the share of ASEAN exports destined for the Asian NICs (see Table 2.1) and in the share of these exports in the total imports of the Asian NICs during the decade. As the petroleum price increases of the 1970s raised the value share of mineral-based goods in the imports of the Asian NICs, the share of petroleum in ASEAN exports to these countries also grew. Consequently, the expansion in the ASEAN share of their total imports extended uniformly across all commodity groups. China, on the other hand, has remained a relatively insignificant destination for ASEAN exports; they constituted only 1 percent more of China's total imports in 1980 than they did in 1970, mostly because of an increase in the ASEAN share of China's imports of manufactured goods.

In their exports to Japan and the United States, the ASEAN countries appear to have performed well. These destinations combined take more than 40 percent of ASEAN exports (see Table 2.1), and the ASEAN share of the imports of both Japan and the United States doubled in the

1970s. Although their share increased in both markets across all five commodity groups, a principal factor in the gains was the expansion of petroleum exports from Indonesia and Malaysia. In the case of the United States, however, another important factor was a tenfold increase in ASEAN's share of total imports of technology-intensive goods — primarily electronic components. These exports have expanded as a consequence of direct investment, primarily by Japanese and American firms, in the ASEAN countries. In general, technology is not the location-determining factor in the production of these components. Local subsidiaries carry out the labour-intensive stage in the production of electronic goods which are ultimately exported for consumption or further assembly in the United States (Yamazawa et al., 1983).

These gains to the ASEAN countries came chiefly at the expense of Australasia and Canada, whose share of Japanese imports fell from 14 percent to 9 percent and whose share of United States imports fell from 30 percent to 18 percent, and of the EEC, whose share of Japanese imports fell from 8 percent to 5 percent and whose share of United States imports fell from 23 percent to 15 percent (see Table 2.1).

The loss of share by Australasia and Canada came primarily in their exports of mineral-based goods — their petroleum content was low relative to that of ASEAN mineral-based exports. When the relative prices of petroleum products increased, the value share of these exports declined. This is not surprising when it is considered that mineral-based products constitute 60 percent of Japan's total imports and 40 percent of the total imports of the United States. The loss of share by the EEC, on the other hand, is the result of declines in its shares of Japanese and United States imports of manufactures.

In Japanese imports, these declines in the EEC share were in labour- and technology-intensive goods, where the corresponding gainers were China and the Asian NICs. In imports by the United States, the losses fell principally in the labour- and human-capital-intensive commodity groups. In this case the corresponding gainers were again the Asian NICs.[18]

Constant market share analysis of ASEAN exports

The results are summarized in Table 2.8. Although the analysis has been carried out for all five commodity groups and all five ASEAN countries, only the all-ASEAN results are presented here.[19]

As the results of Table 2.7 lead us to expect, the share of ASEAN exports in the imports of its principal trading partners expanded in almost all periods, the one exception being ASEAN exports to Japan in the years

1973-76, when the share of petroleum in Japan's total imports grew rapidly. Since ASEAN exports at the time also contained petroleum, the commodity composition effect for total exports to Japan is high for that period. The loss of ASEAN market share was caused by a loss in the minerals category, showing that Indonesia and Malaysia were slow to increase the volume of their petroleum exports in response to the 1973 price increase.

These gains in the ASEAN share of the imports of major trading partners and partner country-groups are not all the result of overall competitiveness, however, as the results listed in Table 2.8 indicate. After 1973, ASEAN was uncompetitive relative to the rest of the world in exporting to the Asian NICs and to China.

In the former case, the good overall performance of ASEAN exports during the decade was the result of positive commodity composition and market distribution effects. Four-fifths of this trade was in natural-resource-based goods such as timber, rubber and sugar. Although they retained their share of total imports by the Asian NICs, ASEAN exports of this commodity group lost competitiveness on average throughout the decade.

ASEAN exports to China are similarly dominated by agriculture-based goods. Between 1973 and 1976, when China's imports of this commodity group were declining, ASEAN exports continued to expand. As in the case of their exports to the Asian NICs, this gain was owing to commodity composition rather than to competitiveness. During this period, however, exports of labour-intensive goods from ASEAN (mainly Singapore) to China were strongly competitive. It was over this period that the large increase in the ASEAN share of China's labour-intensive imports shown in Table 2.7 was achieved. But after 1976 China's total and agricultural imports expanded fourfold. The commodity composition of its agricultural imports shifted away from that of ASEAN exports, resulting in a loss of market share. As for the trade in labour-intensive goods in this period, Singapore's exports to China kept pace with their competitors despite a decline in competitiveness.

In all the destination countries and country groups, ASEAN exports of the three groups of manufactured products remained competitive throughout the decade, although the sizes of the competitiveness residuals were generally higher in the earlier intervals, when these exports were expanding their shares from low bases. ASEAN labour-intensive exports were particularly competitive in all the markets identified, except after 1976 in those of the Asian NICs, China and Japan. In the former two cases, ASEAN shares held their ground by virtue of their commodity composition. In Japan their share declined in that period.

Table 2.8

ASEAN Exports to the Pacific Basin and the EEC—"Competitiveness" Residuals from Constant Market Share Analysis[a]

	MERCHANDISE INTENSIVE IN:[b] (PERCENTAGE)					ALL MERCHANDISE
	AGRICULTURAL RESOURCES	MINERAL RESOURCES	LABOUR	TECHNOLOGY	HUMAN CAPITAL	
TO A,NZ,C[c]						
1970–73	56	−43	341	3004	319	50
1973–76	23	33	146	0	412	54
1976–80	26	308	75	41	−17	108
TO CANADA	(54.6)[e]	(2.0)[e]	(18.9)[e]	(10.0)[e]	(8.1)[e]	(.65)[f]
1970–73	44	−59	34	8994	473	59
1973–76	11	−295	118	−48	366	−21
1976–80	14	530	180	61	−27	40
TO K,T,HK[d]						
1970–73	−125	37	137	347	91	−78
1973–76	−99	31	25	37	32	−66
1976–80	−154	−13	−5	84	161	−81
TO CHINA						
1970–73	283	6883	—	763	7397	296
1973–76	−1128	301	528	132	−197	−1060
1976–80	−2	−1280	−346	7542	81862	−69
TO JAPAN						
1970–73	19	37	461	376	260	31
1973–76	28	−131	48	260	190	−44
1976–80	−12	125	−63	−6	72	65

TO USA					
1970–73	7	–125	145	653	710	10
1973–76	5	235	–11	74	85	72
1976–80	–8	–54	80	129	190	–4
TO EEC-9					
1970–73	33	–7	321	559	457	45
1973–76	20	–6	287	35	111	31
1976–80	8	178	91	63	133	35

a. These terms indicate the average degree to which trade in individual commodities would have expanded had the commodity composition and the distribution across destination countries conformed to that of imports by each destination country group from the world as a whole.

b. See footnote d to Table 2.4.

c. See footnote b to Table 2.4.

d. See footnote c to Table 2.4.

e. The shares of each commodity group in Canada's imports from ASEAN as of 1980 are given in

Either ASEAN labour-intensive manufactures were uncompetitive relative to those of the Asian NICs in the Japanese market, or they suffered from discriminatory commercial policies and marketing practices in Japan. Nevertheless, the strong overall performance of the ASEAN countries as exporters of natural-resource-based and manufactured goods is borne out by the CMS analysis.

V. SUMMARY AND CONCLUSION

As interdependence through merchandise trade has increased among Pacific Basin countries, the ASEAN countries have increased the shares of their trade with other Pacific Basin countries, especially Japan and the Asian NICs. ASEAN has assumed a growing significance in the imports and exports of Australasia, the Asian NICs and the United States. Of the more rapidly growing imports to ASEAN, however, only the exports of the Asian NICs achieved a significant expansion in their shares during the 1970s. The relatively slow-growing economies of Australasia and Canada had declining shares of ASEAN imports, as did Japan. Except as a destination for the exports of Japan and the Asian NICs, the significance of the EEC declined greatly during the decade as a trading partner for Pacific Basin countries in general, and for ASEAN in particular.

The changes in total ASEAN imports during the 1970s were characterized by a significant increase in the importance of intra-ASEAN trade and a decrease in the share of total imports to ASEAN from the EEC. The United States has increased its share of ASEAN technology-intensive imports at the expense of the EEC, while Japan has increased its share of ASEAN human-capital-intensive imports at the expense of both the United States and the EEC. In imports of labour-intensive goods there has been an expansion in the importance of intra-ASEAN trade and of the Asian NICs, both replacing Japan, whose share of ASEAN labour-intensive imports fell by almost half. The role of intra-ASEAN trade may, however, be overstated by the data, given the importance of entrepôt trade, particularly with Indonesia and Malaysia, in Singapore's total trade.

The share of Australasia and Canada in ASEAN imports fell slightly (to 5 percent), the principal loss being in human-capital-intensive goods. All of Australia's manufactured exports suffered a considerable loss of competitiveness after 1973, partly because of the "Dutch disease" effect of the commodity boom on the cost of production and Australia's exchange rate between 1973 and 1980 Finally, despite rapid growth in China's total exports, its share of ASEAN imports remained very small throughout the decade. China's export expansion appears to have been concentrated to date in the markets of Japan and the United States.

The results from constant market share analysis go beyond changes in the commodity group shares and indicate where aggregate gains are the result of differences in commodity composition or market distribution rather than competitiveness. As for the export performance of the trading partners of ASEAN, the general pattern of the competitiveness residuals corresponds with that of the gains in aggregate shares of ASEAN imports. Exceptions late in the decade are the manufactured exports to ASEAN of the United States and Japan, the good performance of which depended mostly upon specialization within the technology- and human-capital-intensive commodity groups and the distribution of these exports among ASEAN countries. The good performance of ASEAN exports during the decade similarly corresponded with high competitiveness residuals for all destinations except the Asian NICs and China, whose imports have so far been of relatively minor importance for ASEAN.

Of special significance for the trading partners of ASEAN are the trends in trade specialization that occurred during the 1970s. The pattern of ASEAN export specialization came to be dominated by petroleum, but non-mineral exports shifted markedly away from agriculture-based goods towards manufactures. The share of agriculture-based goods in non-mineral exports fell from 87 percent to 61 percent, while that of manufactures rose correspondingly from 13 percent to 39 percent. Future trends in the overall pattern of ASEAN export specialization will depend upon the degree to which growth in domestic demand diminishes the petroleum surplus and upon movements in the world prices of petroleum products. Nevertheless, as the capital endowments of the ASEAN countries continue to rise, these countries should specialize increasingly in manufactured exports. Relative to their principal trading partners, the ASEAN countries have a growing comparative advantage in labour-intensive goods. Relative to China, however, their comparative advantage remains in natural-resource-based goods. In the world market for labour-intensive manufactures, China may be a formidable competitor (Findlay et al., 1985; Tyers et al., 1985). The degree to which ASEAN manufactured exports are labour-intensive may depend, therefore, on the pattern and growth of China's exports.

As for the pattern of ASEAN import specialization, petroleum imports also increased in share. But, again, there were major changes in the pattern of ASEAN non-mineral-based imports. While technology- and human-capital-intensive goods retained stable shares of ASEAN imports overall, their shares of non-mineral imports increased from 62 percent to 72 percent. The share of agriculture-based goods in total ASEAN imports fell from 21 percent to 14 percent and in non-mineral imports from 25 percent to 19 percent. The corresponding shares of labour-intensive manufactures also fell, from 11 percent to 6 percent and from 13 percent to 8 percent, respectively. Although future trends in overall import specialization will depend upon movements in petroleum prices as incomes and capital endowments grow in ASEAN countries, the trends away from agriculture-based and labour-intensive goods can be expected to continue. Among exporters to this rapidly expanding market, these trends will favour Japan, the United States and the Asian NICs over exporters with relatively large endowments of agricultural resources or labour, such as Australia, Canada and China.

Finally, while the emphasis of this paper has been on the fundamental forces affecting the international distribution of factor endowments and the changes in the pattern of international trade which occur in response to these forces, the continuation of the observed trends into the 1990s will depend substantially upon government policies. The low intra-Pacific resistances to trade which have been primarily responsible for the pre-eminence of Pacific Basin destinations in the exports of ASEAN and other Pacific countries are partly the result of close political ties and the exchanges of direct investments which accompany them. Still greater significance would accrue to Pacific Basin trading partnerships should further steps be agreed upon to integrate the Pacific economy (Crawford, 1981; Anderson et al., 1984). More important still, however, are unilateral policies which distort the pattern of trade directly. World trade in agricultural goods is increasingly influenced by high levels of protection in Europe and East Asia. Subsidized exports are adversely affecting the market shares and the terms of trade facing some ASEAN countries and the traditional food exporters of the Pacific Basin (Tyers and Anderson, 1985). This trend should encourage the shift in ASEAN export specialization away from agriculture-based goods and into manufactures.

The expansion of ASEAN manufactured exports will also depend on policies adopted in ASEAN countries and their principal trading partners. Within ASEAN, governments have attracted investment by improving the skill levels of their labour forces and actively inhibiting labour monopolies. These policies are generally entrenched and should continue to foster growth. Outside ASEAN, however, export prospects for manufactures depend not only on the recent policy changes in China and her entry into world markets for labour-intensive manufactures but also on the access of Pacific developing countries to markets in industrial countries. Slow economic growth in Europe and the United States combined with the effects of the strong United States dollar have increased political pressures for protection (Salvatore, 1985). The effects of this "new protectionism" have been largely sidestepped by the Asian NICs, however (Hughes and Waelbroeck, 1981). While the resurgence of protectionist sentiment in the industrialized world may retard the growth of the shares of ASEAN and other developing countries in world manufactures trade, its determinants are fundamentally different from those of agricultural protection, which has increased steadily in most industrialized countries as agriculture's shares of income and employment have declined to relative insignificance. World trade in manufactures is much more important as a determinant of global economic growth. Accordingly, the larger industrialized countries cannot afford to inhibit too greatly the changes in structure within manufacturing sectors and in the international division of labour which have underlain the trade patterns analysed in this paper.

NOTES

* This paper is based on research conducted as part of the ASEAN Australia Economic Relations Joint Research Project. The authors are indebted for helpful discussions and comments to Kym Anderson, David Lim and Hal Hill.

1. Canada's long border with the United States results in a significant amount of intra-industry trade, stimulated primarily by the relatively low cost of internal transportation. In this respect, Canada must be considered a special case.
2. In section II, all merchandise is classified on the basis of its intensity in the primary factors of production which most determine where production takes place. These primary factors include natural resources, labour, human capital and technology.
3. In 1970 ASEAN was a net exporter of petroleum and petroleum products worth US$0.4 billion. By 1980, the value of these net exports had risen to US$5.5 billion.
4. In this discussion, the Pacific Basin is defined as including the Western Pacific market economies and the United States and Canada.
5. See Ojala and Rae (1983), Table 3. Ojala and Rae also note that agricultural trade represents about a sixth of Pacific Basin imports and exports. That portion of agricultural exports directed to other Pacific Basin countries grew be-

tween 1965 and 1980 from 48 percent to 55 percent, while the corresponding share of imports rose from 70 percent to 77 percent.

6. Some of the recorded increase in intra-ASEAN trade is the result of poor recording of entrepôt trade between Malaysia and Indonesia and non-ASEAN countries via Singapore.

7. The intensity-of-trade index was used first by Kojima (1964) and then by Drysdale (1969). It has more recently been applied to measure Pacific Basin interdependence by Anderson (1983) and Ojala and Rae (1983). It is defined for country i's exports to country j as the share of i's exports going to j relative to the share of j's imports in world imports net of i's imports.

8. The indexes for exports to Australia from ASEAN and the Asian NICs almost double, while those from other Pacific Basin countries show more moderate increases; see Tyers and Phillips (1984a).

9. Australasia is the sum of Australia and New Zealand.

10. Even at this level of factor aggregation, the model does have considerable predictive power; see, for example, Hamilton and Svensson (1982).

11. The accuracy of the revealed comparative advantage index has been criticized in a recent article by Bowen (1983). It has intuitive appeal, however, as an index of specialization across exporters.

12. Throughout this paper, the ASEAN group of countries is considered as a single entity. Clearly, natural resource endowments vary considerably among ASEAN countries, and the patterns of trade specialization observed for ASEAN as a whole do not necessarily reflect those of individual ASEAN countries. Singapore is a case in point; it has more in common with the other Asian NICs than with its ASEAN partners. While Singapore's pattern of trade specialization relative to the other ASEAN countries reflects its scarcity of natural resources, its exports are more natural-resource-based than those of the Asian NICs. This is primarily because of entrepôt trade and petroleum processing—points to be discussed further in later sections.

13. In Canada, tertiary students made up 4 percent of the total population and 37 percent of the population aged between 20 and 24 in 1975. In Australia the corresponding statistics were 2 percent and 26 percent, respectively, and in New Zealand they were 0.4 percent (1976) and 29 percent, respectively.

14. The constant market share (CMS) results are further detailed in Tyers and Phillips (1984b).

15. China's trading partners are the only source of data on China's international trade. Without the cross-check provided by export data, the results presented here are vulnerable to under-reporting of imports from China by the ASEAN countries.

16. The competition between the United States and Japan for shares of ASEAN technology-intensive and human-capital-intensive imports is discussed in detail by Krause (1982). He indicates that the United States has performed

comparatively well in its exports to ASEAN of relatively small-unit-value, homogeneous, and therefore price-sensitive, items such as electronic components. In its exports of larger technology-intensive goods, the demand for which is less price-sensitive, the United States has performed less well— especially in Indonesia and the Philippines, where commercial policies are perceived by Krause as weakly administered. He indicates that this may be due in part to changes in United States law and government practices overseas, such as the Foreign Corrupt Practises Act, the taxation of American citizens abroad, and the introduction of human rights criteria into Exim Bank lending.

17. The U.S. dollar eventually floated upwards against the yen, following the surge in the real interest rate in the United States that began in 1978, but this rise in the dollar did not begin until after 1980.

18. As their patterns of revealed comparative advantage have become more similar (Table 2.4), the intensity of trade between Japan and the United States has declined (Table 2.2), as has the share of each in the other's imports. Although this has been mostly caused by the increased petroleum component of these imports, the United States lost share in Japanese imports of all three categories of manufactures. Correspondingly, Japan lost share in United States imports of labour-intensive goods but achieved modest gains in its share of United States imports of technology-intensive and human-capital-intensive goods.

19. For a comprehensive set of CMS results, see Tyers and Phillips (1984b).

REFERENCES

Anderson, K., (1983) "Intensity of Trade between Pacific Basin Economies, *Economic Papers*, 2: 58-67.

Anderson, K., and B. Smith, (1981) "Changing Economic Relations between the Asian ADCs and Resource Exporting Advanced Countries of the Pacific Basin," in W. Hong and L.B. Krause (eds), *Trade and Growth of the Advanced Developing Countries in the Pacific Basin*, Seoul: Korea Development Institute.

Anderson, K., P. Drysdale, C. Findlay, P. Phillips, B. Smith, and R. Tyers, (1984) "Pacific Economic Growth and the Prospects for Australian Trade,"

Discussion Paper No. 85/02, Economic Planning Advisory Council, Government of Australia, Canberra (November).

Balassa, B., (1965) "Trade Liberalization and Revealed Comparative Advantage," *Manchester School of Economics and Social Studies* 33: 99-124.

Balassa, B., (1977) "A 'Stages' Approach to Comparative Advantage," in I. Adelman, *Economic Growth and Resources*, Proceedings of the Fifth Congress of the International Economic Association, Tokyo, vol. 4, pp. 121-56 (London: Macmillan).

Bowen, H.P., (1983) "On the Theoretical Interpretation of Indexes of Trade Intensity and Revealed Comparative Advantage," *Weltwirtschaftliches Archiv*, Band 119, Heft 3: 464-74.

Branson, W.H., and H. Junz, (1971) "Trends in U.S. Comparative Advantage," *Brookings Papers on Economic Activity* 2: 285-346.

Branson, W.H., and N. Monoyios, (1977) "Factor Inputs in US Trade," *Journal of International Economics* 7: 111-31.

Corden, W.M., (1982) "Booming Sector and Dutch Disease Economics," *Working Papers in Economics and Econometrics* No. 79, Australian National University, Canberra (November).

Corden, W.M., and P.J. Neary, (1982) "Booming Sector and De-industrialization in a Small Open Economy," *Economic Journal* 92 (368): 825-48.

Crawford, Sir John (ed.), assisted by G. Seow, (1981) *Pacific Economic Cooperation: Suggestions for Action*, Heinemann Asia, for the Pacific Community Seminar.

Dixit, A., (1981) "The Export of Capital Theory," *Journal of International Economics* 11: 279-94.

Drysdale, P., (1969) "Japan, Australia and New Zealand: The Prospects for Western Pacific Integration," *Economic Record* 45 (III): 321-42.

Drysdale, P., and R.G. Garnaut, (1982) "Trade Intensities and the Analysis of Bilateral Trade Flows in a Many-Country World," *Hitotsubashi Journal of Economics* 22 (2): 62-84.

Findlay, C., P.R. Phillips, and R. Tyers, (1985) "China's Merchandise Trade: Composition and Export Growth in the 1980s," *ASEAN-Australia Economic Papers*, No. 19, Australian National University, Canberra (May).

Garnaut, R.G., and K. Anderson, (1980) "ASEAN Export Specialization and the Evolution of Comparative Advantage in the Western Pacific Region," in R. Garnaut (ed.), *ASEAN in a Changing Pacific and World Economy*, Canberra: Australian National University Press.

Goodman, B., and R. Ceyhun, (1976) "U.S. Export Performance in Manufacturing Industries: An Empirical Investigation," *Weltwirtschaftliches Archiv*, Band 112, Heft 3.

Gregory, R.G., (1976) "Some Implications of the Growth of the Mining Sector," *Australian Journal of Agricultural Economics* 20: 71-91.

Gruber, W., D. Mehta, and R. Vernon, (1967) "The R & D Factor in International Trade and Investment of United States Industries," *Journal of Political Economy* 75: 20-37.

Hamilton, C., (1983) "Australian Manufacturing Industry During the 1970s: An International Comparison and Implications for the ASEAN Countries," Seminar Paper No. 255, Institute for International Economic Studies, University of Stockholm.

Hamilton, C., and L.E.O. Svensson, (1982) "Testing Theories of Trade Among Many Countries," Seminar Paper No. 209, Institute for International Economic Studies, University of Stockholm.

Hickman, B.G., Y. Kuroda, and L.J. Lau, (1977) "The Pacific Basin in World Trade," Working Papers Nos. 190, 191 and 192, National Bureau of Economic Research, San Francisco.

Hiemenz, I.V., and S. Naya, (1983) "Changing Trade Patterns and Policy Issues: Prospects for East and Southeast Asian Developing Countries," Paper presented at East-West Center Conference on Patterns of Growth and Structural Change in Asia's NICs and Near-NICs in the Context of Economic Interdependence, Honolulu, Hawaii, 3-8 April.

Hufbauer, G.C., (1970) "The Impact of National Characteristics and Technology on the Commodity Composition of Trade in Manufactured Goods," in R. Vernon (ed.), *The Technology Factor in International Trade*, National Bureau of Economic Research, Columbia University Press.

Hughes, H., and J. Waelbroeck, (1981) "Can Developing Country Exports Keep Growing in the 1980s?" *The World Economy*, Vol. 4., No. 2, pp. 127-47.

Johnson, H.G., (1968) *Comparative Cost and Commercial Policy Theory for a Developing World Economy*, Stockholm: Almqvist & Wiksell.

Jones, R.W., (1971) "A Three Factor Model in Theory, Trade and History," in J. Bhagwati et al. (eds), *Trade, Balance of Payments and Growth*, Amsterdam: North Holland.

Keesing, D. B., (1966) "Labour Skills and Comparative Advantage," *American Economic Review* 56: 249-58.

Kenen, P., (1965) "Nature, Capital and Trade," *Journal of Political Economy* 73: 437-60.

Kojima, K., (1964) "The Pattern of International Trade among Many Countries," *Hitotsubashi Journal of Economics* 5 (1): 16-36.

Krause, L.B., (1982) *U.S. Economic Policy Toward the Association of Southeast Asian Nations—Meeting the Japanese Challenge*, Washington, D.C.: The Brookings Institution.

Krueger, A.O., (1977) "Growth, Distortions and Patterns of Trade Among Many Countries," *Princeton Studies in International Finance*, No. 40, Princeton University (February).

Krueger, A.O., (1978) "Alternative Trade Strategies and Employment in LDCs," *American Economic Review* 68 (2): 270-74.

Leamer, E.E., and R.M. Stern, (1970) *Quantitative International Economics*, Boston: Praeger.

Morall, J.F., (1972) *Human Capital, Technology and the Role of the U.S. in International Trade*, Gainsville, Florida: University of Florida Press.

National Science Foundation, (1980) *Research and Development in Industry, 1978,* Washington, D.C.

Naya, S., (1980) "ASEAN Trade Development and Cooperation: Preferential

Trading Arrangements and Trade Liberalization,'' Report of the UNCTAD, UNDP and UNESCAP Project RAS/77/015/A/40, New York: United Nations.

Ojala, E.M., and A.N. Rae, (1983) ''Trade and Dependence in the Pacific Basin,'' Discussion Paper No. 2, Centre for Agricultural Policy Studies, Department of Agricultural Economics and Farm Management, Massey University, New Zealand.

Richardson, J.D., (1971) ''Constant Market Shares Analysis of Export Growth,'' *Journal of International Economics* (1) 2: 227-39.

Salvatore, D., (1985) ''The New Protectionism and the Threat to World Welfare: Editor's Introduction,'' *Journal of Policy Modelling*, Vol. 7, No. 1, pp. 1-22.

Stern, R.M., and K.E. Maskus, (1981) ''Determinants of the Structure of U.S. Foreign Trade, 1958-1976,'' *Journal of International Economics* 11: 207-24.

Tan, G., (1982) ''Trade Liberalization in ASEAN: An Empirical Study of Preferential Trading Arrangements,'' Research Notes and Discussions Paper No. 32, Institute of Southeast Asian Studies, Singapore.

Tyers, R., and K. Anderson, (1985) ''Economic Growth and Agricultural Protection in East and Southeast Asia: Implications for International Grain and Meat Trade,'' *ASEAN-Australia Economic Papers* No. 21, Australian National University (August).

Tyers, R., and P.R. Phillips, (1984a) ''Australia, ASEAN and Pacific Basin Merchandise Trade: Factor Composition and Performance in the 1970s,'' *ASEAN-Australia Economic Papers* No. 13, Australian National University (December).

Tyers, R., and P.R. Phillips, (1984b) ''ASEAN Merchandise Trade with the Pacific Basin: Factor Composition and Performance,'' *Pacific Economic Papers*, No. 116, Australia-Japan Research Centre, Australian National University (December).

Tyers, R., P.R. Phillips, and C. Findlay, (1985) ''ASEAN and China Exports of Labour-Intensive Manufactures: Performance and Prospects,'' Paper presented at the Workshop on China's Entry into World Markets, University of Adelaide, 26-28 August.

Vernon, R., (1966) "International Investment and International Trade in the Product Cycle," *Quarterly Journal of Economics* 80 (2): 190-207.

van Dijk, P., and H. Verbruggen, (1981) "A Constant Market Shares Analysis of ASEAN Manufactured Exports to the EEC," Paper presented to the Conference on ASEAN-EEC Relations, Institute of Southeast Asian Studies, Singapore, 6-8 August.

Wells, L.T., Jr., (1968) "A Product Life Cycle for International Trade?", *Journal of Marketing* 32: 1-6.

World Bank, (1982) *World Development Report 1982*, Oxford University Press.

Yamazawa, I., K. Taniguchi, and A. Hirata, (1983) "Trade and Industrial Adjustment in Pacific Asian Economies," *The Developing Economies*, Vol. XXI, No. 4, pp. 281-312.

3

Investment, Growth and Employment in Thailand: From Agriculture to Rural Industry

THEODORE PANAYOTOU

I. INTRODUCTION

Thailand, like other developing countries in the Pacific Rim in the 1980s, finds itself at the crossroads in its development strategy. Agriculture, which receives the lion's share of development assistance, faces absorptive capacity constraints at home and depressed prices abroad. Industrial exports, which enjoy generous promotional privileges, face increasing protectionism from developed countries, at a time when foreign exchange earnings are needed to service a rising foreign debt and to contain a growing balance of trade deficit. Equally disturbing is the growing employment deficit at home. Agriculture is increasingly becoming labor-saving as it shifts from the extensive to the intensive margin while urban-based industry is becoming increasingly capital-intensive because of factor-price distortions and promotional incentives, at a time when the labor force is growing faster than ever before because of the historically high population growth rate of the 1960s.

The development policy challenge is to identify new investments with high employment generation, unconstrained market demand, and low capital requirements to bridge the employment gap while minimizing the adverse effect on the budget deficit and balance of payments.

The present study makes the case for investment in the development of labor-intensive rural industry to support and supplement agricultural development which faces absorptive capacity constraints and to compete with the capital intensive urban-based industry which has been over-promoted with little regard to employment, market demand and balanced growth.

It is not an argument for abandonment of agriculture which is the backbone of the Thai economy but a call for rationalization of the development effort in the light of emerging constraints and the scarcity of investment funds. The growth of agriculture at its historically high rate of 4 to 5 percent would be ensured more by reform of restrictive price policies than by additional development funding. Agriculture is shown to be receiving as much funding as it can possibly absorb while it releases labor to the capital-intensive, urban-based industry beyond the latter's absorptive capacity. Because of administrative constraints at the Ministry of Agriculture and the political supremacy of Bangkok industrial elites, little can be done to either enhance agriculture's absorptive capacity or reduce industry's capital intensity. However, at the margin, development funds can be directed to rural industry, which has been neglected despite its potential contribution to employment and growth and its strong linkages with agriculture. The conclusions reached are of relevance not only to Thailand but also to other developing countries in the region, such as the Philippines, Indonesia and Malaysia which have been following similar development strategies.

The study is organized into 8 sections. After a brief overview of the Thai economy (section 2) we review the investment funding and absorptive capacity of agriculture (section 3) as well as its development constraints and sources of future growth (section 4). In section 5 we estimate the employment gap by projecting and comparing the growth of the labor force to the expansion of agricultural and non-agricultural employment. In section 6 we relate employment to growth in the context of the national development objectives. In section 7 we assess the potential contribution of rural industry to additional employment and more equitable growth. The study ends with concluding remarks (section 8).

II. THE THAI ECONOMY AND THE DOMINANCE OF AGRICULTURE

In a study of this breadth and time frame it is not possible to reduce the analysis to a set of testable (and tested) hypotheses or a limited number of fully documented propositions. Neither the time and space, nor the data available would suffice. It would be, therefore, helpful to clear as much ground as possible right from the start by distilling a set of generally accepted (if not indisputable) stylized facts about the Thai economy which do not require detailed documentation yet are essential to the argument which follows. Some 18 relevant facts have been identified and are listed below:

1. Over the past two decades, the Thai economy has been growing at an impressive rate (7 to 8 percent per annum in real terms), one of the highest in the world.

2. Thailand is one of the very few developing countries which are major net food exporters. Thai food and foodstuff exports include rice, maize, sugar, cassava, pineapple, fish and livestock products.

3. Agriculture has dominated and continues to dominate the Thai economy in terms of Gross Domestic Product, employment and exports. However, agriculture's relative contribution to the economy has been diminishing steadily while its absolute contribution continues to rise.

4. Manufacturing, which has been growing faster than agriculture (9.9 percent compared to 4.5 percent during 1970-81), is about to surpass agriculture in terms of contribution to GDP, while it lags far behind agriculture in terms of employment (9 percent compared to 76 percent in 1980).

5. Labor productivity in agriculture is very low since agriculture employs over 70 percent of the labor force but produces less than 25 percent of GDP. However, agriculture is indirectly ''responsible'' for about 50 percent of all manufacturing trade and services in the sense of backward and forward linkages with these sectors.

6. Most of the past agricultural growth has been attained through expansion into new lands (mainly in reserved forests) rather than through productivity improvements.

7. Agricultural yields have been stagnant, at best. Productivity increases in some areas have been barely sufficient to offset declines in other areas. Fertilizer application in Thailand is among the lowest in the world and so are crop yields.

8. Thai farmers are known to be very responsive to economic incentives except for a socio-cultural preference for producing rice for their own consumption.

9. It is generally recognized that the limits to the land frontier are being approached and that future agricultural growth will have to come from productivity improvements (higher yields per unit of land).

10. It is also generally recognized that the rapid expansion into watershed areas and marginal lands has brought about second-generation problems (erosion, floods, droughts) which pose a threat to the resource base and hence to the sustainability of Thai agriculture.

11. Partly for historical reasons and partly because of the availability of an open-access land frontier for expansion, neither land tenancy nor landlessness have been serious problems in Thailand. For the same reasons, insecurity of ownership has been and continues to be a serious problem affecting more than 50 percent of the agricultural land. With the frontier land approaching exhaustion and the increasing commercializa-

tion of agriculture, both tenancy and landlessness have been increasing in recent years and are expected to accelerate with the intensification of agriculture.

12. Poverty has been substantially reduced over the past two decades. However, a not insignificant twenty percent of the population, over ten million people, continue to live in "absolute" poverty despite the impressive growth of the past 20 to 25 years.

13. Regional, sectoral and rural-urban inequalities have generally been widening with much of the country's wealth being concentrated in Bangkok and the outlying central region.

14. There is a large and rising flow of seasonal and permanent migration from rural areas to urban centers, especially Bangkok, which is about fifty times larger than the next largest city in the country. In recent years, Bangkok has undergone a dramatic growth with consequent overcrowding and serious problems which make further expansion undesirable.

15. While Thailand has succeeded in reducing the population growth rate from over 3 percent in the late 1960s to under 2 percent in the early 1980s, the number of new entrants into the labor force is still rising because of the earlier rapid population growth.

16. While there is little unemployment in the western sense (of people actively but unsuccessfully searching for jobs) and the labor market is known to function fairly efficiently, there is substantial underemployment and seasonal unemployment as well as pockets of labor shortage during the planting and harvesting peaks of the agricultural season.

17. Thailand has chronic balance of trade and payments deficits which would have been substantially larger, and perhaps unmanageable, without agriculture's steadily rising balance of trade surplus.

18. The net effect of government policies amounts to a taxation of agriculture and other rural activities and a subsidization of large-scale urban-based industry. Government investment expenditures in agriculture and related activities have been heavily biased in favor of large-scale irrigation infrastructure in the central region of Thailand. There is currently a shift towards small irrigation projects in northeast Thailand, and a more diversified allocation of the agricultural development budget.

In conclusion, agriculture has played a dominant role in the Thai economy and, despite the gradual decline in its contribution to GDP, it will continue into the foreseeable future to be a major employer of the Thai labor force and a net contributor to foreign exchange earnings in addition to being the supplier of food to 50 million people.

III. INVESTMENTS IN AGRICULTURE: FUNDING AND ABSORPTIVE CAPACITY

Given the continuing importance of agriculture to the Thai economy, it is necessary to ensure that agriculture receives sufficient attention and funding to continue growing despite the approaching exhaustion of frontier land. This will require investments in irrigation, research, and extension as well as in land development and land improvement to raise agricultural productivity.

Table 3.1 shows planned development expenditures by sector during the past four and the current fifth Five-Year Development Plans covering the twenty-six-year period from 1961 to 1986. The development expenditures in agriculture are seen to have increased from under 5 billion baht[1] during the First Plan (1961-66) to over 122 billion baht during the Fifth Plan (1982-86). This is a tremendous increase by any measure whether in absolute or relative terms, whether by comparison to the rate of inflation (which averaged six percent per annum over the period) or to the growth rate of the agricultural sector or by comparison to other sectors. As a recipient of development expenditures, agriculture is second only to education.

Over time, the share of agriculture in planned development expenditures has increased from 13.5 percent during the First and Third Plans to 15.5 percent during the Fourth and Fifth.[2] In absolute terms, the most spectacular increase in agricultural development expenditures was the recent increase from 39 billion baht during the Fourth Plan (1977-81) to 123 billion baht during the Fifth Plan (1982-86), a 215 percent increase in a time of one-digit inflation. These figures do not include funds (four billion baht during the Third Plan and twelve billion during the Fourth Plan) which have not been specified as agricultural but were, in fact, used for agriculture. Moreover, the Fifth Plan, unlike earlier plans, has earmarked twenty-four billion baht for rural development, a significant part of which is allocated for agricultural activities in backward areas; namely, projects on food production for nutrition, upland rice production, soil improvement, Northeast saline soil development, agricultural credit for rural poor, water resource development, etc.

On an annual basis and in relation to other economic sectors, the growth of expenditures in agriculture has been remarkable. As seen in Table 3.2, the share of agriculture in the total government budget allocated to economic services rose from under 10 percent in the late 1960s and early 1970s to over 40 percent in the late 1970s and early 1980s. In absolute amounts, the government expenditures in agriculture rose from

Table 3.1

Planned Development Expenditures[a] During Thailand's First, Second, Third, Fourth and Fifth National Economic and Social Development Plans (Million Baht)

SECTOR	FIRST PLAN (1961-66)	SECOND PLAN (1967-71)	THIRD PLAN (1972-76)	FOURTH PLAN (1977-81)	FIFTH PLAN (1982-86)
1. Agriculture & Cooperatives	4,622	10,645	13,965	39,100	122,630
2. Industry, Mining & Commerce	2,563	1,277	2,350	3,605	20,070
3. Transportation & Communication	10,230	17,393	19,745	37,175	117,520
4. Energy	4,329	6,084	7,875	15,950	102,360
SUB-TOTAL	21,744	35,398	43,395	95,830	362,580
5. Public Welfare & Community Development	1,154	1,659	2,700	8,620	22,560
6. Public Facilities	4,344	6,099	14,930	33,335	94,110
7. Public Health	3,178	2,290	6,340	19,380	56,280
8. Education	2,491	6,387	32,910	95,285	237,610
9. Others	1,560	3,876	–	–	2,210
10. Rural Development	–	–	–	–	23,990
GRAND TOTAL	34,471	55,712	100,275	252,450	799,340

Source: National Economic and Social Development Board, Division of Economic and Fiscal Planning ''Unpublished Data Sheets.''
a. From all sources: Central government, local government, foreign loans, and foreign grants.

Table 3.2
Total Budget Expenditures for Economic Services and the Share of the Ministry of Agriculture and Cooperatives (Million Baht)

YEAR	TOTAL BUDGET EXPENDITURES	ALLOCATED TO ECONOMIC SERVICES		ALLOCATED TO MINISTRY OF AGRICULTURE AND COOPERATIVES		
		AMOUNT	as % of total	AMOUNT	as % of economic services	as % of total expenditures
1967	19,239.2	5,791.0	30.1	490.6	8.5	2.6
1968	21,249.3	6,247.3	29.4	583.7	9.3	2.7
1969	23,929.4	6,843.8	28.6	637.9	9.3	2.7
1970	27,324.7	7,869.5	28.8	643.3	8.2	2.3
1971	28,598.5	7,664.4	26.8	671.5	9.8	2.2
1972	28,987.2	6,580.2	22.7	647.7	9.8	2.2
1973	30,603.2	6,793.9	22.2	2,384.9	35.1	7.8
1974	39,081.3	7,503.6	19.2	2,847.8	0.4	7.3
1975	50,457.9	12,715.4	25.2	4,258.4	33.5	8.4
1976	62,670.4	12,722.1	20.3	5,451.9	42.9	8.7
1977	68,790.1	14,583.5	21.2	6,805.2	46.7	9.9
1978	80,786.9	16,076.6	19.9	7,008.8	43.6	8.7
1979	92,152.3	17,785.4	19.3	7,691.8	43.2	8.3
1980	114,743.3	24,096.1	21.0	9,431.6	39.1	8.2
1981	140,102.2	31,943.3	22.8	11,926.1	37.3	8.5
1982	161,063.7	32,857.0	20.4	13,587.0	41.4	8.4
1983	177,326.7	33,869.4	19.1	15,131.3	44.7	8.5

<u>Source</u>: Bureau of Budget

less than a billion baht (or 2 percent of total expenditures) in the early 1970s to over 15 billion baht in 1983.

The public funds for development expenditures come from a number of sources. As shown in Table 3.3, of a total development budget of 800 billion baht for the Fifth Plan, 67 percent was from the national budget, 17 percent from foreign loans, and 2 percent from foreign grants with the balance coming from self-financed government agencies (8 percent) and local government (5 percent). Agriculture relies more heavily on the national budget (73 percent) and on foreign loans (22 percent) than all other sectors combined (65 percent and 16 percent respectively), which might be one of the reasons why the Thai government is reluctant to borrow more for agriculture (although the loan component for energy exceeds 50 percent). The foreign grant component in agriculture (4 percent) is also larger than in other sectors (under 2 percent) but the contribution of self-financed government agencies is negligible and that of local governments non-existent.

Thus, agriculture, far from being neglected, has attracted and continues to attract increasing attention and funds from both the government and foreign donors. Productivity-augmenting activities such as irrigation, soil improvement, and research and extension receive the lion's share of the agricultural development budget. Agriculture receives as much funding for research as do all other sectors combined (industry, energy, transportation, health, education, defense, utilities), a share which is twice as high as agriculture's contribution to GDP.

Yet, this is not a sufficient reason for not investing additional funds in agriculture in general, and agricultural research in particular, if the expected return from such investments exceeds the opportunity cost which is the foregone return from alternative investments.

Unfortunately, even at the current level of funding of agriculture, the government is facing serious absorptive capacity constraints in designing, implementing and evaluating projects. During the 1960s and the early 1970s the funding for agriculture kept pace with the absorptive capacity of the Ministry of Agriculture. However, as the funding accelerated during the 1970s and the 1980s, the Ministry has found it increasingly difficult to design and implement a sufficient number of projects to absorb the entire development budget allocated to agriculture. As seen in Table 3.4, during the first two development plans (1961-71) the actual development expenditures in agriculture amounted to 91 percent of the planned development expenditures for the sector. While the economy as a whole continues to absorb over 85 percent of the planned expenditures, agriculture's absorptive capacity (defined as the ratio of actual to planned development expenditures) fell from 91 percent to 80

Table 3.3

Planned Development Expenditures for Thailand's Fifth Plan Period (1982–86) (Classified by Source of Funds in Million Baht)

	NATIONAL BUDGET	SELF-FINANCED GOVERNMENT AGENCIES	LOCAL GOVERNMENT	FOREIGN LOANS	FOREIGN GRANTS	TOTAL
Agriculture & Cooperatives	89,940	2,500	n.a.	27,070	5,120	122,630
Industry & Commerce						
Mining	4,800	3,980	n.a.	6,770	260	15,810
Commerce	3,730	530	n.a.	n.a.	n.a.	4,260
Transportation & Communication	68,750	21,430	n.a.	27,210	130	117,520
Energy	10,660	34,360	n.a.	56,580	760	102,360
SUB-TOTAL FOR ECONOMIC SERVICES	175,880	62,800	n.a.	117,630	6,270	362,580
Public Welfare & Community	20,250	110	n.a.	n.a.	2,200	22,560
Public Facilities	29,310	2,790	50,640	11,370	n.a.	94,110
Public Health	52,760	n.a.	n.a.	1,760	1,760	56,280
Education	232,700	n.a.	n.a.	2,710	2,200	237,610
SUB-TOTAL FOR SOCIAL SCIENCE	335,020	2,900	50,640	15,840	6,610	410,560
Rural Development	22,100	n.a.	n.a.	1,890	n.a.	23,990
Other	n.a.	n.a.	n.a.	n.a.	2,210	2,210
TOTAL DEVELOPMENT BUDGET	533,000	65,700	50,640	135,360	14,640	799,340

Source: NESDB, Division of Economic and Fiscal Planning, unpublished data.
n.a. – figures not available

percent during the Third Plan (1972-76) and to 64 percent during the Fourth Plan (1977-81). That is, of the thirty-nine billion baht planned for agricultural development during 1977-81, only twenty-five billion baht (or 64 percent) were expended by the end of 1981.

With the dramatic increase of the planned agricultural development expenditures during the Fifth Plan (1982-86) from 39 to 122 billion baht, it is likely that the absorptive capacity of agriculture will fall below 50 percent. The government is, therefore, legitimately reluctant to borrow additional funds for agricultural development when the share of agriculture in foreign loans (22 percent) is already above that for the economy as a whole (17 percent) and the Ministry of Agriculture is unable to absorb the existing development funds.

The absorptive capacity limits of the Ministry of Agriculture are partly the result of the rapidity with which the annual development budget of the Ministry has expanded (from less than one billion baht to about twenty-five billion baht within two decades) and partly the result of institutional, administrative and personnel constraints. For example, the Office of the Permanent Secretary of Agriculture which is responsible for the implementation of donor-assisted agriculture projects is understaffed by at least 30 percent; that is, 30 percent of the authorized positions remain vacant.

Despite the absorptive capacity constraints of the public sector which had limited the actual development expenditures in agriculture to 64 percent of the planned level, during the Fourth Development Plan the capital formation in agriculture proceeded at a faster rate than during earlier plans because of the contribution of the private sector which accounts for about 70 percent of all capital formation in agriculture.[3] The gross investment of the private and public sector combined averaged 6.5 billion baht and the capital stock in agriculture reached 87 billion baht in 1981, the last year of the Plan (see Table 3.5). The average annual growth of the agricultural capital stock during the Fourth Plan was 5.6 percent, which is 60 percent higher than the growth rate during the Third Plan (3.5 percent).

The capital stock embodies all (net) investments in Thai agriculture whether private or public, domestic or foreign. Private foreign investment in agriculture is usually very limited except in plantations, which are not common in Thailand. Yet, in recent years, Thai agriculture began to receive non-negligible amounts of private capital inflow. For example, during 1980-82 Thailand received 413 million baht of foreign private investment in agriculture compared to twenty-one million during the preceding three-year period. While this is less than one percent of the total private capital inflow into Thailand, it is, nevertheless, indicative of

Table 3.4

Discrepancy Between Actual and Planned Development Expenditures in Thailand as an Indicator of Absorptive Capacity Limits

Plan/ Period	AGRICULTURE			INDUSTRY: COMMERCE MINING			ECONOMY AS A WHOLE		
	Planned(P)	Actual (A)	P/A	Planned (P)	Actual (A)	P/A	Planned (P)	Actual (A)	P/A
First Plan (1961-66)	4,622	4,203	0.91	2,563	2,572	1.00	34,471	27,617	0.80
Second Plan (1967-71)	10,645	9,735	0.91	1,277	868	0.68	55,712	65,937	1.18
Third Plan (1972-76)	13,695	10,961	0.80	2,380	2,419	1.03	100,275	91,548	0.91
Fourth Plan (1977-81)	39,100	25,032	0.64	3,605	5,552	1.54	252,450	219,007	0.87
Fifth Plan (1982-86)	122,630	-	-	20,070	-	-	699,340	-	-

- Figures not available yet.
Source: National Economic and Social Development Board, Division of Economic and Fiscal Planning ``Unpublished Data Sheets.''

Table 3.5
Capital Formation in Thailand's Agricultural Sector (at 1972 Prices in Million Baht)

YEAR	PRIVATE SECTOR		PUBLIC SECTOR		TOTAL	
------	gross investment	stock of capital	gross investment	stock of capital	gross investment	stock of capital
1961	588	29,348	340	16,249	928	45,597
1962	712	29,033	453	16,134	1,165	45,166
1963	953	28,969	578	16,147	1,531	45,118
1964	1,218	29,173	625	16,207	1,843	45,381
1965	1,242	29,395	704	16,344	1,946	45,733
1966	1,546	29,912	818	16,591	2,364	46,503
1967	2,371	31,236	969	16,980	2,340	48,218
1968	2,455	32,597	1,076	17,462	3,531	50,059
1969	2,204	33,660	1,142	17,993	3,346	51,653
1970	2,153	34,635	1,817	19,181	3,970	53,816
1971	2,405	35,828	1,463	19,972	3,868	55,800
1972	1,979	36,553	1,125	20,398	3,104	56,951
1973	2,627	37,900	889	20,573	3,516	58,473
1974	3,547	40,121	615	20,468	4,162	60,569
1975	3,538	42,225	1,175	20,926	4,714	63,162
1976	3,651	44,428	1,775	21,968	5,426	66,396
1977	4,396	47,288	1,789	22,988	6,185	70,257
1978	4,704	50,318	1,807	24,091	6,611	74,409
1979	5,403	53,960	1,910	25,158	7,313	79,118
1980	5,200	57,272	2,089	26,367	7,289	83,639
1981	4,566	59,834	2,068	28,711	6,634	87,347

Source: General Economic Research Section, Department of Economic Research, Bank of Thailand, "Unpublished Data Sheets."

the maturity of Thai agriculture and its healthy and highly diversified sources of funds. Availability of capital does not appear to be a severe constraint on agricultural growth and productivity improvement in Thailand; misallocation and maldistribution of resources, including capital, is. The allocation of the development budget including foreign assistance has been skewed in favor of the better-off areas. Until recently, little has been expended on irrigation and research for rainfed areas and little productivity improvement has been achieved outside the central region and the irrigated areas of the north.

IV AGRICULTURAL GROWTH: CONSTRAINTS AND PROSPECTS

If there is no scarcity of development funds for agriculture, what can explain the stagnation of agricultural yields in Thailand? First, the aggregate yields are somewhat misleading because they are averages of areas such as the central plain where yields have been rising and areas such as the northeast where yields have been falling. Second, the effect of development investment in irrigation and technology has been more to expand the dry season cultivation (in the central plain) rather than to increase yields. Third, the existence of an easily accessible land frontier (in the form of ''reserved'' forests) for the expansion of the cultivated areas has eased the need for intensification, which would have been inevitable with the growth of population and export demand. As Table 3.6 shows, as much as 90 percent of the past growth in agricultural production has been accomplished through expansion of the cultivated area rather than through yield increase.

Fourth, fertilizer prices have been among the highest and fertilizer use among the lowest in Asia because of misguided government intervention, the oligopolistic structure of the central fertilizer market and the uneconomic compound fertilizers used. Fifth, the irrigated area is limited to the central plain and parts of the north, irrigation structures are poorly maintained and irrigation water, which is provided free of charge, is wastefully used, limiting the effectively irrigated area. Sixth, insecurity of ownership affecting over 50 percent of the agricultural land (World Bank, 1982, p. 30) deprives the owners of both the means (e.g., credit) and the incentive to undertake the investments and purchase the inputs necessary for agricultural intensification. Seventh, as a consequence of relentless encroachment of watersheds and high-slope lands, there have been increasing problems of floods, droughts and soil erosion which have depressing effect on yields in certain areas.

Last, but equally important, Thailand "has long pursued agricultural price policies and, more recently, industrial trade policies which sharply distort producer incentives against agriculture and in favor of capital intensive . . . manufacturing" (World Bank, 1983, p. 16). The World Bank has estimated the direct income impact on farmers of rice taxation to be between 8,400 and 14,500 million baht annually and of rubber taxation 3,300 million baht, and concluded that "these direct income effects of the pricing policies alone take out about as much or more from the rural areas as the combined rural development expenditures for agriculture and non-farm activities" (World Bank, 1983, p. 16).

The industrial trade policies also tax agriculture (and rural industry) by increasing the prices of production inputs and consumer goods purchased from urban areas. Undoubtedly, a combination of low crop prices, high input prices, and high consumer prices (i.e., adverse terms of trade for agriculture) are potent disincentives for agricultural growth, unless it is attainable through inexpensive expansion of the cultivated area. Indeed most (90 percent) of the agricultural growth of the past twenty years was attained through expansion of area rather than increase in productivity (see Table 3.6).

Thus, it is not lack of investment in irrigation and agricultural research and extension which held yields low in Thailand—indeed lower than any comparable Asian country—but institutional failures (insecurity of land ownership, open-access forest land, unpriced irrigation water), market imperfections (fragmented capital markets, an uncompetitive fertilizer market at the import/wholesale level) and, above all, misguided government policies (export taxes, quotas, and industrial trade policies). Investment in irrigation and research has not been a binding constraint and additional investment funds in these areas would do little to increase yields unless: (a) institutional and policy constraints are removed; and (b) the absorptive capacity of the Ministry of Agriculture is enhanced to accommodate additional projects.

What promises to be more effective in the area of irrigation and research is an increase in the effectiveness of existing funds through reallocation away from large irrigation structures to research for rainfed agriculture and water control in the northeast. Such a shift has been initiated within the Fifth Plan, but more could be done in this direction. Unfortunately, the Ministry of Agriculture faces its most severe staff constraints in its northeast regional office. Moreover, institutional constraints, market imperfections and policy distortions tend to affect more seriously the more remote and backward areas which are, in addition, disadvantaged by transportation costs, information gaps and agroclimatic conditions.

Table 3.6
Growth Rates of Production, Planted Area and Yield of Major Crops, Thailand, 1975/76–1982/83 (Percentage)

	WET SEASON RICE			DRY SEASON RICE[a]			MAIZE			CASSAVA[b]		
	Prod.	Area	Yield	Prod.	Area	Yield	Prod.	Area	Yield	Prod.	Area	Yield
1975/76	13.2	11.3	1.7	28.6	14.0	12.8	14.5	5.8	8.0	29.8	23.8	4.8
1976/77	-3.4	-4.5	1.5	15.3	16.0	-0.6	-6.6	-2.1	-4.6	25.2	17.7	6.3
1977/78	-9.8	5.1	-14.1	13.9	8.9	4.5	-37.3	-6.2	-33.0	22.0	37.2	-11.0
1979/80	23.3	9.2	12.6	42.7	42.7	0.0	66.5	14.7	44.4	21.6	5.2	15.6
1980/81	5.2	0.1	5.0	78.5	53.4	15.2	4.7	-6.0	11.7	49.0	37.2	8.6
1981/82	0.2	-0.9	2.9	2.8	10.9	-7.2	15.0	9.3	5.1	7.3	9.5	-2.0
1982/83	-6.2	-0.4	-5.7	4.4	10.8	-5.9	-12.9	7.1	-18.8	0.2	-2.7	2.9
TOTAL	18.8	13.5	3.1	136.0	106.1	19.2	46.5	32.6	5.5	128.9	100.5	18.7
Average	2.4	1.7	0.4	17.0	13.3	2.4	5.8	4.1	0.7	16.1	12.6	2.3

Source: Office of Agricultural Economics, ''Agricultural Statistics of Thailand,'' MOAC, Bangkok (various issues).
a. 1979/80 corresponds to 1980, 1980/81 to 1981, 1981/82 to 1982, and 1982/83 to 1983.
b. 1979/80 corresponds to 1979, 1980/81 to 1980, 1981/82 to 1981, and 1982/83 to 1982.

If the frontier for further expansion of agricultural land is being exhausted, and if additional development assistance for agriculture is unlikely to produce dramatic increases in yields within our time horizon (1985-90), what are the likely sources of agricultural growth during the rest of the 1980s? This is a key question because of the significance of agriculture to the Thai economy as a source of employment, income, foreign exchange and growth linkages to other sectors.

The very factors which have constrained agricultural growth in the past are also the most promising sources of agricultural growth in the future. The approaching exhaustion of easily accessible new land is certain to put pressure on farmers to use existing land more efficiently and more intensively, utilizing existing seed-fertilizer-water technologies.

Since Thailand has been among the slowest adopters of the new technology in Asia, there is still considerable potential for increasing yields with existing technology and infrastructure given appropriate incentives. According to the World Bank (1978), "in the case of irrigated agriculture there is a substantial backlog of known technology and improved practices which could raise yields" (p. 96).

Large gains in yields are also to be expected from increased fertilizer use following a reduction in the cost and increase in the effectiveness of fertilizer, to be accomplished through: (a) the promotion of competition among importers/wholesalers of fertilizers, (b) availability and promotion of low-cost (unsubsidized) single-nutrient fertilizer, (c) effective quality control, and (d) improved water control. According to the World Bank (1982), "one of the most urgently needed means to improve productivity in Thailand is to reduce the farm cost of fertilizer application by substantially increasing the availability of single-nutrient fertilizer and thus doubling the incremental value/cost ratio for many crops" (Vol. IV, Annex 6, p. 18). Based on farmer-field trials the Bank has found that the use of cheaper (unsubsidized) sources of nitrogen, such as urea instead of the mixed fertilizers like ammonium phosphate currently in use, would more than double the value/cost ratio for rice, maize, sorghum, cassava, kenaf and cotton. With value/cost ratios between 2.5 and 5 (compared to current ratios of about 1.5 or lower) a dramatic increase in fertilizer use and yield can be expected.

If, in addition to lowering the cost of fertilizer and improving its quality, the government allows the prices of crops to rise to their competitive market levels, the value/cost ratio of using fertilizer and other yield-augmenting inputs will increase further. For example, elimination of rice export taxes in 1981 would have increased the value/cost of fertilizer by 60 percent, inducing additional fertilizer use. As we have seen earlier in this section, the tax burden on the rice sector alone exceeds eight billion baht. Domestic and trade restrictions which include price control, export taxes, export premiums and quotas reduce farm prices and production incentives especially for rice, rubber and feedstuff. Again, according to the World Bank (1982), "relaxation of trade restrictions is likely to be the most efficient way of attaining Government's objective of increasing production" (Vol. II, p. 27).

Other sources of agricultural growth which are now in operation and will continue to gather momentum during the rest of the 1980s and well into the 1990s include: (1) improved maintenance and management of existing irrigation systems and improved water control in rainfed areas; (2) a higher percentage of cultivated area under secure ownership; (3) modest reduction in idle land and increased cropping intensity; (4) increased use of improved seeds of available varieties and pest and disease control; (5) reduction of damaged crop area and improvement in the resource base of agriculture through a combination of measures such as soil improvement, land development, replanting of watersheds and creation of alternative employment opportunities for forest squatters; (6) some success of current efforts to produce improved crop varieties and more intensive cropping systems for rainfed areas; and (7) continued funding of agriculture at the current level (in real terms) and an increasing shift of emphasis (and funding) to rainfed areas.

Assuming a minimum performance of the most likely of these growth sources, it is safe to conclude that agriculture will continue to grow at its historical rate (around 4 percent) throughout the next decade without additional development assistance (see Table 3.7). In the light of absorptive capacity constraints of the Ministry of Agriculture, additional development assistance is unlikely to increase agricultural growth beyond the projected rates.

V GROWTH AND EMPLOYMENT

We have, thus far, established a number of facts and made some projections about Thai agriculture: (a) agriculture has played and continues to play a dominant, though gradually declining, role in the Thai economy; (b) agriculture, in general, and productivity-augmenting investments (irrigation and research and extension), in particular, receive strong support and growing funding from the government, foreign development agencies and the private sector; (c) the absorptive capacity of the Ministry of Agriculture, in general, and of the project-implementing departments, in particular, is being taxed by existing project commitments to the point that additional development assistance for agriculture is

Table 3.7

Projected Annual Growth Rate of Thai Agriculture by Subsector 1981-86, 1986-80 (Percentage)

GDP IN CONSTANT PRICES	1960-70	1970-75	1975-80	FIFTH PLAN 1982-86	WORLD BANK MISSION PROJECTIONS 1981-86	WORLD BANK MISSION PROJECTIONS 1986-90
Crop	4.7	5.2	3.3	4.7	4.2	4.3
Livestock	3.5	7.6[b]	5.5	4.2	5.0	5.2
Fisheries	20.7	4.7[b]	-3.1[c]	5.4	3.7	4.4
Forestry	4.1	2.9	0.3	0.3	0.3	0.2
Agriculture	5.5	5.1	0.5	4.5	4.1	4.3

Source: World Bank (1982), Vol. II, p 56.
a. Semi-log trend regressions: 1960-70 is at 1962 constant prices and 1970-90 is at 1972 constant prices.
b. 1970-77.
c. 1977-80.

unlikely to be put to effective use; and (d) the all-important growth of the agricultural sector throughout the 1980s and early 1990s is ensured more by policy reforms than by additional development assistance.

Two issues remain to be tackled. First, if additional direct assistance to agriculture faces absorptive capacity constraints, is there scope for effective development assistance in other sectors of the economy which by their virtue of strong linkages with agriculture can enhance the growth potential of agriculture beyond its projected rate? Second, is agricultural growth as *sufficient* as it is necessary for the attainment of the national objectives of respectable growth, reduction of inequality and enhancement of political and social stability? According to the Fifth National Economic and Social Development Plan (1981-86):

> national development must create national stability and economic justice. . . . This is vital for the maintenance of future political stability and national survival. . . . [The Fifth Plan] stresses "the adjustment of economic structure" rather than "economic growth" . . . [and] "equality" in national economic and social development effort by aiming to disperse income and economic activities to provincial areas . . . rather than simply allowing the benefits of national development to remain in certain areas or in the hands of certain groups of people as in the past (NESDB, 1981, pp. 2-3).

The Thai planners are convinced (and the available evidence seems to support their conviction) that "past development efforts have benefited only certain parts of the country." Development benefits were not evenly dispersed as a large part of the country and population did not benefit from past development efforts and are still living in absolute poverty. It is estimated that there are ten million people in the rural areas who are in this category (NESDB, 1981, pp. 1-2). When the benefits from development do not trickle down sufficiently, when land reform and other efforts at asset redistribution are too slow, ineffective or politically unpalatable, and when income transfers are inoperative, employment emerges as the single most promising means of access to development benefits. Productive and gainful employment is not only rewarding to the individual, but it also generates social benefits in the form of full utilization of the country's human resources, multiplier effects from increased income, reduced social tensions and enhanced political stability.

Agriculture and related activities have been for centuries the main sources of employment for the rural population. The availablity of open-access land and other common-property resources such as fisheries and forests has ensured gainful employment and adequate food supplies for a relatively small and slow-growing population. The old Thai saying "in the water there is fish and in the field there is rice and who wants to trade trades" is an expression of contentment with the prevailing availability and distribution of resources and opportunities.

Since the land frontier is being exhausted and open-access natural resources depleted and since agriculture is becoming more intensive and market-oriented, employment opportunities in primary production are declining. On the other hand, the increased agricultural output generates related activities such as marketing, storage, transport, processing and distribution as well as demand for additional agricultural inputs which may be supplied by labor-intensive, secondary (agro-industry) and tertiary (services) sectors. Whether, on balance, more or less employment opportunities are available is an empirical question, to which we turn in the next section. Here, it suffices to say that even if it can be shown that the labor absorption by agriculture and related activities will not diminish in the foreseeable future, there may still be an employment problem if indeed there is underemployment and seasonal unemployment or if the labor force is growing faster than it has in the past.

Thus, the thrust of the remainder of the study is twofold. First, to determine the dimensions of the employment problem over the next decade and to establish the need for additional employment creation outside (but not unrelated to) agriculture in line with the national objective of equity and political stability. Second, to show that rural industry and rural employment are complementary to and have strong linkages with agriculture to be considered as indirect investments toward sustainable agricultural growth.

VI THE EMERGING EMPLOYMENT GAP

In this section we attempt to project the supply and demand for labor in order to determine the dimensions of the employment problem during the rest of the 1980s and early 1990s and the extent to which additional labor creation will be needed.

Thailand has succeeded in reducing its population growth rate from over 3 percent in the late 1960s to under 2 percent in the early 1980s, a 43 percent reduction in the growth rate in less than fifteen years. In 1983, the population growth rate was 1.8 percent per annum, and it was expected to decline to 1.5 percent by 1986, the last year of the Fifth Plan. This reduction, being the net result of concurrent reductions in birth and death rates, brought about a change in the age structure of the population: between 1970 and 1980 the percentage of the population of a working age (15-64) rose by 7.7 percent for males and by 6.6 percent for females. During the Fifth Plan (1981-86), it is projected that the population of pre-school children (0-4) would decrease by 1 percent, of school-age children (5-25) to increase by 1.4 percent and of the working-age population (26-64) to increase by 3.2 percent (see NESDB, 1981, p. 177).

This change in the age structure of the population means larger numbers of new entrants into the labor force than in the past. In the early 1970s, the growth of the labor force was slower than that of the population (because of the low population growth rate in the 1950s). Since the mid-1970s the growth rate of the labor force has exceeded that of the population because of the high population growth rate in the 1960s compared to the present rate (see Figure 3.1). Today, the labor force grows at an average annual rate above 3 percent and is projected to grow at this rate through to 1990; that is, the labor force is growing today at a faster rate than in any other time in Thailand's past or foreseeable future. In absolute numbers, the labor force is projected to grow by over six million during the 1980s compared to five million during the 1970s and 3.4 million during the 1960s. The total labor force today (1984) exceeds twenty-five million and is expected to rise to twenty-seven million by the end of the Fifth Plan and to reach thirty million by 1990. Not only are the new entrants more numerous, they are also more educated and skilled.

The question is whether the Thai economy in its current slowly changing structure would generate sufficient numbers of additional jobs to employ the new entrants of the 1980s and early 1990s. Given the projected rate of agricultural growth of 4 to 5 percent and the gradual structural change of the sector, will agriculture generate increased employment in proportion to the projected growth of the labor force of 3 percent per annum? Will the non-agricultural sector grow fast enough to absorb the balance?

During the past two decades, agricultural employment averaged a growth rate of less than 2 percent with a tendency to fall over time. Based on recent trends, we expect agricultural employment to grow at the rate of 1.2 percent during the 1980s and below 1 percent during the 1990s. Based on a baseline of fifteen million persons employed in agriculture in 1980, we project agricultural employment at 15.9 million in 1985 and 17.1 million in 1990. However, to the extent that the structural change in agriculture during the 1980s is expected to be faster than during the 1970s, these figures overestimate the growth in agricultural employment.

As we have seen in the preceding section, unlike the 1970s when 90 percent of the agricultural growth came from expansion into new land, during the 1980s at least 50 percent of the growth must come from intensification, i.e., increased use of improved seed and appropriate ferti-

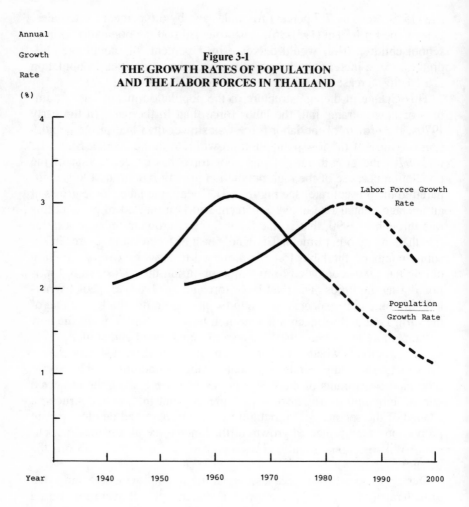

Annual Growth Rate (%)

Figure 3-1
THE GROWTH RATES OF POPULATION
AND THE LABOR FORCES IN THAILAND

Labor Force Growth Rate

Population Growth Rate

Year 1940 1950 1960 1970 1980 1990 2000

lizers, improved efficiency of water use, increased cropping intensity, land improvements, etc. Some of these inputs and activities require additional labor input (for application of fertilizers and pesticides, for weeding, land preparation, double cropping, etc.) while others such as mechanization of tilling and threshing are displacing labor.

While often thought of as labor saving, the high yielding varieties and improved cultivation practices are not necessarily so and could, in fact, be labor using. It all depends on the type of technology and the relative prices of capital, labor and other inputs. Whether crop intensification in

Thailand, on balance, would increase or reduce the demand for labor is an empirical question.

Because of lack of detailed data, we use a rather crude approach to obtaining a measure of the employment effect of the expected growth and intensification of Thai agriculture during the 1980s and early 1990s. First, we know that Thai agriculture has become increasingly intensified (albeit at a slow pace) at least since the early 1970s. A comparison of the agricultural labor/output[4] ratio between the early and the late 1970s will give us some idea as to whether agriculture is becoming more or less labor intensive over time. As seen in Table 3.8, the labor/output ratio has declined from 0.234 in the early 1970s to 0.219 in the late 1970s, a 6.5 percent decrease in labor per unit of output produced as the output per unit of land increased by 12 percent. But how can we be certain that the fall in the labor/output ratio is related to intensification rather than extensification since much more of the latter than the former has been taking place?

In Thailand, virtually all intensification took place in the central region and the north while most of the expansion into new areas took place in the northeast. If intensification is more labor-intensive than extensification, the central region should have a higher (than the northeast) and rising labor/land ratios. Table 3.8 indicates that the reverse is true. The labor/land ratio of the central region is the lowest in the country, 0.112 and falling, while that of the northeast has risen considerably since the early 1970s, from 0.128 to 0.152. The north has the highest labor/land ratio because of a more labor-based intensification (in the Chiangmai Valley) as well as because of expansion into new areas requiring clearing and manual harvesting which are labor-intensive activities. However, even in the north the labor/land ratio is falling.

Consistent with our hypothesis that intensification as practiced in Thailand is, on balance, labor saving, is the fact that the central region has the lowest labor/output ratio, 0.112, down from 0.127 in the early 1970s (an 11 percent fall). In contrast, the northeast has the highest ratio of 0.394, down only 2.7 percent from its 1971-73 level of 0.405. The north and the south are intermediate cases as one would expect. Unfortunately, we have no figures on capital by region; but few would doubt that the capital/output and capital/labor ratios are highest in the central region (especially if one was to include irrigation systems and other social infrastructure provided free of charge) and lowest in the northeast. However, even in the central region, agriculture remains more labor-intensive than the non-agricultural sector. Yet, under present market conditions, agricultural intensification in Thailand is likely to be more labor-saving than labor-using following the central region pattern

Table 3.8
Labor/Output, Labor/Land, and Output/Land Ratios of the Agriculture and Non-Agricultural Sectors in Thailand 1971-80

	LABOR/GDP		LABOR/LAND		GDP/LAND	
	1971-73	1977-80	1971-73	1977-80	1971-73	1977-80
WHOLE KINGDOM						
Agriculture	0.234	0.219	0.135	0.142	578	648
Non-agric.	0.037	0.030	-	-	-	-
NORTH						
Agriculture	0.254	0.240	0.177	0.161	684	673
non-agric.	0.071	0.044	-	-	-	-
NORTHEAST						
Agriculture	0.405	0.394	0.128	0.152	315	386
non-agric.	0.076	0.042	-	-	-	-
CENTER						
Agriculture	0.127	0.112	0.106	0.102	838	916
Non-agric.	0.034	0.030	-	-	-	-
SOUTH						
Agriculture	0.169	0.149	0.136	0.145	802	970
Non-agric.	0.058	0.042	-	-	-	-
BANGKOK/THONBURI						
Non-agric.	0.021	0.012	-	-	-	-

Source: Calculated based on the GDP figures reported in Rijk and Meer/ADB (1984), the employment figures reported in World Bank (1983) and the land figures reported in World Bank (1982).

which is to some degree a precursor of the intensification in the rest of the country, subject, of course, to variations in the agroclimatic conditions and relative prices.

It is, therefore, not unreasonable to expect the rate of growth of agricultural employment to fall further as a result of the approaching limits to the land frontier and the mounting pressures and opportunities for intensification. Conservatively, we project the agricultural employment growth rate to be around 1 percent per annum, which is considerably higher than the rate experienced in the central region; in fact, agricultural employment in this region fell in absolute terms between 1977 and 1980. Based on this modified rate, agriculture employment is expected to reach 15.7 million in 1985 and 16.7 million in 1990; at any rate, it is unlikely to exceed 17 million by 1990.

However, agriculture's contribution to employment is not limited to agriculture. Agricultural growth has powerful forward, backward and consumer demand linkages (to transport, processing, production inputs, consumer goods, etc.) which create additional employment in non-agricultural sectors.

While we do not have access to complete input-output tables or social accounting matrices to measure all the backward and forward linkages from a 4 to 5 percent rate of agricultural growth and technical change, we may project non-agricultural employment following recent trends taking into account what we know about structural change during the 1980s. Over the past decades non-agricultural employment grew by 5 to 6 percent because of rapid economic growth of 7 to 8 percent. With planned economic growth of 6.6 percent during the Fifth Plan and a falling employment/GDP ratio for both the agricultural and the non-agricultural sectors (see Table 3.8), non-agricultural employment is not expected to grow faster than 5 percent per annum. According to the Asian Development Bank, a scenario of annual growth rates of non-agricultural employment of 5 percent over the 1980s and of 4 percent over the 1990s "is ambitious and its realisation will depend on foreign demand for Thai industrial and agricultural products and on whether sufficiently high economic growth rates can be achieved to generate new employment for the 1980s at that rate" (Rijk and Meer/ADB, 1984, p. 144).

Using a baseline figure of seven million persons for 1980[5] and an annual growth rate of 5 percent, we project non-agricultural employment at nine million in 1985 and twelve million in 1990. (ADB's projections for 1990 range between 11.7 and 12.9 million.)

Summing up our projections of agricultural and non-agricultural employment, we arrive at a total employment figure of 24.7 to 25 million by 1985 and 28.7 to 29 million by 1990. Recall that the labor force has been projected to reach 26 million in 1985 and 30 million in 1990. These projections imply a shortfall of employment by one million at best and 1.3 million at worst, or a 3 to 5 percent "unemployment" rate. This is hardly a worrisome figure; many developed countries are accustomed to unemployment figures twice as high. A number of reasons, however, make this figure particularly worrisome for Thailand. Firstly, Thailand has had little experience with unemployment; historically, unemployment figures in Thailand rarely, if ever, exceeded 2 percent in the urban areas and 1 percent in the rural areas.

Secondly, Thailand, like other developing countries, has no income transfer mechanisms such as unemployment and social insurance to deal with the problem.

Thirdly, and more importantly, the official statistics are unlikely to register such a "high" (by Thai standards) unemployment figure since, in the absence of unemployment compensation, few people can afford to remain unemployed for prolonged periods of time. Open unemployment is likely to increase only moderately, perhaps to 2 percent as predicted by the Fifth Plan. The rest would be translated into disguised unemployment and underemployment in agriculture and the informal sectors especially in Bangkok, as has been the case in the past. Fourthly, any additional underemployment during the 1980s would be added to the existing high rates of underemployment and seasonal unemployment especially in the northeast.

In total, the employment problem in Thailand has at least three dimensions of which only one, open unemployment, fits the conventional western definition of unemployment (persons searching but unable to find work). Open unemployment is expected to average no more than 2.5 percent of the labor force or 0.50 to 0.75 million[6] persons throughout the 1980s. At least one-third of the openly unemployed would be in the twenty to twenty-nine age group, many of them with secondary or higher education residing in Bangkok or the provincial urban centers.

Seasonal "unemployment," defined as the difference between employment during the peak (wet) and the slack (dry) agricultural seasons, has ranged between 22 and 35 percent of the labor force, or three and six million persons, during 1975-81 (according to the Labor Force Survey) and is expected to continue at least at this level. Seasonal unemployment consists mainly of unpaid family members (mainly young or female) waiting for the agricultural season, not all of whom would take up employment during the slack season, if such existed. However, the fact that seasonal unemployment is highest in the northeast where employment opportunities during the slack season are most scarce, while it is lowest in the central region where employment opportunities are relatively abundant, suggests that a large proportion of those waiting for the agricultural season would be willing to take up employment if such existed. It is difficult to estimate this proportion but, if one was to assume that two-thirds of the males and half of the females among the seasonally unemployed would be willing to work, over three million additional jobs would have been necessary during the dry season of 1981. Seasonal unemployment increased from 3.1 million in 1975 to 5.6 million in 1981, that is, at a rate several times larger than the growth rate of the labor force. The intensification of agriculture beyond the central region is expected to slow down the growth of seasonal unemployment but it cannot reverse it because rainfed agriculture will continue to dominate the economy of the northeast and the north in the years to come.

While it is not known under what conditions (wage rates, work type and location) the seasonally underemployed would accept additional work, they do remain idle because the prevailing wage rate is below their reservation price, which brings us to the third and most serious dimension of the employment problem: underemployment. Underemployment may be defined in one of three (complementary) ways: (a) persons working in occupations not matching their qualifications; (b) persons working less than a certain number of hours per week; and (c) persons earning less than a certain minimum level of income. The Labor Force Survey defines as 'underemployed' an unpaid family member who works less than twenty hours a week and wants to work more, or an employed person who works less than thirty-five hours a week; underemployed in terms of income is an urban dweller earning less than the minimum wage, a rural household earning less than the minumum wage, or a rural household earning less than 250 baht per head (see Hongladarom and Charsombut, 1984). Underemployment in terms of hours worked has been relatively low, 3 to 5 percent of the labor force during 1977-81; it is most severe in the northeast among male adults, mainly farmers with low educational levels. Underemployment in terms of mismatch between occupation and education has been generally less than 1 percent and is found mainly in Bangkok among males twenty to twenty-nine years of age with vocational or university education. Most important was underemployment in terms of income which ranged between 14 and 34 percent of the labor force during 1977-81 (see Table 3.9). It was important in the rural areas, particularly· of the northeast and the north; it affected equally both sexes and was most severe among farmers, 30-59 years of age and of low educational level. In 1981 there were as many as 3.2 million people in rural areas and 1.0 million in urban areas earning less than 3,000 baht (US$130) per year compared to a per capita GDP of 17,630 baht (see Hongladarom and Charsombut, 1984, p. 25).

Table 3.9
Rate of Underemployment in Municipal and Non-Municipal Areas in Thailand (Percentage)

		MUNICIPAL AREAS		NON-MUNICIPAL AREAS	
Years	Type	Dry Season	Rainy Season	Dry Season	Rainy Season
1977	Hour work	1.4	1.4	5.4	4.1
	Income	15.5	14.5	26.2	34.2
	Mismatch	0.1	0.2	a	a
1979	Hour Work	2.2	1.8	3.3	2.4
	Income	15.3	14.5	20.7	28.3
	Mismatch	0.4	0.3	a	a
1981	Hour Work	2.3	1.5	3.5	1.8
	Income	27.9	28.8	13.3	15.1
	Mismatch	0.6	0.7	a	a

Source: The National Statistical Office, Report of the Labor Force Survey, Whole Kingdom (round 1 and 2), 1977, 1979, 1981 and 1982 (quoted from Hongladarom and Charsombat).
a. Less than 0.1

Related to the employment situation is the stagnation of real wages for unskilled labor and the widening of rural-urban income differentials. If indeed the labor market is not tight, i.e., there is considerable under-employment (as well as other forms of underutilization of labor), we would observe stagnation of real wages for that part of the labor force which experiences the highest rates of underemployment, that is, the un-skilled workers. Indeed, as seen in Table 3.10, between 1965 and 1977 the agricultural real wages in the northeast and the north remained vir-tually unchanged but increased somewhat in the central region. Simi-larly, between 1977 and 1980 there has been no sustainable rise in real wages anywhere in the country except perhaps in the non-municipal areas of Bangkok-Thonburi, as shown in Table 3.11. (Tables 3.10 and 3.11 are not comparable because of differences in the sample population and in the base year of the deflator; moreover, the figures in Table 3.11, unlike Table 3.10, are adjusted to a standard eight-hour day.)

Another observation from Table 3.10 is that wages in the rural north-east are only two-thirds of the wages in the rural central area and in the

Table 3.10
Agricultural Wage Trends in Thailand by Region, 1965–1977 (In Baht/Day)

	NORTH	NORTHEAST	CENTRAL	CPI (CENTRAL)
1965–67	8	8	10	100
	(8)ᵃ	(8)	(10)	
1972	9–10	9–10	12–13	119
	(7.6–8.4)	(7.6–8.4)	(10.1–10.9)	
1976–77	20	16	27	192
	(10.4)	(8.2)	(14.1)	

Source: World Bank, 1977, p. 38.
a. Figures in parentheses are real wages computed by using the CPI for the central region (1965–67 = 100).

urban northeast. This is an indication of the persistent wage differentials among regions and between rural and urban areas. Wages also vary between seasons. The World Bank (1977) reports that in the central region the nominal wage rate in the 1976/77 crop year rose from 20 baht in the slack season to 30 baht in the peak agricultural season. In the northeast, where even in the peak season there is a relative abundance of labor, the nominal wage rate rose from fifteen baht in the slack season to seventeen baht in the peak season. In the north, with features of both the central region and the northeast, the nominal wage rose from fifteen baht in the slack season to twenty baht in the peak season.

The seasonal variations in wage and employment indicate that wages are responsive to changes in the demand for labor and that labor supply is not infinitely elastic. On the other hand, the larger seasonal variation in labor supply with a small variation in wage rates in the northeast indicate a more elastic labor supply in this region than elsewhere in Thailand.

While the seasonal variations in wages indicate a well-functioning labor market, the persistence of regional variations in wages seems to indicate just the opposite: a segmented labor market which contradicts one of our stylized facts (section 1) according to which labor in Thailand is mobile and the labor market efficient. However, the persistence of regional wage differentials can, in fact, be explained by the lack of scope for permanent migration and the high cost of temporary migration. For the better paid activities, such as sugar cane and paddy harvesting, there is considerable rural-rural migration, but it is never sufficient to equalize wages because the economic and psychic cost of movement of farmers is

Table 3.11

Average Daily Nominal and Real Wages[a] For Male Private Employees (Hourly, Daily and Other Paid), Age 20–59, with Lower Elementary Education, Thailand, July–September, 1977–1980 (Baht/Day)

	NON-MUNICIPAL				MUNICIPAL			
	1977	1978	1979	1980	1977	1978	1979	1980
NORTH	29.5 (27.4)	28.0 (24.1)	33.3 (26.1)	40.0 (25.6)	36.1 (33.6)	44.9 (38.7)	43.9 (34.4)	52.3 (33.5)
NORTHEAST	23.6 (22.1)	28.4 (25.4)	28.9 (22.6)	38.1 (24.4)	36.5 (33.9)	45.2 (38.9)	43.2 (33.9)	48.8 (31.3)
SOUTH	38.0 (35.4)	43.2 (37.2)	50.4 (39.5)	54.6 (35.0)	36.5 (33.9)	40.7 (35.1)	40.5 (31.7)	50.3 (32.3)
CENTER	36.0 (33.5)	38.5 (33.2)	47.7 (37.4)	53.7 (34.4)	42.7 (39.6)	44.1 (38.0)	52.7 (41.3)	61.1 (39.2)
BANGKOK-THONBURI	36.5 (33.9)	42.9 (37.0)	48.3 (37.3)	62.9 (40.3)	49.6 (46.1)	48.3 (41.6)	58.4 (45.8)	67.5 (43.2)

Source: World Bank, 1983, p. 108. The real wages (in parentheses) were computed using the consumer price index for the whole country. Obtained from the Department of Business Economics, Ministry of Commerce.
a. Adjusted to a standard 8-hour day. Figures in parentheses are the corresponding real wages (using CPI 1976 = 100).

likely to be higher than that of purely wage laborers who are a rarity in rural Thailand.

There is also evidence which indicates that even in the non-agricultural sectors, the real wage rates of unskilled workers have stagnated as they did in the agricultural sector (a fact which supports the hypothesis that the labor market in Thailand operates efficiently). According to the World Bank (1977), during 1962-76 non-agricultural wages (particularly manufacturing) remained stagnant or increased slightly in nominal terms and declined in real terms. More recently, wages in manufacturing, construction and other formal, non-agricultural sectors have been influenced by minimum wage legislation and, to some extent, by trade unions, and therefore they cannot be used as indicators of the tightness of the labor market.

From the above discussion, four seemingly contradictory findings emerge: (a) the economy grew rapidly; (b) the labor market operates efficiently; (c) unskilled real wages stagnated; and (d) regional wage differentials persist. The apparent contradiction disappears when one considers the rapid increase in population and the decrease in land availability, which meant that increasing numbers of poor families have been willing to supply labor at the same supply price. This is not the same as an infinitely elastic supply of labor; it is rather a case of the labor market loosening up over time as supply rises while demand fails to keep pace. Double cropping in the central region and parts of the north succeeded in tightening the market and raising real wages but neither have such opportunities been available to the northeast nor has the wage differential been high enough to warrant the necessary movement costs. In other words, the migration costs are too high to expect equalization of wages across the board.

It is not only the real wages of the unskilled workers that remained stagnant, but also the returns to marginal farmers and the non-wage urban sector, which constitute the sources of unskilled labor. This situation is expected to continue and intensify during the 1980s because of the higher growth rate of the labor force and lower availability of land for expansion and self-employment at the extensive margin. The implications are clear: poverty will persist and income distribution will deteriorate while economic growth continues at historically high rates. But there is more to this than just the welfare of the ten million ''poor'' of the northeast and parts of the north. In the absence of more rewarding employment opportunities, the clearing of watersheds for land and the migration to Bangkok for work will intensify. The end result is easy to predict: further degradation of agriculture's resource base and growth potential and further congestion of Bangkok and deterioration of social infrastructure with consequent political, social and economic instability.

What should the right response be? Are there any alternative labor de-mand and income-augmenting policies? Since agricultural investments face tight absorptive capacity constraints and urban industry (which means basically Bangkok-based industry) generates little employment and attracts much undesirable migration into Bangkok, there is only one alternative left: investment in non-agricultural rural activity, that is, rural industry in a broad sense to include food processing, transportation, commerce, and other rural services. Other alternatives such as employ-ment generation through public projects or income enhancement through transfer payments have already been proven either ineffective or inopera-tive.

VII INVESTMENT IN RURAL INDUSTRY: POTENTIAL FOR GROWTH AND EMPLOYMENT

Our conclusion that rural industry might hold the key to additional em-ployment, growth, and equity raises more questions than can be possibly answered in the context of this study. What types of rural industry? What are the binding constraints to rural industry and what can the government do about them? What specific investments or interventions are likely to work, at what cost and within what time frame? How much employment would be generated per dollar spent and how would growth and income distribution be affected? What is the expected impact on agriculture?

It is beyond the scope of the present study to attempt to answer all these questions. Instead, we will focus on the last two; that is, the em-ployment generation potential of the rural industry, its likely effects on growth and equity, and its potential linkages to agriculture.

Rural industry, in a broad sense, is a generic term used here for all non-agricultural activities taking place outside the greater Bangkok metropolitan area and the outlying provinces of Nontaburi, Pathumtani and Samutprakan. In a narrow sense, rural industry refers to rural manu-facturing such as food processing, textiles, and cottage industries. Unless indicated otherwise, we will be using the term in its broader sense. What we do not mean by rural industry is public job creation projects (which have been tried with little success) or large-scale government projects such as the Eastern Seaboard Industrial Project which are capital in-tensive and cannot be expected to provide much rural employment.

It should also be stated categorically at the outset that the promotion of rural industry is not presented as an alternative to agricultural growth which is a *sine qua non* for virtually any other economic activity in rural Thailand; it is, rather, a necessary complement to the projected agricul-

tural growth in recognition of (a) the inadequacy of agricultural employment (direct and indirect) to absorb a labor force growing at unprece-
dented rates; (b) the absorptive capacity limits to public investments in
agriculture beyond current levels; and (c) the potential linkages between
rural industry and agricultural growth.

A last qualification concerns the meaning of "promotion." By promotion of rural industry we do not mean subsidization, but improvement in
the allocation of resources and creation of an environment conducive to
competitive operation of rural industry through intervention in areas
where there are market failures or policy distortions (i.e., credit, infrastructure, extension of technology, training, market information) that
prevent the realization of existing growth potential. Even when the objective is distributional, a rural industrial strategy should be pursued only
if it is the most cost-effective avenue for achieving a given reduction in
poverty or improvement in income distribution. We do not advocate import substitution, but rather rural industries for which there is either local
demand (arising from the projected agricultural and income growth) or
export demand (e.g., textiles, handicrafts); rural industries which have
comparative advantage by virtue of the locally available materials (food
and fiber), relatively inexpensive labor and little foreign exchange requirements. Whether there is a potential for further expansion of such industries or establishment of new ones is an empirical question to be answered by another study. However, there are *a priori* reasons and some
evidence suggesting that opportunities for further expansion of rural industry do exist.

According to the World Bank (1983), the government's industrial
trade and investment promotion policies have sharply distorted incentives against rural areas and in favor of capital-intensive, large-scale enterprises via rigid cut-off points on the size of industrial plants eligible
for subsidies and other incentives. These policies must have seriously
hampered the growth of rural non-farm activities and employment. Agricultural price policies, such as the rice and rubber taxation, have further
distorted the incentives against both agriculture and rural industry.

In contrast, very little is being returned to the rural areas in terms of
development assistance, loans and promotional policies. A summary of
the government policies in favor of the rural areas is given in Table 3.12.
From this table and our earlier discussion of development expenditures
(section 3), a number of observations may be made. First, "the major
transfers in favor of the rural areas are specific agricultural investment
programs in irrigation, extension and research (roughly B 8.5 billion)"
(World Bank, 1983, p. 14) which, as we have seen earlier, are largely
spent in the central region. Second, rural employment creation through

public projects received another 3.5 billion baht. Third, rural industry received virtually no attention; special regional incentives are negligible and Small Industry Finance Office (SIFO) loans to rural industry are next to nothing. The World Bank estimates that the tax effects of the industrial and trade policies "exceed the income transfers implied in special rural industrialization efforts many-fold" (1983, p. 17) and concludes that these policies discriminate against labor-intensive industries with depressing effects on wages.

A similar view of Thai industrial policies is expressed by Narongchai Akrasanee of the Industrial Finance Corporation of Thailand (IFCT):

> [The] industrial policy of the government so far has not had favorable impact on the development of either village or town industries. For industry in general, the industrial incentive system and the availability of basic infrastructure in fact have the effect of being biased in favor of Bangkok [and nearby provinces] location and thus against location in provincial towns. The government so far has few activities which are of a real help to [small] town industry. . . .The private sector and the donor countries and agencies have played a very small role in the promotion of village and town industries (Akrasanee et al., 1983, p. 176).

If rural areas are being discriminated against by government policies, the first-best course of action for restoring the rural area's true comparative advantage would be a sweeping reform of government policies and correction of market imperfections and distortions. Such a first-best alternative, however, is unlikely to be adopted in full or to any significant degree in the foreseeable future because of political reasons and administrative constraints. Agricultural price policies stand a better chance of being reformed appreciably within the coming years. (A beginning has already been made with fertilizer prices, maize quotas and rice premiums.) The current industrial promotion and trade policies are likely to persist throughout the 1980s because of the vested interest of the politically powerful Bangkok establishment.

Given the dimensions and the urgency of the employment and poverty problems and the untapped potential of rural industry, a pragmatic second-best policy would be development assistance to labor-intensive rural industry to restore its comparative advantage *vis-à-vis* the highly protected and promoted Bangkok-based capital-intensive industry. Such assistance, combined with the on-going investments and policy reforms in agriculture, is likely to increase the proportion of input and consumer demand supplied by labor-intensive rural activities, to generate addi-

Table 3.12
A Summary of Government Policies in Favor of Rural Areas, Thailand

	SUBSIDY ELEMENT (million baht)
1. Commercial bank loans to agriculture: Interest differential of 2-5 percent on about B 10 billion	200-500
2. Commercial bank loans to agribusiness: Voluntary lending exceeds quota	none
3. BAAC loans to agriculture Interest subsidy of 5-10 percent on about B 10 billion	500-1,000
Loss of Capital from overdues, 10-20 percent of loans outstanding per year	1,000-2,000
4. IFCT loans to food and tobacco Interest subsidy of 5-10 percent on B 400 million	20-40
5. SIFO loans outside Bangkok Interest subsidy of 5-10 percent on about B 80 million	4-8
6. Special regional incentives Reduce capital costs by only about 10 percent relative to urban areas	negligible
7. Rural Employment Generation Program (1980)	3,500
8. Agricultural Development Expenditures on irrigation on extension on research	7,165 917 515
TOTAL OF QUANTIFIED EFFECTS	13,821-15,645

Source: World Bank, 1983, p. 15.

tional demand and to exploit any unutilized export potential (e.g., textiles and handicrafts). That is, for any given rate of agricultural growth, more rural industry output and employment would be generated if rural industry is put on a more equal footing with Bangkok-based industry. Even more important would be the catalytic and dynamic effects of such a stategy: modest development assistance could demonstrate the potential of rural industry in the absence of discriminating policies, thereby facilitating the reform of current industrial policies.

How much additional employment would the promotion of rural industry generate? The answer depends on the extent of the promoted industries as well as on the general economic conditions, particularly the growth of agriculture. Wattanavitukul et al. (1980) reports an employment elasticity for (rural) industry with respect to GDP of 0.98 compared to only 0.3 for agriculture. Rural industries are usually small and more labor-intensive than Bangkok-based industries for a good reason: labor is cheap and capital expensive. Any assistance to rural industry, especially with credit, and the consequent expansion would alter the relative prices of capital and labor and the labor intensity of the industry.

The prevailing factor intensity in a given industry is due partly to technological reasons and partly to economic reasons (e.g., relative prices). Economic factors may reflect distortions. In urban areas we observe relatively high wages because of unions and minimum wage legislation *and* low cost capital because of subsidized interest and investment promotion. In the rural areas we observe low wage rates because of seasonal unemployment and underemployment, imperfect mobility, no minimum wage, or unions *and* high cost capital, informal credit, etc.

To the extent that the labor intensity of rural industry is caused by price distortions, a correction of these distortions or lowering of the cost of capital (through credit) to the rural industry would reduce rural industry's contribution to employment through substitution. On the other hand, the rural industry would expand, generating more employment as a result of its increased profitability. The net effect on employment would depend on the relative size of (a) the elasticity of substitution between labor and capital, (b) the production elasticity of labor (or employment elasticity), (c) the elasticity of output with respect to the price of capital, and (d) economies of scale. Empirical work is needed to obtain estimates for these important parameters before the net effect of alternative policies on employment can be precisely assessed. On balance, however, we can reasonably expect rural employment to increase appreciably.

Table 3.13 shows the present regional distribution of industrial activity: the central region, essentially the greater Bangkok area, accounts for 88 percent of the total value added compared to 4 percent by each of the other three regions where two-thirds of the Thai population live. This distribution is partly the result of comparative advantage and partly the result of a policy bias against the rural industry and in favor of Bangkok. With modest but catalytic development assistance to rural industry with gradual reform of industrial trade and investment promotion policies, it should be possible to stimulate rural industry or disperse some of the existing activity to regional centers and provincial towns and to increase its labor-intensity. The rising transportation cost is an added factor working in favor of production near the source of raw materials and the market as 90 percent of the consumers live outside Bangkok.

To be successful, the promotion of rural industries should be built on the basic features of the rural areas: the availability of raw materials, the seasonality of labor supply and the dispersion of the market. The emphasis should be on restoring the comparative advantage of the rural areas

Table 3.13
Statistics of Regional Industries in Thailand

	Year	Central	South	North	Northeast	Total
1. Population (million persons)	1976	14.1	5.3	9.0	14.8	43.2
	1982	16.3	6.0	9.8	16.7	48.8
2. GDP From manufacturing	1976	54.8	1.9	3.3	3.0	63.0
	1980	118.1	4.9	5.4	6.1	134.5
3. Distribution of manufacturing Value added by region (%)	1976	87.0	3.0	5.2	4.8	100.0
	1980	87.8	3.6	4.0	4.6	100.0
4. Growth rates of manufacturing Value added (%)	1976–1980	21.2	26.7	13.1	19.4	20.9
5. Share of manufacturing value added in regional GDP (%)	1976	25.7	5.0	6.1	6.1	18.7
	1980	27.1	6.0	5.9	6.4	19.6
6. Distribution of products by region (%)						
6.1 Office of The Board of Investment	1960–1982	84.7	7.1	5.6	2.6	100.0
6.2 IFCT	1960–1981	76.8	7.2	7.9	8.1	100.0
6.3 SIFO	1964–1981	63.9	7.2	12.5	16.4	100.0
7. No. of factories	1973	14,654	4,258	6,202	10,743	36,057
(Percent)		(41.2)	(11.8)	(17.2)	(29.8)	(100.0)
	BKK	8,293	–	–	–	–
(Percent)		(23.0)				
	1979	27,718	6,797	10,885	22,336	67,736
(Percent)		(40.9)	(10.0)	(16.1)	(33.0)	(100.0)
	BKK	14,337	–	–	–	–
(Percent)		(21.2)				
8. Ranking of Industries (based on No. of factories)						
Rank 1		Processed foods	Wood products	Tobacco	Processed foods	
Rank 2		Textiles	Rubber & rubber products	Processed food		
Rank 3		Chemical products & wood	Processed food	Wood products	Textiles & non-metalic mineral products	

Source: NESDB (quoted from Akrasanse 1983)

(rather than subsidizing any particular line of production) *vis-à-vis* Bangkok by improving infrastructure, making credit available at competitive cost, providing technical assistance and market information and assisting in skill development. What industries are likely to have a comparative advantage? Two obvious candidates are agri-based industries which are favored by raw material availability and transport cost, and cottage industries which are small and do not require expensive machinery and, therefore, can be operated on a seasonal basis. Finally, export oriented, labor-intensive industries, such as textiles and handicrafts, might have a comparative advantage if based near town centers and linked to a reformed export promotion policy which is not biased in favor of Bangkok. (For more details, see Akrasanee, 1983.)

The rural industry's contribution to the national objectives of equity and stability lies in its potential to increase the demand for labor in the rural areas, particularly the northeast and the north. A stronger demand for labor is expected to have two related effects: increased rural employment especially during the slack season, and upward pressure on unskilled and semi-skilled wages.

Additional rural employment at higher wages is certain to improve rural incomes both in absolute terms and *vis-à-vis* Bangkok and central region incomes. Both equity and alleviation of poverty would have been served since the landless and the small farmers are likely to benefit more than other socio-economic groups from a rural employment strategy. Equally important is the effect on socio-economic and political stability. Availability of year-round rural employment at above-subsistence wages is certain to stem the destablilizing flow of landless and marginal farmers into watershed areas, marginal lands and the Bangkok slums. The long-term sustainability of Thai agriculture is intimately linked to the condition of the watersheds, which has been deteriorating in recent years at an alarming rate (see Panayotou, 1983). This raises the issue of linkages between rural industry and agriculture.

The important linkages from agriculture to rural industry and employment in Thailand have been well documented (see World Bank, 1983). However, little attention has been paid to the equally important linkages from rural industry and employment to agriculture: (a) the increased demand for agricultural products as inputs (raw materials) for industry; (b) the increased demand for agricultural products for consumption resulting from the increased incomes (e.g., more employment at higher wages) of rural poor with high income elasticity of demand for food; (c) increased supply of agricultural inputs such as implements, containers, transport and repair and service of agricultural machinery; (d) generation of cash income, the subsistence farmer's most scarce resource, for the purchase of inputs such as fertilizer, seed, and pesticides needed for agricultural intensification; (e) reduction of risk aversion resulting from the increase in income and the diversification of its sources leading to adoption of modern agricultural technologies and increased input use; and (f) improvement of agriculture's water and soil resource base by attracting squatters out of the watersheds and marginal lands thereby reducing the incidence and severity of floods and droughts, soil erosion and sedimentation of irrigation systems.

How strong these linkages are is an empirical question requiring further study. However, we can identify the factors on which the strength of these linkages would depend: (a) the employment coefficient of rural industry; (b) the food and fiber input of rural industry; (c) the income elasticity of those who gain additional employment; (d) the magnitude and distribution of income generated; (e) the farmer's attitude towards risk at different income levels and the yield variability of new technologies; and (f) the mobility and responsiveness of marginal farmers to economic incentives outside agriculture. The available evidence on these parameters suggests that the linkages from rural industry and employment to agriculture are likely to be anything but trivial.

With strong linkages running both ways, we expect a mutually supporting and reinforcing relationship between rural industry and agriculture. The current level of funding of agriculture, appropriately complemented with a modest development assistance for rural industry and a gradual reform of government policies to put rural Thailand on equal footing with the center, provides hope that the national objectives of sustainable growth, improved income distribution and stable government and society can be attained.

VIII CONCLUSION

The purpose of this study has been to identify the most appropriate investment strategy for Thailand during the second half of the 1980s and the early part of 1990s. To do this, we considered a large number of parameters: (a) the dominance of agriculture in the Thai economy and its gradual structural change; (b) the current level of funding for agriculture compared to its absorptive capacity; (c) the growth prospects of agriculture in the absence of additional public investment beyond current levels; (d) the dimensions of the employment problem in the light of projected growth rates of the labor force and of agricultural and industrial employment; (e) the bias of agricultural and industrial policies against the rural areas and the likelihood of policy reform; and (f) the potential of rural industry for growth and employment generation and linkages with agriculture.

Our findings suggest that agriculture is generously funded beyond its absorptive capacity and has excellent growth prospects throughout the 1980s, despite the approaching limits to land expansion, provided that current efforts at agricultural policy reform continue. An intensified agriculture, however, is expected to generate little additional employment for the rapidly growing labor force. For political reasons, the Bangkok-based industry is expected to continue to receive generous promotional privileges and protection, thus maintaining its capital intensity in the face of relatively abundant low-cost labor. Of the remaining options, rural industry, which has received little assistance thus far, and has been heavily discriminated against by government policies, holds the greatest promise for additional rural growth and employment generation in line with the national objectives of growth with equity.

Rural industry, being intrinsically labor-intensive, would generate more employment per dollar invested than either agriculture or industry, thereby narrowing the employment gap without increasing significantly the budget deficit or the foreign debt. In fact, if the promoted rural industries are carefully selected to have a low import component and a high export value, the balance of trade/payments might improve as a result. Judiciously administered, a modest level of development assistance to rural industry not only promises to generate additional growth and employment but it is also likely to have catalytic effects on industrial policy reform. It is encouraging that the Thai government has included rural industry and employment among its priority areas for the Sixth National Economic and Social Development Plan now under preparation.

NOTES

1. During the Second Plan, agriculture's share in planned total development expenditures was 19 percent but its share in actual total expenditure fell below 15 percent.
2. Data for the Fifth Plan are not avaliable.
3. As we will see later the contribution of the private sector to capital formation in agriculture is adversely affected by capital market distortions and government policies that discriminate against agriculture.

4. The labor-output ratio is the amount of labor in persons per one thousand constant baht (1972 prices) worth of output.
5. A compromise figure between 6.581 million (World Bank, 1983, p. 174) and 7.709 million (Rijk and Meer/ADB, 1984, Annex L).
6. Based on the Labor Force Surveys, open unemployment rose from 85 thousand persons in 1972 to 457 thousand persons in the wet season of 1982 (see Hongladarom and Charsombat, 1984, p. 19).

REFERENCES

Akrasanee, N., (1983) "The Role of Government in Off-Farm Income and Employment Promotion," Akrasanee et al. (eds.), *Rural Off-Farm Employment in Thailand*, USAID/IFCT, Bangkok.

Hongladarom, Chira, and Pradit Charsombat, (1984) "Current Employment Situation with Specific Reference to Rural Employment." A paper prepared for a seminar on Employment Problems and Rural Credit in Thailand at Dusit Thani Hotel, March 31.

NESDB, (1981) *The Fifth National Economic and Social Development Plan (1982-1986)*, National Economic and Social Development Board, Office of the Prime Minister, Bangkok, Thailand.

Panayotou, Theodore, (1983) "Renewable Resource Management for Agricultural and Rural Development in Southeast Asia: Research and Policy Issue." A paper presented at the Fifth Biennial Meeting of the Agricultural Economics Society of Southeast Asia (AESSEA), Bangkok, November 16-19.

Rijk, A.G., and C.L.J. Van Der Meer, (1984) "Thailand Agricultural Assessment Study," Asian Development Bank, January.

Wattanavitukul, S., et al., (1980) "Labor Absorption in Thai Agriculture: An Exploratory Study," Faculty of Economics, Thammasat University, Bangkok, November.

World Bank, (1977) "Thailand: Special Report on Employment," October 6.

World Bank, (1978) "Thailand, Towards a Development Strategy of Full Participation, A Basic Economic Report," September.

World Bank, (1982) "Thailand Programme and Policy Priorities for an Agriculture in Transition," Volume 1-4, December 3.

World Bank, (1983) "Thailand, Rural Growth and Employment."

4

Hedging Your Great Grandchildren's Bets: The Case of Overseas Chinese Investment in Real Estate Around the Cities of the Pacific Rim[1]

MICHAEL A. GOLDBERG

I. INTRODUCING THE ISSUE AND ITS CONTEXT

The Issue

Generalized fears of foreign ownership of real estate take on specific form in British Columbia where they combine with longstanding xenophobia concerning Asians, particularly the Chinese and the Japanese (Adachi, 1976; Lee, 1976, and Ward, 1978). Thus, there are bold headlines when overseas Chinese in particular acquire visible and important parcels of property, despite the much greater scale of foreign real estate investment in Canada by the British and Germans (Cutler, 1975).

Our inquiry here grew out of a concern arising from the latent and frequently blatant xenophobia relating to people of Chinese ancestry and most recently relating to the increasing scale of real estate investment in Canada by overseas Chinese. Despite the intensity of feeling about the issue of overseas Chinese real estate investment, and despite the duration of the issue (it began in the late 1960s in earnest with the Hong Kong riots), relatively little analysis and serious research has been directed toward the subject. This chapter is a step in reducing some of our ignorance.

The Scope of the Research Problem

Attention below focuses on overseas Chinese real estate investment and its attendant capital flows around the cities of the Pacific Rim. We are interested in why these flows take place, where they flow from and where they are destined, who makes these investments, how investment decisions are made, and what types of real property are sought. The extraordinary growth of Southeast Asian economies has provided fuel for these recent flows and is likely to continue to do so in the future (Chen, 1979; Geiger and Geiger, 1973; Hsia and Chan, 1982; and Hofheinz and Calder, 1982).

In order to set these questions and their answers in a suitable framework, we begin with a detailed discussion of overseas Chinese populations, focusing on land, family and entrepreneurship. Having established the underpinnings of our analysis, the paper proceeds to discuss the study method and geographical areas of interest. Data sources and relevant related research will be reviewed in the third section of this chapter. The fourth section describes the findings of the research and attempts to tie these findings to the discussion of overseas Chinese communities, particularly dealing with land, family and business activity. The concluding section of the study summarizes the argument and the findings and tries to assess critically the strength and generality of the results.

II. THE BACKDROP: THE OVERSEAS CHINESE, AND THE ROLE OF LAND AND THE FAMILY IN CHINESE SOCIETY

The Overseas Chinese: Similarity in Diversity

Overseas Chinese communities have long attracted the attention of historians and China specialists (Purcell, 1965; FitzGerald, 1972; Williams, 1966).[2] More recently the focus has shifted to the anthropology of these communities, and in particular their commercial and cultural links (Wu, 1982 for Papua New Guinea; Omohundro, 1981 for the Philippines; Olsen, 1972 and De Glopper, 1972 for Taiwan; Ward, 1972 and Silin, 1972 for Hong Kong; Ryan, 1961 for Java; and Lau, 1974 for Singapore).

Contacts between China and the rest of Southeast Asia have a very long history dating back to before the Han Dynasty (i.e., the third century B.C.) (Purcell, 1965, pp. 8-22). The heyday of emigration ran for roughly seventy years beginning in 1860. Williams observes that the emigrating Chinese during the period 1860-1930 shared three characteristics. First, they were poor. Second, they were motivated to move by hopes of improving their economic well-being. Third, they viewed themselves as sojourners fully expecting to return to China.

By the end of the 1970s, overseas Chinese entrepreneurs had penetrated most sectors of the national economies where they were resident. The roots of Chinese economic activity in trade and industry are still apparent however as can be seen in Table 4.1.

Table 4.1

Occupational Distribution of Ethnic Chinese in Southeast Asia (Percentages)

	THAILAND (1955)	THE PHILIPPINES (1954)	MALAYSIA (1970)	INDONESIA (date unknown)
Government	0.02	–	–	0.6
Professions	1.59	40.0	–	1.5
Commerce and finance	50.84	41.0	24.0	36.6
Industry and handicraft	19.41	11.0	24.0	20.0
Domestic and other service	9.75	–	5.0	2.7
Agriculture	1.19	–	29.0	30.9
Unskilled	17.21	8.0	18.0	7.7
TOTAL	100.00	100.0	100.0	100.0

Source: Wu and Wu, 1980, p. 137.

Economic well-being laid the foundation for political difficulties for the Nanyang (overseas) Chinese which gave them greater incentive to succeed economically and remain essentially as visitors, hesitant to set down permanent roots for fear of persecution. David Wu's comments in this vein, although made in the framework of Papua New Guinea, conveniently summarize this state of affairs:

> The more the Chinese relied on wealth as their last resort, and the more they were involved in commercial ventures, the more envy or hostility they attracted, particularly after the date of self-government was decided.
>
> It has always been the intention of many of the Chinese to stay in Papua New Guinea, a country of birth. They have attempted to make readjustments on the eve of independence, but the realization of this goal depends now on the sociopolitical environment. Taking into account their new awareness and new identification, it is not improbable that those Chinese who stayed will eventually be accepted in the country. Until drastic measures are taken against the Chinese-Australians as a group, many will hang on to their homes and businesses as long as they can.
>
> After one hundred years of settlement, the Chinese in Papua New Guinea still share the same future of many overseas Chinese in Southeast Asia; that of utmost uncertainty (Wu, 1982, p. 162).

In his comprehensive review of the overseas Chinese in the Nanyang, Maurice Freedman provides an interesting example of the role of education in maintaining Chinese cultural awareness and separateness. His remarks relate specifically to Malaysia, but they have more general relevance to Southeast Asia.

> While Malaya was under British rule and the Chinese were regarded, and largely regarded themselves, as sojourners on foreign soil, their school system was as to form and content modeled on that of China. Chinese school culture then became one of the chief instruments in modern times for the expression of anticolonial sentiment, most dramatically so in Singapore where during the 1950's the Chinese schools formed a major center of ideological ferment and political action. But in independent Malaya, where the state can intervene more decisively in educational policy than its British predecessor and where a Malayan ideology can compete with Chinese, the old purely Chinese school system is already virtually dead. . . . The splendid irony of change has been that, since the withdrawal of the British

from Malaya, it has been English education which has begun to capture the allegiance of the Chinese (Freedman, 1979, pp. 10-11).

Education is seen as central to the continuance of business and commercial success as Omohundro notes with respect to the Chinese of Iloilo, a small town in the Philippines:

> Sons and daughters of the smallest petty merchant and the largest trader alike seek college educations. Filipinos and Chinese have attended college in enormous numbers in the last two decades. The most common specialization for Chinese is commerce, followed by engineering and business administration.
>
> Sons return with these degrees to work for their fathers in the family stores. Fathers say it makes sons better businessmen who know more law and government, accounting, taxes, and economics. But status within the family does not readjust to the graduates because experience is held in greater esteem by the less-educated elders. A college-educated son is rarely, if ever, promoted above an elder brother with only a high school degree.
>
> Daughters are also trained in business but only to the point of assisting the family rather than holding much responsibility (Omohundro, 1981, p. 147).

At several points so far, we have touched on Chinese superiority in business. It is sufficiently important to warrant some discussion here in its own right. Specifically, what are the unique characteristics of overseas Chinese business relations and styles (if any), and how might these be maintained, expanded and transmitted from one generation to the next?

Freedman considers a variety of facets of Chinese enterprises and concludes that the fundamental advantage possessed by Nanyang Chinese was their ability to handle money.

> The vast majority of the men who left southeastern China in the nineteenth century to make their fortune overseas were peasants or artisans. In Southeast Asia great numbers of them took to business; many grew very rich. The general economic success of the Chinese abroad could not have been due to any special business training in China because the commercial class played too small a role in the emigration. The prosperity of a great many of the first generation of Southeast Asian Chinese rested on their industriousness. The peasant Chinese was almost proverbially a hard worker; his patient toiling

habits were so often commented on that we can have little doubt that the capacity of overseas Chinese for regular and sustained work was founded in a discipline acquired at home. But the will and ability of Chinese to work hard could not have been the sufficient cause of their progress in the amassing of riches. They accumulated wealth because, in comparison with the people among whom they came to live, they were highly sophisticated in the handling of money. At the outset they knew not only how to work themselves but also how to make their money work (Freedman, 1979, p. 23).

A great deal of recent attention has been focused on Chinese business characteristics, and the common threads of this body of research will be reconstructed here. Redding and Hicks delineate a variety of traits that, taken together, can begin to differentiate Chinese business styles from those of other peoples.

Its principal characteristics may be tentatively proposed as follows:

1. Smallness of scale
2. Centralized decisionmaking with one key and dominant person
3. Strong family control via the occupancy of key positions
4. Low levels of structuring
5. A generally autocratic (though commonly benevolent) leadership style
6. A lack of formalism in planning, and high flexibility
7. Financial acumen of a high order
8. Reliance on trust in external business relationships (1983, p. 5)

Several points are worth elaborating. First is the degree of familism evident in the centralized control of the dominant person (usually the father or eldest brother) and the reliance on family in key positions. Related to this is the generally small scale of enterprises which is consistent with great flexibility and informality. Evidence for this style can be had from various overseas communities. In Papua New Guinea, for example, Wu (1982, p. 88) found:

Almost without exception, overseas Chinese societies demonstrate a common feature of entrepreneurship: the organization of kinship members in managing a small-scale enterprise which later expands both in terms of the number of kinsmen organized and the volume of business transacted. Business organization built on the basis of kinship has been characteristic of commercial development among over seas Chinese living in both rural and urban areas, in developing and developed countries. Examples of kinship-oriented entrepreneurship have been reported for the Chinese of Indonesia (D. Willmott 1960), Cambodia (W. Willmott 1970), Tahiti (Moench 1963), the Philippines (Omohundro 1973; Amyot 1973); the United States (Barnett 1960), and England (Watson 1975).

The foregoing relate to the internal organization of firms and demonstrate that there does seem to be a Chinese way of running businesses. This impression of a unique Chinese approach is reinforced when the internal organizational style is combined with external relationships with suppliers and customers and kinship ties in business. A key element is trust, and it is manifest in a diversity of ways in the complex web of business and associated social relationships. De Glopper's comments about business ties in Lukang, Taiwan, are of general and specific relevance in this discussion:

> The very first thing to say about the structure of business relations in Lukang is that one does not do business with people one does not know. No one deals with strangers. Business relations are always, to some degree, personal relations. They need not be very close, but both participants in a business relation should be acquainted, familiar, "siek-sai" as the Taiwanese say (cf. Mandarin *shu-ssu*) (De Glopper, 1972, p. 303).

In such personal interactions, success results from far more than cleverness or sharp business practices. It is firmly rooted in the perceptions that business associates hold of each other. Again, De Glopper notes:

> *Hsin-yung* refers to an individual's or a firm's reputation, reliability, credit rating. It is the most important thing in business, a firm's most valuable asset. People say that to start a business one needs capital, but capital isn't enough. One must have *hsin-yung*, and to have *hsin-yung* one must know people, have a good reputation with some set of people, such as the other members of one's trade (De Glopper, 1972, p. 304).

With so much emphasis placed on trust, it is not surprising that the informality noted by Redding and Hicks within Chinese organizations applies among them as well. Little in the way of formal contractual arrangements are made or apparently needed.

Overseas Chinese in the Philippines have traditionally negotiated all business and legal matters verbally or with a minimum of paperwork. These negotiations have been secured by community knowledge of the reputation of the parties involved. Civil suits and even many criminal suits between Chinese have been handled within the community by traditional methods of mediation, family responsibility, and intracommunity sanctions. Recourse to Filipino law and the courts has been extremely rare. But . . . as the Chinese community continues in its isolation from China in the Philippine environment, its members become less exclusively located within it and less dependent upon it. The inevitable outcome is a weakening of community sanctions against wayward members or against unpopular activities. The weakening of sanctions combined with increased competitive pressures in a stagnant commercial environment has led to more recourse to Filipino law and courts (Omohundro, 1981, pp. 74-75).

Of particular importance here is the inculcation of business values in succeeding generations. De Glopper (1972, p. 324) cites a Lukang proverb on the subject: ''It's difficult to raise a child who can do business.'' The process starts when children are very young, as Omohundro illustrates among the Iloilo Chinese:

Chinese in a shopkeeper's family get involved in the store operations almost from the time they start school. As children, they learn to operate the adding machine and the abacus and to write the character script used in accounting. As they grow older, they are expected to fill any role that is needed, from janitor to sales clerk and cashier. They will accompany their father to Manila on purchasing trips and learn about credit and suppliers. As members of the family they will be expected to oversee employees, help at inventory time, load and unload stock, and so eventually participate directly in every aspect of shopkeeping (Omohundro, 1981, p. 146).

Olsen (1972, p. 292-294) also found that Chinese children in Taiwan from business families possess very different values with respect to business, profits, government and competition.

The Family: The Essential Building Block in Chinese Society

One of the most striking features of Chinese societies to non-Chinese observers is the cohesion and importance of the family unit, both in its nuclear and extended forms. The institution of the family in China is a very old and central one. The family was seen as a key element in the Confucian order of a stable and harmonious state dating back roughly 2500 years.

Family relationships were a central facet of societal relationships and were ordered as follows:

1. Ruler/minister
2. Father/son
3. Elder brother/younger brother
4. Husband/wife
5. Friend/friend

Now these Five Human Relationships (*wu-lun*) were arranged in order of priority, and with the exception of the last one were all superior/inferior relationships too; and so they were intended to give guidance as to the correct weight to be put on any relationship. Properly observed there could be no conflict or friction within Chinese society or within the family group, for every member of the family and of society was held tightly in check by the duty and obedience which he owed to another. Properly observed there could be no conflict, because there was no area of human intercourse not covered explicitly or implicitly by one or another of the five clauses (Baker, 1979, p. 11).

Within the family unit, there is also a well-ordered set of relationships that parallel the five noted above. These "three relationships" serve to obviate disputes and reinforce authority within the family units much as the five did at a societal level. The hierarchy to be followed within the family is:

1. Generation
2. Age
3. Sex

When combined with the five relationships, these three imply that every person in classical Chinese Confucian society knew exactly his or her position. Everything was tightly ordered, "harmony" was maintained, and the "mandate of heaven" continued to be bestowed on such a society's rulers. Father-son relationships were particularly critical since they had enormous implications for family businesses and also for the smooth transition of the family (and the family business) from one generation to the next.

It is clear from the foregoing discussion that in any given period, Chinese societal interactions were extremely well ordered. However, over time, it was much harder to keep things so cohesive.

> Time is real. To the Chinese, society came before all. The family was continuous, beginning with dead ancestors and including the yet unborn. The human obligations that preserved the family and the pride in its continuity made it impossible to devalue time. The recluse or the Buddhist might say otherwise, but if he was not simply playing with ideas, then his opinion was regarded as socially destructive (Balazs, 1964, pp. 108-9).

In all this striving for permanence and family continuity in the face of time and change, land plays a special role. Beattie in fact ties continuity of leading families in T'ung-ch'eng county of Anhui Province (eastern China) directly to their holdings of land:

> There can be no doubt moreover that one major element in the survival of the enduring elite of T'ung-ch'eng . . .was its continuous effort to secure its wealth in the form of land. All the great families of the county were built up in their early days on land, and its attractions seem to have been increased, not diminished, by the growing commercialization and monetization of the local economy, especially the increased opportunities to sell rent grain on the market and to multiply the proceeds by usury (1979, p. 130).

Closely allied with land in perpetuating the family line is education. We saw earlier the importance of education in inculcating business values and skills and thus extending the family in time and also in wealth and influence. However, in traditional China, education was to be pursued in its own right since it was the road to power and prestige. China's civil service, nearly two-and-a-half millenia old, was the world's first to be filled through open competitive examination. To be a scholar was to have access to the civil service and the power and security that went with such posts in Imperial China. Indeed some went so far as to directly link learning and land. Beattie makes this explicit when citing patriarch Chang Ying (1638-1708) of T'ung-ch'eng country, Anhui Province.

> The key to the dual process of prolonging the lineage organization and maintaining its prestige was indeed Chang Ying's favourite prescription of land and study. Some inalienable property, no matter

how small, was essential to the group, or else it would have been impossible to keep up its corporate activities and its aid to members. Private landholding seems likewise to have been considered of vital importance to individual members, hence all the attempts to encourage its acquisition and to regulate its disposal. Educational traditions had to be perpetuated, both privately by individuals and publicly by lineage sponsorship, for without it there was a risk that the vital elite nucleus might become attenuated or even disappear (1979, p. 126).

Land and education are key elements in preserving the family lineage and keeping kinship relationships intact over time. In an urban setting, however, such as the ones that most overseas Chinese find themselves in today, land is replaced by the family business as the means to maintain the family through time. However, unlike land, which is viewed as permanent, business is riskier and more difficult to perpetuate. Omohundro (1981, p. 145) cites a common saying among overseas Chinese in Iloilo, Philippines to the effect that "No third generation stays rich."

Thus, in a non-rural environment, business takes the place of land as the means to sustain the family line. Business becomes much more than making a living; it is the perpetuation of the family and the Chinese family tradition, and thus overseas Chinese business skill and success must be seen against the background of the family and all its importance and not just as a means for achieving prestige and wealth in the short run. Chinese business relations, as we saw earlier, are heavily oriented toward long-run relations and *hsin-yung* (trust), completely in keeping with the long-run view of the family and the need to keep its line functioning over many generations.

Land: Its Historical and Cultural Significance

Essentially, this substitution of business for land is a product of the last one hundred years at most. However, even in urban settings in the Nanyang, the Chinese have not lost their penchant for real estate.

Land holds a central position in a rural society:

Throughout its history, China remained basically rural. The security of the family depended on the land it owned. To sell family land was like participating in a fraction of the family's death, and to buy land for the family was like holding a wedding, with its promise of fruitfulness and strength (Scharfstein, 1974, p. 5).

In his classic history of China, Eberhard traces the evolution of the modern importance of land to the end of the Chou period (third century B.C.) when land could be held by an individual family head and family units. (See also Balazs, 1964, pp. 101-25.) Eberhard suggests:

> As long as the idea that all land belonged to the great clans of the Chou prevailed, sale of land was inconceivable; but when individual family heads acquired land or cultivated new land, they regarded it as their natural right to dispose of the land as they wished. From now on until the end of the medieval period, the family head as representative of the family could sell or buy land. However, the land belonged to the family and not to him as a person (1962, p. 54).

We are reminded once again of the land-lineage we encountered above in looking at the Chinese concern with sustaining the family through many generations. In his study of family and kinship Baker makes the land-kinship connection rather forcefully:

> Land was the basis of family wealth and the most important form of property in traditional China. It had symbolic as well as economic value, and families would relinquish their holdings only when there was no other option for survival left to them (1979, p. 3).

In a system without primogeniture, where males of each generation share in the family's wealth (the land primarily in agrarian historical China), male progeny soon outstrip the ability of the family to increase landholdings and maintain their social and economic position. Thus, over time, family holdings grow and dissipate with succeeding generations. This rise and fall of family status and wealth, however, also kept the family unit vital and poised over the ages to reassert its ascendancy, paving the way for the economic vigour that typifies overseas Chinese business activities up to the present time.

> What this process of rise and fall in family fortunes meant was a society like a seething cauldron, with families bubbling to the top only to burst and sink back to the bottom. When they burst they shattered their land-holdings too, and the patch-work quilt effect caused by the constant fragmentation and re-agglomeration of land-holdings was a distinctive feature of the Chinese landscape. This very process of constant flux within families, while at the same time each family was fiercely competitive with others around it, ensured a kind of social control through a fluid balance of power (Baker, 1979, pp. 133-134).

Synthesis: Pulling the Disparate Pieces Together

We have explored a range of topics including: the family, business and economic activity and culture; education; land; social and economic cohesiveness and distinctiveness; and uncertainty and fear about the future of Nanyang Chinese communities and wealth.

These various elements were not readily separated. In fact, there were extremely close ties between the family and business competitiveness. Both of these were related to the legendary Chinese thirst for education. Finally, all of these in turn were closely interconnected with both the historical institution of land and property in China and with present day needs for acquiring and sustaining wealth by family units.

Behind all of these connections and complexities is the threat of being uprooted and/or discriminated against and, in the extreme, of facing physical violence. This fear, combined with the overpowering Chinese desire to provide for succeeding generations, yields an environment within which capital flows and investments will likely take place across national borders. Business know-how and connections provide the sufficiency conditions for these flows, while fear provides the necessary condition.

Against this backdrop, we can now move on to the details of the present study and explore the investment behaviour of overseas Chinese with respect to real estate investment in cities around the Pacific Rim. We begin by outlining the methods used in the work and then move on to set out the findings of the study and its basis in the background materials discussed.

III. THE METHOD

Initially, it had been hoped that there would be sufficiently detailed information to allow a rigorous quantitative analysis of capital flows among Pacific Rim countries, identified both by country of origin and destination and by source and use of funds. While such an analysis is possible within Canada (or the United States), it quickly became obvious that no such data source existed. Moreover, it became clear that there were virtually no hard data available on the subject of Pacific Rim capital flows for real estate purposes, let alone any detail on overseas Chinese sources. No comprehensive picture exists of such capital movements around the Pacific, though there are several "guestimates" for specific cities and regions such as Cutler's (1975) for Canada in general and Vancouver in particular, Daly's (1982) estimates for Sydney, Australia, Thrift's (1983) summary of Asian real estate investment in Australia (notably Sydney and Melbourne), and finally Zagaris' (1980) and Barak's (1981) figures of Asian investment in U.S. real estate.

After detailed discussions with colleagues in the university and with business people involved in Asian property markets and after reviewing the literature, a structure was arrived at for interviewing investors, real estate agents, and others. With the benefit of these beginnings, a decision was made to visit Hong Kong, Singapore, Kuala Lumpur and Bangkok during the month of May 1983. Contact was made with nearly forty individuals in these four cities in advance of the interviews. All in all, more than seventy people were interviewed, roughly distributed as follows: Hong Kong 35, Singapore 15, Kuala Lumpur 10, and Bangkok 10.

IV. THE FINDINGS

Circumstances vary dramatically among the four cities where interviews were conducted. These cities and their respective nations (Hong Kong excepted, of course) drew their Chinese populations from different parts of China. Thailand overwhelmingly received emigrants from northeast Guangdong (Teochiu-speaking people from the Swatow region), while Hong Kong is dominated by Cantonese speakers from southern Guangdong. Singapore and Malaysia, in contrast, drew large proportions of their Chinese population from southern Fujien province (Hokkien speakers). The widely varying regional backgrounds of the overseas Chinese in the four cities implies major differences in business and social practices.

It is useful to summarize the scale and role of Chinese economic activity in the four areas of interest. (Singapore and Hong Kong are essentially Chinese *in toto*, and Malaysia and Thailand are clearly dominated by Chinese businesses.) In their recent study of the overseas Chinese contribution to Southeast Asian economies, Wu and Wu (1980) provide a number of interesting estimates that illustrate the importance of the overseas in the region. They also provide some interesting information on Chinese enrolments in universities, which as we saw previously is of utmost importance to the Chinese and, as we will see shortly, is of great concern today where Chinese access to Malaysian universities is restricted through a quota system, the quality of Thai universities is increasingly suspect, and the scale of Hong Kong post-secondary institutions so limited as to preclude all but the most gifted and energetic. Singapore alone appears to provide a scale and quality of education at the university level to satisfy Chinese demands.

Returning to the data, Table 4.2 provides estimates of Chinese capital in Southeast Asia from 1930 through 1975, and shows a fourteenfold growth of such capital in four decades. The 1969 estimate is disaggregated in Table 4.3 to show the distribution by sector. The tertiary sector dominates such investment, undoubtedly because of massive overseas Chinese banking activity, followed by the secondary manufacturing sector. Primary activities (agriculture, forestry, fishing and mining) are less important, comprising less than 15 percent of total investment in Southeast Asia in 1969. (Note these figures exclude Hong Kong and Taiwan and therefore considerably understate investment.) Finally, Table 4.4 gives some idea as to the extent of Chinese banking activities in Southeast Asia and beyond.

This banking activity is of particular interest to us here both because of its magnitude and geographic scope, and because of the business connections that it implies around the Southeast Asia region. By extension, this skill with financial matters should also be of utmost relevance in understanding the flows of real estate capital specifically about the Pacific Basin. We are reminded again of Freedman's earlier observations concerning the historical antecedents of this financial acumen among the Chinese in the Nanyang.

The Interviews and Their Settings

Given the previously discussed differences in the Chinese communities of Hong Kong, Singapore, Malaysia and Thailand, we report on the results of the interviews city-by-city where we see different factors emerging as being most important. At the conclusion of this report we draw together some common themes that reappeared in the interviews in each city.

For consistency and to assist in comparison among the four cities, we report the findings under the following four headings.

A. Investment Flows and Their Origins and Destinations
B. Investment Criteria
C. Information Sources and Methods of Analysis and Evaluation
D. Methods of Investing

The most interesting of these are the first three since they vary most dramatically among the four cities and turn up some of the most surprising insights. In contrast, it turned out that there was relatively more homogeneity with respect to methods of investing.

Table 4.2

Selected Estimates of Chinese Capital in Southeast Asia (Current US $)

	VIETNAM	CAMBODIA	LAOS	THAILAND	MALAYSIA AND SINGAPORE	THE PHILIPPINES	INDONESIA	BURMA	TOTAL
Shozo Fukuda (1930)	126.9	–	–	251.3	264	101.3	333.3	–	1,077.4
H.G. Callis (1937)	80	–	–	100	200	100	150	14	644
China Yearbook (1948)	0.5	–	–	212.8	1,761.3	–	-550.3	100.5	2,625.4
Wu Ku (1960)	150	–	–	600	1,200	400	900	70	3,320
Yu Chung-hsun (1968)	80	–	–	700	1,200	500	400	50	2,930
Ho I-wu (1969)	430	55	40.1	412	1,470	573.5	704	135	3,819.6
Wu and Wu (1975)	–	–	–	3,737	7,845	1,289	2,570	–	15,441

Source: Wu and Wu, 1980, p. 32.

Table 4.3
Total Chinese Capital Investment in Southeast Asia, 1969 (Value in US $ Million)

	THAILAND		MALAYSIA		THE PHILIPPINES		INDONESIA		SINGAPORE		SOUTH VIETNAM		CAMBODIA		BURMA	
	Value	Percent	Value	Percent	Value	Percent	Value	Percent	Value	Percent	Value	Percent	Value	Percent	Value	Percent
Primary	73.0	17.7	250.0	35.7	10.0	1.7	-	-	70.0	9.0	100.0	23.3	5.0	9.1	-	-
Secondary	125.0	30.3	150.0	21.4	288.7	50.4	230.0	32.7	200.0	26.0	150.0	34.8	10.0	18.2	50.0	37.0
Tertiary	214.0	52.0	300.0	42.9	274.7	47.9	474.0	67.3	500.0	65.0	180.0	41.9	40.0	72.7	85.0	63.0
Total	412.0	100.0	700.0	100.0	573.4*	100.0	704.0	100.0	770.0	100.0	430.0	100.0	55.0	100.0	135.0	100.0

	TOTAL ASEAN		TOTAL SOUTHEAST ASIA	
	Value	Percent	Value	Percent
Primary	403.0	12.76	508.0	13.44
Secondary	993.7	31.45	1,203.7	31.85
Tertiary	1,762.7	55.79	2,067.7	54.71
Total	3,159.4	100.00	3,779.4	100.00

Source: Wu and Wu, 1980, p. 33
a. The figure for the Philippines includes as Chinese only those who are not citizens.

Table 4.4
Ethnic-Chinese Banks in Hong Kong and ASEAN, 1979

LOCATION OF HEAD OFFICE	TOTAL NO.	BANKS WITH FOREIGN BRANCHES (BASED ON LOCATION OF HEAD OFFICE)	PRIVATE AND COMMERCIAL BANK WHOLLY OR PARTIALLY OWNED BY ETHNIC CHINESE LOCATION OF OVERSEAS BRANCHES											
			Sing.	H.K.	Mal.	Indo.	Phil.	Thai.	Taiwan	U.S.	U.K.	Japan	Other	Total
Singapore	14	6	–	7	64	–	–	1	–	–	3	3	1	79
Hong Kong	24a	16	1	–	1	–	–	2	–	9	3	3	1	20
Malaysia	19	4	31	–	–	–	–	1	–	–	–	–	–	32
Indonesia	44	–	–	–	–	1	–	–	–	–	–	–	–	1
Thailand	12	2	1	2	1	1	–	–	1	1	1	2	–	10
Philippines	11	2	–	–	1	–	–	–	1	1	–	–	–	2
Total	124	30	33	9	66	1	–	4	2	11	7	8	2	143

Source: Wu and Wu, 1980, p. 99
a. Excluding thirteen PRC-controlled banks.

1. HONG KONG: BORROWED PLACE, BORROWED TIME ON RECALL[3]

Hong Kong investor thinking was so dominated by the lease renewal question that it was virtually impossible to separate investor behaviour from that all pervasive issue. My visit to Hong Kong in December 1982, followed closely on the heels of Mrs. Thatcher's abortive visit of September 1982, while the May 1983 visit, during which the bulk of the interviews were conducted, corresponded to the precipitous fall of the Hong Kong dollar, the continued plummeting of stock prices (especially property shares), and the further slide of the property market (Hong Kong Rating and Valuing Department, 1983; Lethbridge, 1980; Youngson, 1982; and Yung, 1982).

Nonetheless, most of the people interviewed had been through severe downturns before, and they were able to look beyond the short-run calamity to a longer run future. The result is a set of responses that both reflect short-term fears and economic uncertainty and a longer term view based on the need to diversify and preserve assets.

A. Investment Flows

In the initial interviews it was stressed that real estate investment flows are anything but one-way out of Hong Kong. Subsequent talks with people in Singapore, Kuala Lumpur and Bangkok confirmed this initial impression. Hong Kong was seen as an attractive destination for much overseas Chinese money within Southeast Asia.

Looking at outflows, North America, particularly the West Coast, was the most frequently cited destination. (New York and Toronto were seen as very attractive locations as well, but generally it was the West Coast with its relatively good access to Hong Kong which was preferred.) Australia, a popular destination previously, was seen as less attractive in view of restrictions through the Australian Foreign Investment Review Board (FIRB) on overseas real estate ownership. Australia also lost some of its attractiveness when it tightened its admissions regulations for overseas students (primarily overseas Southeast Asian ethnic Chinese) into its universities. Lastly, Singapore was seen as a most active real estate market and had attracted much Hong Kong investment in the face of the looming development of the Singapore Mass Rail Transit (MRT), then in the final planning stages. Much of this enthusiasm for Singapore has cooled recently with the glut in hotels and office buildings that is visible at the present time (Kaye, 1984).

B. Investment Criteria

It was noted previously that several people stressed that Hong Kong and the high growth areas of Southeast Asia (Fung-shuen and Mera, 1982) are the places to make money. The kinds of capital flows of concern here accordingly place less stress on capital appreciation and more on capital preservation (or capital conservation as it has come to be known in the trade). Overseas Chinese investors are not a homogeneous group by any means and a word of caution needs to be inserted at this point as different investors have quite different criteria.

The very largest investors, often in real estate or manufacturing, have a large diversification element in their investment behaviour. In contrast, smaller investors (who themselves still might be quite wealthy by any standard with assets in the CDN$5 to 10 million range), and many large investors also, are often less willing to take risks and therefore will trade-off considerable potential return for low-risk situations, whereas the true diversifier is willing to accept individual projects with reasonably high risk since it is the total portfolio that provides risk protection. Smaller investors will place a premium, in general, on safety, and relatively low returns on investment result.

Looking at the time horizon within which the investments are being made, it is not unreasonable to generalize here for both small and large investors and to note that investments abroad are almost always long term (ten years and longer). Thus, short-term profits will be sacrificed for long-term growth prospects and stability. This long-term view implies relatively lower levels of leverage (gearing is the Southeast Asian and British term) than would commonly be encountered in North America. Lower leverage implies lower risk and is certainly more suitable for long-term holdings and preservation of assets.

Over and above normal economic investment criteria relating to risks and returns, there is an enormously complex array of non-economic criteria at work here. Among the most important non-economic factors was the presence of family in the city where the real estate investment is to be made. Friends and business acquaintances were also seen as important. An unexpectedly important aspect of all this is the connection between education and real estate investment overseas, a connection that follows directly from the desire to invest, if possible, in conjunction with the location of family members abroad. Sending children to study abroad at the university level is almost a necessity because of the lack of university space in Hong Kong. It is interesting in this regard to note that both the United Kingdom and Australia have recently tightened up considerably and raised the costs of university education for foreign (largely overseas Chinese) students. This has incurred the wrath of overseas Chinese in all the cities where interviews were conducted and will quite likely have an impact on overseas Chinese investment plans in both those countries. Several contacts in Hong Kong mentioned that having the children at university encouraged personal visits, which increased the familiarity with the potential investment destination. Also, quite often small real estate investments were made to house the children while at university and/or to provide foreign source income to pay for schooling and living abroad. A spin-off of these small investments was stated to be that they gave the children experience in doing business and managing their own business affairs. All of this is remarkably in keeping with the discussion earlier about inculcation of business values (Omohundro, 1982; Silin, 1972; and Wu, 1982) and about education (Omohundro, 1981; Beattie, 1979; Wu, 1982; Purcell, 1965, and Williams, 1966) both in traditional China and among the Nanyang Chinese.

It is particularly interesting to observe here that one of the reasons given for interest in Canadian real estate was the enormous number of Hong Kong residents who had attended universities in Canada. (An estimate by the Commission for Canada in Hong Kong put the number of Hong Kong-based Canadian university alumni at close to sixty thousand people).

Political stability was another factor of concern, and English-speaking democracies, particularly those with growth potential, were seen as being superior locations. Canada, the United States and Australia were attractive for this reason.

Immigration policy is increasingly of interest to Hong Kong people. At the minimum, having children establish themselves as citizens in a stable democracy such as Canada or the United States is seen as an essential means for perpetuating the family unit.

Finally, there are several criteria that are not strictly economic nor completely devoid of economic content. They are not central criteria, but they do matter at the margin. Tax treatment of overseas investors is important, and foreign withholding taxes and other specifics are of concern. Inheritance taxes similarly play some role, though apparently a surprisingly minor one. Foreign ownership legislation is another matter of concern for two reasons: first, because it is indicative of attitudes toward foreign investment, and second because of the costs and difficulties in working within its regulations.

C. Information Flows and Evaluation Methods

Family members, friends and business associates were the most important information sources by far. The earlier observation about the Lukang

Chinese to the effect that one does not do business with someone he does not know is borne out here (De Glopper, 1972). Once again, education plays a significant part since the children (or other family members) studying abroad provide valuable information sources in their own right. Moreover, visits to foreign countries to see the family members while in university provide additional opportunities for potential investors to make contacts.

Real estate brokers play a relatively smaller role, except for very large investments, though once contacts have been made, brokers move out of this general category of impersonal business acquaintances and into the category of business associates, *if* they have performed honestly and well. Virtually all interviewees spoke negatively about the "carpet-bagger" real estate fairs that have been promoted in Hong Kong by off-shore real estate agents during the past few years.

Finally, one cannot underestimate the value of such periodicals as the *Asian Wall Street Journal* and especially *Asiaweek* and the authoritative *Far Eastern Economic Review*. One is consistently impressed by the level and accuracy of detail about Pacific Rim property markets and economic conditions that they present. Worldwide real estate agencies such as Jones, Lang Wootton and Collier's International also publish rather detailed reports on Pacific Rim property markets and the economies of the region, as does the Hong Kong Shanghai Bank's Economic Research Department. Taken together, there is a remarkable amount of information about the whole region published regularly and widely available.

Turning to how this information is evaluated, we see once again a central role for trusted family and friends and business associates, including local lawyers and accountants who are resident in the city where the prospective investment is located. Personal visits are also extremely common, and a virtual necessity for larger and more complex transactions. All sources suggested rather simple investment rules for evaluating the information with a heavy dose of "gut-feel" and past experience. The highly centralized family and business organization that we saw in our previous discussion (Ward, 1972; De Glopper, 1972; Omohundro, 1981; and Wu, 1982) is at work here as well.

D. Methods of Investing

In keeping with the security motive and risk aversion criterion, low leverage seems to be a generally followed rule. Only large and sophisticated investors appear to buy properties by using funds borrowed abroad. Low leverage, long-term time horizon and safety (capital conservation) typify the investments in overseas real estate.

Two other facets of overseas Chinese real estate investing are noteworthy. First, is the ease with which funds could be transferred. Using telegraphic funds transfer (T/T), monies can be moved across international boundaries within hours. Second, once funds are so moved, they tend to stay abroad, building a larger capital base for additional investment in the long term.

2. SINGAPORE: A RETURN TO THE AGE OF CITY STATES?

In May 1983 Singapore was just at or a bit past the peak of its most recent real estate boom. Subsequently the market has fallen rather sharply in hotels, offices and retail facilities (Kaye, 1984). However, there was concern, but not gloom, differentiating Singapore from Hong Kong. There was another basic difference between Hong Kong and Singapore, and for that matter between Singapore and the other cities we are looking at. It is the only city or state where the resident overseas Chinese are dominant and have significant control over their own political destinies.

A. Investment Flows

Flows of real estate investment capital into Singapore were extremely large. Not only were Hong Kong people taking advantage of Singapore's rapid growth, but so also were Malaysian and Indonesian Chinese. The last two groups are located very close to Singapore, have many business ties and invest in Singapore real estate accordingly. The education connection also looms large here, Singapore being the destination of Indonesian Chinese students, particularly, but also ethnic Chinese from the Philippines and Malaysia. Indonesia, especially, lacks credible secondary schools and universities, and the proximity and excellence of Singapore's schools attract Indonesian and Malaysian Chinese in large enough numbers so that the National University of Singapore has had to limit foreign student enrolments from these countries.

To date, capital outflows from Singapore have been relatively modest, especially to North America. The investment that has occurred so far has been largely to diversify assets and has been destined for the United Kingdom and Australia. The United Kingdom has lost its glamour as a result of sluggish growth and its education policies (as noted earlier in the context of Hong Kong). Australia is similarly moving out of favour because of the Foreign Investment Review Board and its overseas education policies. Previously, Australia's relative proximity (six hours to Perth by frequent non-stop air services and nine hours to either Melbourne or Sydney by equally frequent service) and close business ties with Singapore meant that Australia was an ideal location for diversification.

With the fall from grace of both the United Kingdom and Australia,

Singaporeans are beginning to look seriously at North America. Preferred locations are on the West Coast because of travel time considerations.

B. Investment Criteria

Given the relative security and growth possibilities in Singapore, investment motives are quite different from those in Hong Kong. Diversification is the prime motive. All respondents said that Singapore was the best place to make money because of its long-term growth. They did, however, feel the need to diversify because of the small scale of the island state. A subsidiary reason for investing is rooted in capital preservation and perpetuation of the family. A final determinant is based on "where the kids go to school." It was suggested that a couple of apartments "were a good way to earn tuition for the kids, provide them with good housing, and give them a little experience to look after the investment." Exchange and foreign ownership controls are also important. This works against investment in Australia, but very much in favour of Canada and the United States. Canada, moreover, was seen as an exceptionally safe place to live and to send children to university.

C. Information Flows and Evaluation Methods

Given Singapore's distance from North America, information flows are somewhat restricted. Previous population movements from China to North America established pools of friends and family, largely from Guangdong, and provided a good set of information linkages for Hong Kong residents. Singaporeans trace their roots largely back to Fujien province, and relatively fewer Fujienese moved to North America; thus, Singaporeans lack the extensive North American networks of information that are typical of Hong Kong.

Investment opportunities are brought to the attention of investors primarily by real estate brokers with international connections. Banks also serve as information sources. Family and friends, as always in Chinese communities, provide additional useful information. Newspaper advertisements of properties abroad are increasing as are the real estate seminars that have annoyed people in Hong Kong, but they remain a minor element. It appears that no one information channel is dominant, but rather all serve different potential investors at different times in Singapore.

As for evaluation criteria, several individuals pointed out that Singapore investors are much less sophisticated than those in Hong Kong. Examples were given of several Singapore companies that have been very badly hurt in the United States in their eagerness to get into West Coast markets in the absence of adequate information and analysis. All this can be expected to change significantly as Singaporeans obtain more experience in overseas real estate investment and analysis and become more familiar with these markets.

D. Methods of Investing

Because overseas real estate investment by Singaporeans is still relatively new, the methods for investing are reasonably conventional. Low leverage is again the rule, and T/T is the vehicle for moving the funds to purchase the desired property. Several people pointed to an interesting rule which set the leverage as a function of the cash flow that the investment could generate. Here the question is how much money must be paid in cash up front so that the resulting mortgage payments can be covered by cash flow from the property.

3. KUALA LUMPUR, MALAYSIA: CHINESE ANXIETIES ARE GROWING

In Malaysia, we see up close the kinds of problems that the overseas Chinese have faced with respect to indigenes, despite the fact that Malaysian Chinese constitute nearly 40 percent of the population. Under the New Economic Policy, there must be 30 percent bumiputra (Malaysian indigenous people) ownership of Malaysian corporate wealth (Tasker, 1983). In many instances this has led to confiscation of Chinese wealth in functional terms, since Malaysian Chinese have had to take on bumiputra partners to meet NEP requirements at costs to the bumiputra far less than market value. Combined with some restrictions on holding political office, Islamic fundamentalism on the fringes of the Islamic state religion, quotas on Chinese students at universities, and more general concerns about education in Malaysia and particularly education in the Chinese language, we have almost a prototype of the kinds of problems Wu and Wu (1980, pp. 173-193) catalogue so succinctly to show what the overseas Chinese minorities have had to cope with in Southeast Asia. Despite their significant numbers and overwhelming importance to the Malaysian economy (or perhaps because of these very strengths), the Chinese of Malaysia find themselves having to be alert to heightened discrimination and threats to their continuity.

A. Investment Flows

Malaysia is the recipient of only very modest inflows of real estate investment. The flows that do come into Malaysia are largely from Chinese in Indonesia, Thailand and Singapore. Recent restrictions on foreign investment have meant that investment over M$1 million must be cleared in advance by the Foreign Investment Review Committee.

As for outflows of capital, they have largely been destined for Hong Kong when it was booming, for Singapore during its recent growth phase and because of its proximity and historical ties with Malaysia, and increasingly for North America. Canada is relatively less known than the United States as a destination for capital. Sunbelt cities seem preferred (e.g., West Coast, Mountain and southern states). Australia and the United Kingdom used to be important places to invest, but both are now on the wane for reasons cited earlier.

B. Investment Criteria

Diversification is the prime criterion. Accordingly, good locations are sought with minimum risk, yet with the possibility of capital gains in the longer run. Low leverage in overseas investments is a concomitant of such a diversification objective.

In light of anti-Chinese feeling in Malaysia, safety and security for the family is a consideration, perhaps one of growing importance, though at present largely in the backs of people's minds. Fears of potential Vietnamese aggression, the possibility of Thailand succumbing to insurgents from Vietnam and Cambodia, and the shrinking likelihood of return of ideological rule in China all influence decisions at the margin.

Other criteria that were mentioned in several instances included immigration possibilities tied to investments. Given the recent emphasis on the Bahasa Malay language and the downplaying of Chinese language and education, there is a growing concern about the quality of education, and the need to send children abroad for schooling is once more linked to possible investments and to immigration.

The longer run nature of these concerns was stressed repeatedly. In the short run it was felt that Malaysia presented the best opportunities for economic growth and prosperity (not unlike what had been repeated frequently in Hong Kong). However, the need to think in the long-term (very much a Chinese need) did imply looking abroad and employing criteria such as those mentioned here.

C. Information Flows

Again, unlike Hong Kong where personal contacts abroad dominated information flows, Malaysian investors relied on a broad range of sources. Real estate brokers from around the world provide much information. So do bankers, especially large international banks with real estate departments. Newspaper advertisements and unsolicited letters with information about overseas properties have become increasingly common, though both were held in low esteem. Good leads came from brokers, bankers, friends, and business associates with whom one had good contacts. These broker and business ties seemed to be the most important. Family ties and sources were less important since there are fewer Malaysian emigrants and therefore fewer family connections abroad. As with both Singapore and Hong Kong, the real estate fairs (mostly sponsored by Australians in Kuala Lumpur) are held in low regard.

Evaluation of the information varied tremendously. Common to all was the need to visit the property first hand to inspect it and assess the reliability of the preliminary information presented to the investor. Larger and more experienced investors relied on more sophisticated tools and more detailed site visits and analyses. For most, however, simple rules of thumb were used. Given the low leverage that seemed to characterize all of these investments, there was really little need to do much analysis other than to be assured that the property was well situated and would maintain or increase its value because of location.

D. Methods of Investing

Investments are carried out in the same kind of direct manner seen in both Hong Kong and Singapore. There is a difference in Malaysia though, since foreign exchange movement between M$10 thousand and M$2 million must be registered. Above M$2 million, permission must be sought from the central bank to move money legally. This is a minor inconvenience apparently at this point, but a consideration nonetheless.

Funds are moved by T/T as elsewhere. Monies are left abroad and not repatriated, particularly given the exchange control situation and the possibility that it can get tighter. As with investors from other cities, foreign companies are frequently created using local nominees both for tax purposes and often for anonymity as well.

4. BANGKOK: THE CHINESE AFTER A CENTURY IN RESIDENCE

After more than a century, the Chinese have become absorbed into Thai society. The last anti-Chinese race riots were in 1956, and they are largely forgotten now. Despite their dominance of the Thai economy and their visibility, the Chinese in Thailand, while eternally wary, appear relatively secure. Aside from latent resentment against their economic dominance of the country, some concerns were voiced about Vietnam and military threats, though interestingly, it was the Chinese Communists in Beijing, the bane of Thailand only two decades earlier, who are now often seen as stabilizers of Southeast Asian politics. In this setting, a relatively low level of overseas investment is given prominence, although several sources suggested that there may well be more importance to the subject than people were willing to admit.

A. Investment Flows

There are modest flows into Thailand by overseas Chinese for real estate investment. The sources are mostly ASEAN countries (notably Indonesia and the Philippines) and some from Hong Kong. Outflows are more significant and are directed toward Hong Kong (slowed by recent political and economic events), the People's Republic of China (particularly such special economic zones as Shenzhen in Guangdong near Hong Kong), the America West Coast (Los Angeles and San Francisco most notably), and Vancouver in Canada. Australia's role has declined for reasons noted elsewhere. Thailand is the only country in the group that is not in the Commonwealth. It was all the more intriguing to find education in an English-speaking country to be of such importance. This is consistent with earlier discussions about the centrality of education to the Chinese. More interestingly, one can infer that English education also carries with it some special attributes relating to its utility in international trade and overseas business transactions, as well as access to certain types of education, such as business administration, that are dominated by English texts and research material.

B. Investment Criteria

It was noted by several contacts that risk and leverage were acceptable ways to earn money in Thailand. However, to retain income, putting money abroad in low or no leverage situations was preferred. As in other cases, diversification is closely allied with preservation both of capital and the family line.

Because of the relatively long tenure of the Chinese in Thailand, there seemed to be some interesting differences between older Thai Chinese who have led rather sheltered lives and younger people, many of whom were educated abroad. The older generation seems more conservative (in contrast with Hong Kong) and more interested in staying with those economic activities that have served them well. The younger and frequently foreign-trained generation was said to be more innovative. However, both agreed on the need to invest abroad; the older group because of memories of past difficulties, the younger cohort because of its ties and experiences abroad.

Schooling is a consideration as well, though it was much less important than in the other cities discussed here. However, where children do attend schools abroad, particularly universities, these educationally based ties do come into play in the investment process.

C. Information Flows and Methods of Evaluation

Nominally, exchange controls make it illegal to invest directly abroad without permission. Thus, newspaper advertisements in Thai papers are not supposedly an information source. However, foreign newspapers and periodicals do provide a wealth of information on the existence of investment opportunities and brokers. Brokers from abroad are quite active in Thailand, and they do develop some limited business from direct solicitation. Local brokers are also relatively limited in their activities because the Thai market itself is small. By far the most important sources of information are from business associates, friends, travel and, again, children attending university abroad.

Evaluation of the information takes similar forms to those discussed earlier. Visits to see the property in question seemed to be the most common means to evaluate prospects. Friends and family are also normally called in to help evaluate the data and the property. Often assistance from overseas bankers is sought as well. Rather simple rules appear to apply. For example, if the property carries itself with a large downpayment, and if it is likely to maintain its value, then it should be purchased. We return thus to the preservation criterion with low leverage and a long-term investment horizon.

D. Methods of Investing

The mechanics of investment once again appeared to be very straightforward. The only problem revolved around the exchange controls that are in place since, in theory, no money can leave Thailand legally. However, several sources stated that the spread between the official rate of exchange and the black market rate was at most 1/4 percent for large transactions over US$10 thousand and that transactions in virtually any amount (well into the millions of dollars US) could be handled in less than a day, indicating a vigorous black market and an almost completely ineffective system of exchange control. Once the funds were moved out of the country, they would be forwarded anywhere in the world by T/T as elsewhere.

V. SUMMARY AND CONCLUSIONS, NEEDED EXTENSIONS, AND POLICY CONSIDERATIONS

1. Summary and Synthesis of the Findings

Trying to summarize and synthesize the foregoing findings runs the risk of blurring over important differences in the quest for useful generalizations. In some areas the risk is worth taking, while in others the differences are too important to overlook. However, for the sake of brevity, Table 4.5 serves as a convenient summary.

2. Extensions

Several extensions follow logically. First, the scope can be expanded geographically by adding such countries as Indonesia, the Philippines and Taiwan, and such cities as Penang, Jahore Bahru and Malacca in Malaysia, and Chiang Mai in Thailand. It can also be expanded by developing additional contacts in the cities visited in this study. Finally, conditions have changed since these interviews were conducted, so moving the study ahead in time would provide very useful insights.

A second source of extensions deals with methodology. A number of detailed case studies could be undertaken in various cities using different types of investments and investors. Comparing across case studies could also lead to generalizations against which the present findings could be contrasted.

3. Policy Implications

There is enormous scope for government policy to influence and shape the nature of overseas Chinese real estate investment in Canada. If we want to curtail it, this can be accomplished through legislation concerning foreign investment (as has been done in Australia) and through closing down entrepreneurial class immigration. However, if we want to encourage such investment, then a number of policies would seem in order.

1. We should continue the entrepreneurial immigrant class to attract leading overseas Chinese entrepreneurs to broaden our entrepreneurial and economic base.

2. Given the importance of education, we should encourage each province to certify private secondary schools so that potential students have assurances that these are *bona fide* and good quality educational institutions. We should also inform overseas Chinese about the fees that can be paid for access to our excellent public secondary school system. At the

university level, we should continue wide access and, if necessary, charge differential fees only for those who can afford to pay.

3. Lastly, we should promote greater access by air with Pacific Rim nations and their airlines. As well we should provide prospective investors with as much information as possible about doing business in Canada through our trade commissioner services in Southeast Asia.

4. Broadening the Picture: World Cities, Circuits of Capital, The Changing Economic Order, and The Context of Overseas Chinese Real Estate Around The Pacific Rim and Its Emerging World Cities

Major changes are currently wrenching the world economy. Three changes are worth stressing here. First, there has been a shift away from producing goods and processing materials toward the production and processing of information and services. The impacts on cities have been particularly profound and unlikely to abate in the coming decade. Stanback and Noyelle (1982) explore several U.S. cities in this regard; Kwok (1982) looks at information and its role in the Hong Kong economy of the future; and Jacobs (1984a and 1984b) raises the issue with respect to cities in general across the globe.

Second, out of these changes have emerged a number of "world" cities. Financial transactions and expertise in moving capital internationally are of particular importance here and in the evolution of the changing system of world cities (McGee, 1984; and Thrift, 1983). Looking into the future, Cohen suggests:

> These trends, since they place more pressure on corporations and financial institutions in developed nations, will probably tend to further concentrate corporate and financial decision-making in present world centers, drawing decision-making activities away from national or regional centers. This would exacerbate uneven urban development in developed nations, particularly since the continued movement of productive activities overseas would further erode urban blue-collar jobs (1981, pp. 310-11).

The third change of relevance to our discussions is the emergence of the Pacific Rim as a major economic region. Gazing into the future, Hofheinz and Calder assert:

> it is one thing to doubt whether Eastasia can continue to grow at the same phenomenal rate, and quite another to believe that its fortunes

Table 4.5

Overseas Chinese Investment—Summary of Interview Findings

	HONG KONG	SINGAPORE	KUALA LUMPUR	BANGKOK
METHODS OF INVESTING				
Use Retained Foreign Earnings Abroad	1[a]	1	1	1
Telegraphic Funds Transfer	1	1	2	3
Shell Companies	2	2	2	2
Direct Investment/Equity Ownership	1	1	1	1
INFORMATION SOURCES AND METHODS OF ANALYSIS				
Direct Mail Advertising	3	2	2	2
Financial Institutions	3	2	2	2
Real Estate "Fairs"	3	3	2	3
Mass Media and Magazines	3		2	
Real Estate Agents	2	1	1	2
Site Visit/Inspecton	1	1	1	1
Trusted Friends and Business Associates	1	1	1	1
Family (incl. Children)	1	2	2	2
INVESTMENT CRITERIA				
Location of Family, Friends, Trusted Business Ties	1	1	2	2
Potential for Growth	2	2	2	2
Ease of Access from Southeast Asia	2	1	1	2
Linked to Location of Children's University	1	1	1	2
Possible Immigration	1	3	2	3
Capital Conservation	1	2	2	2
Portfolio Diversification	1	1	1	1

ORIGIN AND DESTINATION OF FLOWS

Other (South America, Other Asia)	3	3	3	3
Western Europe	3	3	3	3
Other Southeast Asia	2	2	3	3
Hong Kong	–	1	1	1
Singapore	2	–	1	2
United Kingdom	2	2	2	3
Australia	1	1	1	2
Other Canada/US	2	2	2	2
Western Canada	1	1	1	2
Western US	1	1	1	2

Source: Personal Interviews by Author.
a. 1 = very frequently cited; 2 = frequently cited; 3 = seldom cited

will be reversed. Short of a world war or some other cataclysmic event that interrupts the flow of commerce and raw materials, it is hard to conceive of a dramatic decline in Eastasian growth and performance, and the possibility exists of a considerable and sustained upward thrust. Given the deep-seated ills of Western societies, Eastasia may gain against the West even if, in comparison with past performance, it only stands still (1982, p. 251).

These changes hold special meaning for our focus, overseas Chinese real estate around the Pacific Rim. As the world moves toward economies strongly rooted in both information networks and advanced professional skills for generating and analysing data, Chinese enterprises and families should share disproportionately in this movement in view of their extensive international commercial ties and their past and continued heavy emphasis on education, particularly in the professions. Second, the growing importance of international finance, and its increasing focus on "world cities" (Thrift, 1983, pp. 2-9) again implies an expanded role for overseas Chinese in the development of world cities and the accompanying world financial dealings. Their traditional skills and experience with money (Freedman, 1979, pp. 23-26) and in international and regional banking (Wu and Wu, 1980, pp. 96-101; Wu, 1983, pp. 115-16), place the Chinese in an ideal position to take advantage of the kinds of changes that we have been discussing in the world economic and urban order. Third, the expected continued growth of the East Asia region and the surplus capital that such growth is likely to produce implies that there will be considerable additional sources of capital for international real estate and other investment in the future. Fourth, and finally, the continued ascendancy of a relatively limited number of key urban areas around the world implies that much of the international real estate investment will be directed toward these centres.

In summary, the present study, as suggested at the outset, began with modest goals and focus. It has become apparent, however, in the course of this research that we have set foot in an area that is of growing significance. The complexity which characterizes overseas Chinese societies, business practices, family relations, educational objectives, and the need to operate in a frequently hostile and always uncertain world, needs to be further unravelled, analysed and probed. The present effort is a tentative start in the direction of greater understanding. It is a step in any event, and as the great classical sage Lao Tzu observed, "the journey of a thousand begins with a single step." We hope the journey has at least begun here.

NOTES

1. An earlier and longer version of this paper appeared as a Working Paper of the Institute of Asian Research at the University of British Columbia. Financial support for this work was provided by a major grant to the Institute by the Max Bell Foundation of Toronto. The grant made it possible to conduct the interviews and obtain the necessary research assistance to carry out this work. I am particularly indebted to the Institute's Director, Professor Terry McGee, for his counsel and encouragement. The present work also formed the basis for a book, which probes the issues raised here in considerably more depth: Michael A. Goldberg, *The Chinese Connection: Getting Plugged Into Pacific Rim Real Estate, Trade, and Capital Markets* (Vancouver: University of B.C. Press, 1985). Again, this manuscript could not have been undertaken or completed without the assistance of both the Max Bell Foundation and the Institute of Asian Research.

2. One issue that we have carefully avoided is that of precisely defining the overseas Chinese. The authoritative study by Purcell (1965) is equally circumspect. Similarly, Williams (1966, p. 6) deals with the issue with the following broad definition to which we subscribe:

   An overseas Chinese is a person of some Chinese ancestry who views residence abroad as compatible with Chinese cultural identity and less certainly with some remote Chinese political orientation. The overseas Chinese considers his expatriation the result of his own or his forebears' economic strivings. He regards himself as a member of the overseas Chinese people, which is in turn, part of the greater Chinese nation, and is so regarded by those around him.

3. Here we want to make our apologies to the late Richard Hughes (1970) for borrowing from the title to his classic analysis of Hong Kong's political conundrum, *Hong Kong: Borrowed Place, Borrowed Time*.

REFERENCES

Adachi, Ken, (1976) *The Enemy That Never Was*, Toronto, Ont.: McClelland and Stewart.

Amyot, Jacques, (1973) *The Manila Chinese*, Quezon City, Philippines: Institute of Philippine Culture.

Baker, Hugh D.R., (1979) *Chinese Family and Kinship*, New York, N.Y.: Columbia University Press.

Balazs, Etienne, (1964) *Chinese Civilization and Bureaucracy*, New Haven, Conn.: Yale University Press.

Barak, Ronald S., (1981) *Foreign Investment in U.S. Real Estate*, New York, N.Y.: Law and Business, Inc.

Barnett, Milton L., (1960) "Kinship as a factor affecting Cantonese economic adaptation in the United States," *Human Organization*, Vol. 19, No. 1, pp. 40-46.

Beattie, Hilary J., (1979) *Land and Lineage in China*, Cambridge, Mass.: Cambridge University Press.

Chen, Edward K.Y., (1979) *Hyper-growth in Asian Economics*, London, England: The Macmillan Press Ltd.

Cohen, R. B., (1981) "The New Industrial Division of Labor, Multinational Corporations and Urban Hierarchy," in M. Dear and A. Scott, editors, *Urbanization and Urban Planning in Capitalist Society,* New York, N.Y.: Methuen, pp. 287-315.

Cutler, M., (1975) "How Foreign Owners Shape our Cities," *Canadian Geographical Journal,* Vol. 90, pp. 39-48.

Daly, M.T., (1982) *Sydney Boom Sydney Bust*, Sydney, Australia: George Allen and Unwin.

Daly, M.T., (1983) "The Revolution in International Capital Markets: Urban Growth and Australian Cities" (mimeographed), Sydney, Australia: Department of Geography, University of Sydney.

Dear, Michael, and Allen J. Scott, editors, (1981) *Urbanization and Urban Planning in Capitalist Society,* New York, N.Y.: Methuen.

De Glopper, Donald R., (1972) "Doing Business in Lukang" in W. E. Willmott, editor, *Economic Organization in Chinese Society,* Stanford, Ca.: Stanford University Press, pp. 297-326.

FitzGerald, Stephen, (1972) *China and the Overseas Chinese,* Cambridge, England: Cambridge University Press.

Freedman, Maurice, (1979) *The Study of Chinese Society,* Stanford, Ca.: Stanford University Press.

Fung-shuen, Victor Sit, and Koichi Mera, editors, (1982) *Urbanization and National Development in Asia,* Hong Kong: University of Hong Kong.

Geiger, Theodore, and Frances M. Geiger, (1973) *Tales of Two City-States: The Development Progress of Hong Kong and Singapore,* Washington, D.C.: National Planning Association.

Hicks, G. L., and S. G. Redding, (1982) "Industrial East Asia and the Post-Confucian Hypothesis: A Challenge to Economics" (mimeographed), Hong Kong: Department of Management Studies, University of Hong Kong.

Hicks, G. L., and S. G. Redding, (1983) "Uncovering the Sources of East Asian Economic Growth" (mimeographed), Hong Kong: Department of Management Studies, University of Hong Kong.

Hofheinz, Roy Jr., and Kent E. Calder, (1982) *The Eastasia Edge,* New York, N.Y.: Basic Books.

Hong Kong Rating and Valuation Department, (1983) *Property Review, 1983,* Hong Kong: Rating and Valuation Department.

Hsia, Ronald, and Lawrence Chau, (1978) *Industrialisation, Employment and Income Distribution,* London, England: Croom Helm.

Hughes, Richard, (1970) *Borrowed Place, Borrowed Time,* Harmondsworth, England: Penguin Books.

Jacobs, Jane, (1984a) "Cities and the Wealth of Nations," *The Atlantic,* Vol. 253, No. 3, pp. 41-66, March.

Jacobs, Jane, (1984b) "The Dynamic of Decline," *The Atlantic*, Vol. 253, No. 4, pp. 98-115.

Kaye, Lincoln, (1984) "A Sector Much Exposed on the Downside," *Far Eastern Economic Review*, Vol. 123, No. 10, pp. 55-56, 5 March.

King, Ambrose Y. C., and Rance P. L. Lee, editors, (1981) *Social Life and Development in Hong Kong*, Shatin, Hong Kong: Chinese University of Hong Kong.

Kwok, R. Yin-Wang, (1982) "Communication Needs in Hong Kong's Development," Hong Kong: Centre for Urban Studies and Urban Planning, University of Hong Kong.

Lee, C.F., (1976) "The Road to Enfranchisement: Chinese and Japanese in British Columbia," *BC Studies*, Vol. 30, No. 1, pp. 44-76.

Lethbridge, David (editor), (1980) *The Business Environment in Hong Kong*.

McGee, T.G., (1984) "Circuits and Networks of Capital: The Internationalization of the World Economy and National Urbanization," (mimeographed), Vancouver, B.C.: Institute of Asian Research, University of British Columbia.

Moench, R.U., (1963) "Economic Relations of the Chinese in the Society Islands," Unpublished Doctoral Dissertation, Cambridge, Mass.: Harvard University.

Olsen, Stephen M., (1972) "The Inculcation of Economic Values in Taipei Business Families," in W. E. Willmott, editor, *Economic Organization in Chinese Society*, pp. 261-96, Stanford, Ca.: Stanford University Press.

Omohundro, John T., (1981) *Chinese Merchant Families in Iloilo*, Athens, Ohio: The Ohio University Press.

Omohundro, John T., (1973) "Chinese Merchant Society in the Philippines," *Philippine Sociology Review*, Vol. 21, pp. 169-80.

Purcell, Victor, (1965) *The Chinese in Southeast Asia*, Second Edition, Kuala Lumpur: Oxford University Press.

Scharfstein, Ben-Ami, (1974) *The Mind of China*, New York, N.Y.: Dell Publishing Co.

Silin, Robert H., (1972) "Marketing and Credit in a Hong Kong Wholesale Market," in W. E. Willmott, editor, *Economic Organization in Chinese Society*, pp. 327-52, Stanford, Ca.: Stanford University Press.

Stanback, Thomas M. Jr., and Thierry J. Noyelle, (1982) *Cities in Transition*, Totowa, N.J.: Allanheld, Osmun and Co.

Stover, Leon, (1974) *The Cultural Ecology of Chinese Civilization*, New York, N.Y.: Mentor Books.

Tasker, Rodney, (1983) "The Roots of the Problem," *Far Eastern Economic Review*, Vol. 120, No. 18, pp. 21-27, May 5.

Thrift, Nigel, (1983) "World Cities and the World City Property Market: The Case of Southeast Asian Investment in Australia," Canberra: The Australian National University, Department of Human Geography Research, School of Pacific Studies.

Ward, Barbara E., (1972) "A Small Factory in Hong Kong: Some Aspects of its Internal Organization," in W. E. Willmott, editor, *Economic Organization in Chinese Society*, pp. 353-86, Stanford, Ca.: Stanford University Press.

Ward, Peter, (1978) *White Canada Forever*, Montreal, Quebec: McGill-Queen's University Press.

Watson, James L., (1975) *Emigration and the Chinese Lineage: The Mans in Hong Kong*, Berkeley, Ca.: University of California Press.

Williams, Lea E., (1966) *The Future of the Overseas Chinese in Southeast Asia*, New York, N.Y.: McGraw-Hill Book Co..

Willmott, D., (1960) *The Chinese of Semarang: A Changing Minority in Indonesia*, Ithaca, N.Y.: Cornell University Press.

Willmott, W.E. (editor), (1972) *Economic Organization in Chinese Society*, Stanford, Ca.: Stanford University Press.

Willmott, W.E., (1970) *The Political Structure of the Chinese Community in Cambodia*, New York, N.Y.: Athlone.

Wong, John (editor), (1976) *The Cities of Asia*, Singapore: Singapore University Press.

Wu, David Y. H., (1982) *The Chinese in Papua New Guinea: 1880-1980*, Hong Kong: Chinese University Press.

Wu, Yuan-Li, and Chun-Hsi Wu, (1980) *Economic Development in Southeast Asia: The Chinese Dimension,* Stanford, Ca.: Hoover Institution Press.

Wu, Yuan-Li, "Chinese Entrepreneurs in Southeast Asia," (1983) *American Economic Review,* Vol. 73, No. 2, pp. 112-17.

Youngson, A. J., (1982) *Hong Kong Economic Growth Policy*, Hong Kong: Oxford University Press.

Yung, Cheng Tong, (1982) *The Economy of Hong Kong*, Kowloon, Hong Kong: Far East Publications.

Zagaris, Bruce, (1980) *Foreign Investment in the United States*, New York, N.Y.: Praeger.

5

Pacific Ocean Minerals: The Next Twenty Years

CHARLES J. JOHNSON, ALLEN L. CLARK and JAMES M. OTTO

INTRODUCTION

No commercial mining of marine mineral resources has taken place beyond the near-shore, shallow continental margins, even though more than US$300 million has been spent on evaluating deeper-water metal deposits. During the early 1970s, there was substantial optimism that commercial mining of ocean floor manganese nodules would begin in the 1980s. Major industry consortiums were formed to undertake exploration and research to evaluate the potential for commercial production of deep ocean manganese nodules. However, today there is considerable pessimism among private industry representatives who see little prospect for commercial developments of manganese nodules in the foreseeable future.

This chapter brings together the major technical and economic factors useful to nonspecialists interested in evaluating the future of ocean mining in the Pacific. In particular, important new discoveries in recent years of other types of mineral occurrences as well as increased involvement of governments could result in renewed interest in commercial developments during the last half of the 1980s. This chapter is divided into the following five sections: (1) mineral resource characteristics; (2) the economics of ocean mining; (3) the impact of ocean mining on metal markets; (4) the future outlook for ocean mining in the Pacific, and (5) conclusions.

MINERAL RESOURCE CHARACTERISTICS

There are three types of mineral deposits beyond the near shore that may be commercially developed within the next twenty years. The best known deposits are ocean floor manganese nodules (hereafter referred to as nodules), but two other ocean minerals occurrences, cobalt-rich manganese crusts (hereafter crusts) and polymetallic sulfide deposits (hereafter sulfides), have received relatively high levels of interest during the 1980s, primarily by government and academic research groups. Our present understanding of the physical nature of these three resources is summarized in the following section.

Manganese Nodules

Nodules, relatively rich in manganese, iron, nickel, copper, and cobalt, are abundant over vast areas of the deep ocean floor at depths of four to five thousand meters. On average, nodules are potato-shaped, three to six centimeters in diameter, and have average metal grades of approximately 0.75 percent nickel, 0.5 percent copper, 0.25 percent cobalt, and 20 percent manganese. While nodules have been found in all the earth's oceans, the regions of highest potential and commercial interest are located primarily in the Pacific Ocean. The richest known area for possible commercial mining is within the Clarion-Clipperton fracture zone located between Hawaii and Baja California, as shown in Figure 5.1. This area covers about four million square kilometers, half of which contains extensive nodule deposits. Assuming 20 percent of the nodules are recoverable, this area contains approximately two billion dry metric tons of nodules averaging about 1.3 percent nickel, 1 percent copper, 0.22 percent cobalt, and 25 percent manganese. This quantity of nodules could support about thirty mining operations (McKelvey, 1980). If considered as part of the reserve base, the estimated tonnage of recoverable nodules from this area would increase the 1984 U.S. Bureau of Mines estimates of world reserves by 50 percent for cobalt, 25 percent for nickel, and 5 percent for copper and manganese.

Cobalt-Rich Manganese Crusts

Crusts are different from nodules in a number of physical aspects, the most important of which are metal grades, location, and underlying substrate. Table 5.1 compares the typical grades of crusts with grades of nodules.

The average metal grade of cobalt in crusts is more than three times

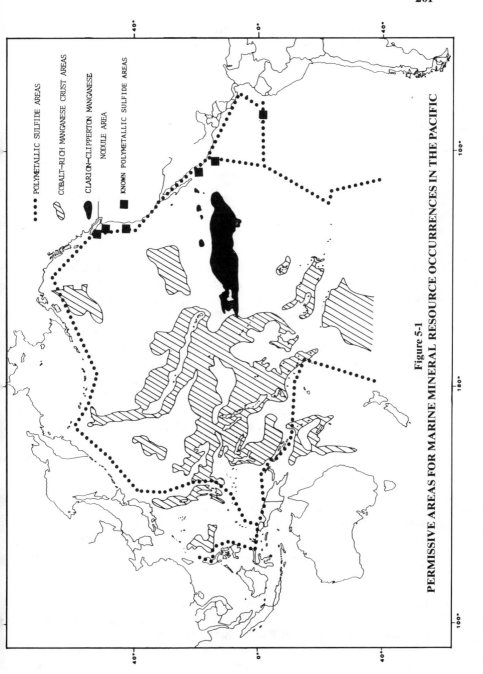

PERMISSIVE AREAS FOR MARINE MINERAL RESOURCE OCCURRENCES IN THE PACIFIC

Figure 5-1

POLYMETALLIC SULFIDE AREAS

COBALT-RICH MANGANESE CRUST AREAS

CLARION-CLIPPERTON MANGANESE NODULE AREA

KNOWN POLYMETALLIC SULFIDE AREAS

Table 5.1
Typical Metal Grades of Nodules and Crusts

METAL	NODULES[a]	CRUSTS[b]
Cobalt (percentage)	0.27	0.90
Copper (percentage)	0.54	0.06
Manganese (percentage)	20.00	25.00
Nickel (percentage)	0.76	0.50
Platinum (gm/tonne)	–	0.40[c]

a. McKelvey et al., 1983
b. Clark et al., 1984 (Note there is considerable variability in grades between sites)
c. Based on a limited number of analyses (Halbach et al., 1984; Halbach, 1984)

that of nodules; the grade of nickel is only one-half to two-thirds that of nodules, and copper grades are about one-tenth the grade of nodules. Manganese grades are typically between 20 and 25 percent for both nodules and crusts. For older crusts, those formed between nine and sixteen million years ago (Halbach et al., 1984), significant platinum values of up to one gram/tonne have been reported. The crusts of greatest commercial interest appear to be at depths of eight hundred to twenty-four hundred meters, compared with nodules located at depths of four to five thousand meters. The largest concentrations of nodules are found on soft ocean floor sediments, whereas most crusts are attached to the hard rock substrate of seamounts. Crusts range in thickness from surface coatings of less than one millimeter and in rare instances to more than ten centimeters. Crust deposits of greatest commercial interest are expected to be associated with seamounts that are twenty-five million years and older.

The most extensive deposit discovered to date was found near Johnston Island in 1984 by scientists on the West German research ship, *Sonne*. This deposit averages three centimeters in thickness and contains in excess of ten million tonnes of crust on a gentle slope between 1,000 and 1,800 meters (Halbach, 1984). Figure 5.1 shows areas of the Pacific where it is likely that seamounts of commercial interest may be located. Table 5.2 gives a relative ranking of the crust potential within the Exclusive Economic Zones (EEZs) of the Hawaiian Archipelago and United States Trust and Affiliated Territories. Research in progress will define the relative potential of all Pacific island nations.

Bottom photographs taken by the U.S. Geological Survey on the *S.P. Lee Guyot* have indicated "several densely-packed nodule fields" (Hein et al., 1985). Nodule concentrations have also been noted in a few

Table 5.2

Estimated total Resource Potential of Crusts Within the EEZs of Hawaii and U.S. Trust and Affiliated Territories

PACIFIC AREA	RELATIVE RANKING[a]
Marshall Islands	High
Micronesia	High
Northern Marianas	Medium
Kingman-Palmyra	Medium
Johnston	Medium
Hawaii	Medium
Belau-Palau	Medium
Wake	Low
Guam	Low
Howard-Baker	Low
Jarvis	Low
Samoa	Low

a. Potential is based primarily on the total area within the 800-2,400 m range on seamounts with an estimated age of 40 million years and older. If younger seamounts or greater depths are included, the potential of each area would increase. The estimates are of in-place resources and, as such, do not indicate either potential recoverability or mineable quantities.

	COBALT[b]	NICKEL[b]	MANGANESE[b]	PLATINUM[c]
High	>5	>2.5	>200	>10
Medium	1-5	0.6-2.5	30-200	2-10
Low	<1	<0.6	<30	<2

b. Million metric tons
c. Million troy ounces

photographs of seamounts taken by the Hawaii Institute of Geophysics within the Hawaiian EEZ. Therefore, it is possible that nodule concentrations of commercial interest may exist in relatively shallow waters within the EEZ of one or more Pacific nations. These seamount nodule concentrations will probably have metal grades similar to seamount crusts.

Polymetallic Sulfides

These deposits are of hydrothermal origin and are found along fracture zones on the ocean floor that are spreading apart at relatively rapid rates (up to fourteen centimeters per year). In general, sulfide deposits occur as vents, similar in appearance to stalagmite cones, and may rise more than thirty meters from the ocean floor. The largest potential deposit discovered to date occurs approximately two hundred nautical miles east of the Galapagos Islands. Within this area a series of coalesced inactive sulfide vents occur intermittently for one km along a fault and within a zone approximately 20 to 200 meters wide (Malahoff, 1982).

Two major deposit types are recognized to date. As shown in Table 5.3, the first type of deposit (Type I), such as found in the Galapagos region, is high in copper but relatively low in other metals. The second type (Type II), such as that found at Juan de Fuca and Guaymas Basin, is high in silver and zinc but low in copper. Minor amounts of cadmium and lead of possible commercial interest are also present (Table 5.3). Estimates by Mottl reported by Broadus (1984) indicate that the largest sulfide deposits will probably be thirty million tonnes.

Relatively little exploration has taken place for polymetallic sulfide vents; thus the aforementioned descriptions may not reflect accurately the potential of this type of mineral occurrence. Exploration for sulfide sites began in the early 1980s, and it is estimated that less than US$20 million had been invested as of 1985. Areas where occurrences are likely to be found are shown in Figure 5.1.

ECONOMICS OF OCEAN MINING

Of the three ocean mineral deposit types discussed in this chapter, it is only for nodules that research and development have advanced to the stage of detailed pilot-scale mining and processing tests. It follows that the economic parameters pertaining to nodule mining are known with a much greater degree of reliability than for either crusts or sulfides. However, even in the case of the heavily studied nodules, existing financial

Table 5.3
Metal Grades of Deep-Ocean Sulfide Deposits[a]

METAL (GRADES)	TYPE I SULFIDES	TYPE II SULFIDES
Cadmium (gm/tonne)	31	n.a.
Copper (percentage)	5	1
Lead	trace	trace
Silver (gm/tonne)	10	300
Zinc (percentage)	0.14	30

Source: Broadus, 1984.
a. Sulfides high in copper concentrations, such as found near the Galapagos, are referred to as Type I in this chapter. Sulfides with high zinc and silver concentrations, such as found at Guaymas Basin and Juan de Fuca, are referred to as Type II.

analyses should be used with caution as they may not reflect accurately the economics of a full-scale commercial operation.

The numerous financial analyses published in recent years agree with the view of the various ocean mining consortia that nodule mining is unlikely to meet the profit criteria of private industry at present metal prices (Nyhart et al., 1983; A.D. Little, 1979). However, as discussed in the section on the future outlook, a number of factors could change that might result in renewed interest in the commercial mining of nodules.

The most likely mining system would include a highly efficient bottom-collecting device combined with a hydraulic system for lifting nodules through a six thousand meter pipe to the mining ship. Such systems have been demonstrated with one-fifth scale mining systems by two mining consortia—Ocean Mining Associates and Ocean Management Incorporated (A.D. Little, 1979). The nodules probably would be transported by 60,000 to 100,000 DWT ships to a shore-based processing plant for recovery of metals.

As shown below, there are at least five nodule processing alternatives "that have either undergone significant bench-scale and pilot-work or are based on a process currently in operation" (A.D. Little, 1984):

    i.   Reduction Ammonia Leach Process
    ii.   Cuprion Process
    iii. Pyrometallurgical Process
    iv.   Hydrometallurgical Acid Leach Process
    v.   Sulfuric Acid Leach Process

Table 5.4

Nodule Mining and Processing Costs[a] (Three Million Tonnes Dry Nodules Per Year)

	MILLION 1984 US$	PERCENT
CAPITAL INVESTMENT		
Mining & Ore Transport	300	21
Processing	1100	79
TOTAL CAPITAL INVESTMENT	1400	100
OPERATING COSTS (ANNUAL)		
Mining & Ore Transport	110	27
Processing Plant		
Energy	170	42
Non-energy	75	19
Employment	25	6
Maintenance/Insurance	25	6
TOTAL OPERATING COSTS	405	100

a. The estimates are a compilation from various published and unpublished sources and are useful in indicating the relative levels for various cost elements. Processing plant costs are for a four-metal integrated pyrometallurgical plant described in A.D. Little, 1984.

It is not possible to predict which processing option will be selected for the first commercial development. The capital and operating cost data presented here are based on a four-metal (cobalt, copper, manganese, and nickel) pyrometallurgical processing option. This process has the disadvantage of being energy-intensive; however, it has the advantage of using a relatively well-known technology.

As shown in Table 5.4, nodule mining and transportation accounts for only US$300 million, or about one-fifth of the total estimated capital investment of US$1.4 billion. About one-quarter of the total operating costs are associated with mining and transport, the remainder being associated with the land-based nodule processing plant.

Therefore, 75 to 80 percent of both capital and operating costs for a nodule project is associated with the land-based nodule processing plant. In addition, the major cost variables that can be readily changed in a nodule project are associated with the processing plant. The siting of the plant is a key variable: capital costs could vary by 10 to 20 percent (about US$100 to US$200+ million), or more, between sites. Annual operating costs can vary by US$50 to US$100 million per year. The main operating cost variable shown in Table 5.4 is the cost of energy, which can vary by more than US$50 million between sites. The main sources of energy for a pyrometallurgical processing plant are coal and coke (about one million tonnes of coal and 0.4 million tonnes of coke per year), and electricity equivalent to about 275 MW of base-load electricity (Callies and Johnson, 1985).

Nodule transport can vary up to about US$25 million per year, depending on the distance from the minesite to the processing plant which will probably be located near a low-cost source of electricity. Labor, although not a major factor in a capital-intensive nodule operation, can vary by US$20 million between a plant sited in a developed country, with high labor costs, and a plant in a developing country (Callies and Johnson, 1985).

Not included in the direct operating cost figures in Table 5.4 are taxes payable on operating profits of the processing plant. Effective tax rates vary widely among nations around the Pacific and will probably rank second after energy in overall impact on operating cost factors influencing the siting of a processing plant (Callies and Johnson, 1985).

Profitability and Risks

As previously stated, published nodule mining estimates indicate that a project will probably have a relatively low level of profitability. An A.D. Little study in 1979 provided estimates for nodule mining with three different processing options. The range in the internal rate of return

(IRR) in constant 1978 US dollars for the various options considered was as follows:

	Internal Rate of Return (percentage)
Pyrometallurgical	6.3 - 12.2
Ammonia Leach with Manganese	3.1 - 9.2
Ammonia Leach without Manganese	2.9 - 8.7

The A.D. Little study states: "Based on our experience and interviews with key mining executives, we are of the opinion that a DCF/ROI [IRR] of 30% (without inflation) is commensurate with the level of risk currently associated with the first ocean nodule projects." Various analyses in recent years and the lack of interest by industry in investments in further nodule research and development (R&D) activities support the widely held contention that nodule mining is not expected to meet commercial project objectives.

However, it is questionable whether such a high IRR can be justified for the entire mining project when only about 20 percent of the project may be at high risk. If the land-based processing plant is designed to allow conversion to use landbased ores (at a modest incremental cost), then a more typical IRR of 12 to 14 percent in constant dollars appears reasonable for the processing plant. The 20 percent investment in the mining portion is high risk and might have a required IRR of 25 to 30 percent. The impact of applying a lower IRR to the 80 percent of investment in processing could result in a reduction of at least US$100 million each year in required after-tax revenues to the investor.

Other combinations may also be considered such as the conversion of existing land-based smelters to processing facilities for nodules. At least one consortium has proposed building a smelter to produce a concentrate that would subsequently be refined at existing plants (Little, 1979). If existing plants can be used to refine the intermediate smelted product, then the total capital cost of a nodule operation might be reduced substantially.

From a financial perspective, a nodule "mining" project is primarily a nodule "processing" project. Substantial opportunities may exist for reducing the costs and risks in "processing;" therefore, more attention to "processing" and the location of processing facilities appears warranted.

Law of the Sea Treaty Implications for Mining Economics and Risk

The United Nations Law of the Sea Treaty signed in 1982 established fairly detailed terms for commercial deep-ocean mining. Private mining consortia have stated that the Law of the Sea Treaty is unacceptable in a number of areas including (1) the requirement that mining technology be transferred to the United Nations-established "Enterprise" and to developing countries when requested, and (2) the lack of assurance that existing investors will be able to mine the sites they have been exploring (U.S. G.A.O., 1982). In addition to complaints voiced by the consortia, private international banks believe the Law of the Sea Treaty would not provide adequate protection to their loans in a number of areas (U.S. G.A.O., 1982).

It is futile to try to predict whether or not private mining consortia will operate under the Law of the Sea Treaty in the future. However, it does appear that the Treaty raises the risks perceived by investors and lenders, and this will be reflected in a higher profitability requirement before investment will proceed.

The discoveries in recent years of major crust deposits within the EEZs of selected Pacific countries may change fundamentally the commercial prospects for deep ocean mining of nodules under the Law of the Sea Treaty. Mining of crusts and, perhaps, associated nodules, may prove to be no more costly than deep ocean mining of nodules. Because of the perceived lower risks of investing within the EEZs of stable Pacific nations such as the United States, private sector investment is more likely to proceed first within the EEZs of these countries.

IMPACT OF OCEAN MINING ON METAL MARKETS

As previously stated, it is not possible at present to predict the timing of the first commercial deep ocean mining operations. However, given the lead time required to establish such a major and complex project, it appears probable that the first commercial mining operation will not occur until the turn of the century (1995-2005). It is possible to examine the impact an individual mining activity might have on future markets. Table 5.5 shows the estimated impact of a single mining operation, for the various deposit types, on the United States, Japanese, and world markets in the year 2000. For the purposes of this chapter, it is assumed that all consumption of metals will grow at an average rate of 2 percent from a 1983 base. Because of wide fluctuations in metal imports during the early 1980s, the 1983 base year was established by averaging annual imports for the 1980 to 1983 period.

Table 5.6 shows the extent to which the United States relies on specific nations for the strategic commodities—cobalt, ferromanganese, and nickel. It is apparent from Table 5.5 that a single nodule or crust operation might play a major role in reducing the supply vulnerability for a

Table 5.5
Impact of a Single Marine Mining Operation on Selected Markets in the Year 2000[a]

| MINERAL | MARKET SIZE IN THE YEAR 2000 ('000 TONNES) | | | MINE OUTPUT AND SHARE OF MARKET | | | | | | | | | | | | | | | | |
| | | | | Nodules | | | | Crusts | | | | Sulfides (Type 1) | | | | Sulfides (Type 2) | | | |
	World	US	Japan	'000 Tonnes	World	US	Japan	'000 Tonnes	World	US	Japan	'000 Tonnes	World	US	Japan	'000 Tonnes	World	US	Japan
Cobalt	37.5	10.0	3.2	5.1	14	51	161	7.7	20	77	241	63.5	1	8	4	12.8	b	2	1
Copper	11130.0	804.0	1635.5	30.6	b	4	2	-	-	-	-	-	-	-	-	-	-	-	-
Lead	4784.5	183.0	280.0	-	-	-	-	-	-	-	-	-	-	-	-	-	-	-	-
Manganese	13249.7	803.0	1719.0	637.5	5	79	37	212.5	2	26	12	-	-	-	-	-	-	-	-
Nickel	927.8	213.0	148.4	35.7	4	17	24	4.3	b	2	3	-	-	-	-	-	-	-	-
Platinum	0.3	0.1	0.046	-	-	-	-	.0003	b	b	1	-	-	-	-	-	-	-	-
Silver	15.0	5.3	2.6	-	-	-	-	-	-	-	-	0.013	b	b	1	0.4	2	7	15
Zinc	8315.7	921.0	686.1	-	-	-	-	-	-	-	-	1.8	b	b	b	382.5	5	42	56

Source:
a. Assumptions: Single marine mining operations would recover: for nodules-3 million tonnes/year; for sulfides-1.5 million tonnes on a dry basis and 85 percent contained metal recovery. Import markets and world mine production estimates are based on 2 percent annual growth projected from a base year of 1983 (average of 1980-1983).
Sulfides high in copper concentrations, such as found near the Galapagos, are referred to as Type 1 in this chapter.
Sulfides with high zinc and silver concentrations, such as found in the Guaymas Basin and on the Juan de Fuca Ridge, are referred to as Type 2. A number of metals of less economic interest are not included.
b. Indicates less than 0.5 percent.

Table 5.6

U.S. Sources of Supply—Cobalt, Ferromanganese, and Nickel (1980–83)
(Country share of U.S. Imports)

COBALT		FERROMANGANESE[a]		NICKEL	
Country[b]	Percent[c]	Country	Percent[b]	Country	Percent[b]
Zaire	48	South Africa	51	Canada	48
Canada	17	Gabon	12	Australia	13
Zambia	12	Mexico	8	Botswana	11
Finland	7	Brazil	8	Philippines	5
Botswana	3	Canada	5	Dominican Rep.	4
Other	13	Portugal	4	South Africa	4
TOTAL	100	TOTAL	100	TOTAL	100

Source: Derived from data in U.S. Bureau of Mines, Minerals Year Book, 1981, 1983.

a. Ferromanganese represents the predominant form of manganese imports.
b. Figures have been adjusted to indicate original country of primary mine production.
c. Country percents are 1980–83 average.

country whose mining industry includes an ocean-mining project.

The implications of a classification of a metal as strategic is that governments are more likely to become involved in one or more of the following:

    i.   Establishing a strategic stockpile;

    ii.   Supporting research to provide substitutes; and/or

    iii.   Providing incentives to develop new sources of supply.

The last point is relevant to nodule and crust mining. To date, the main form of incentive has been government support of research addressing distribution, physical characterization, and mining and processing options. At present, the United States government is actively supporting research with respect to the crust and polymetallic sulfide potential within its 200-mile EEZ for possible leasing to private companies.

With respect to other metals, one nodule mining operation would have a small impact on world markets. However, as shown in Table 5.5 for manganese in particular, and to a lesser extent for nickel, metal supplies from one nodule operation could meet a substantial share of the American and Japanese metal requirements in the year 2000.

Nodules

For a single nodule operation, only cobalt is likely to have a significant impact on the world market; however, as shown in Table 5.5, one mining operation could supply about half of United States' demand and about 160 percent of Japan's demand. As shown in Table 5.7, cobalt is primarily produced in Zaire and Zambia, both of which averaged 62 percent of world mine production during the 1980-84 period. Cobalt is considered by the United States government as one of the most important "strategic" minerals because of (1) the lack of domestic supplies and the relatively high degree of concentration of output from countries that may, for political or economic reasons, restrict supplies, and (2) the critical role of cobalt in high technology and military applications.

Crusts

Because crusts contain more than three times as much cobalt as nodules, impacts on cobalt markets will be higher. Table 5.5 shows that one crust operation, producing one-third as much ore as a nodule operation, would have a substantial impact on world markets (20 percent), a major impact on the United States market (77 percent), and would far exceed Japanese requirements (241 percent). The impact of manganese on

Table 5.7
Average Share of World Mine Production—Cobalt, Manganese, and Nickel
(1980–84)

COBALT		MANGANESE		NICKEL	
Country	Percent[a]	Country	Percent	Country	Percent
Zaire	49	USSR	42	USSR	23
Zambia	13	South Africa	18	Canada	20
Australia	7	Brazil	8	Australia	12
Canada	6	Gabon	8	New Caledonia	9
Finland	4	People's Republic of China	7	Indonesia	6
Other Market	7	Australia	6	Cuba	5
Other Central	15	India	6	Other Market	20
		Other	4	Other Central	4

Sources: Share based on production from 1980–1984 as reported by: U.S. Bureau of Mines, Mineral Commodity Summaries, 1982–1985; World Bureau of Metal Statistics, World Metal Statistics Yearbook, 1984.
a. Columns may not add to 100 because of independent rounding.

world markets would be small but significant with respect to the United States and Japan. Nickel, copper, and platinum would have an insignificant impact on United States, Japan, or world markets.

Sulfides

These deposits do not contain minerals generally considered to be of high strategic potential by the major industrialized nations. The three main metals that would be produced are copper, silver, and zinc. As shown in Table 5.5, only in the case of zinc would there be a substantial impact on the American and Japanese markets. However, as Australia, Canada, and the United States are major producers of zinc, there are no major strategic concerns pertaining to the availability of this metal.

Table 5.8 shows the percentage of annual gross sales revenues from each of the significant metals that might be recovered from a single nodule, crust, or sulfide mining operation. If manganese is recovered as ferromanganese in a nodule operation, it would represent about half the sales revenue; but with existing technologies, manganese recovery from either nodule or crust operations may not add significantly to operating profits. If manganese is not recovered, then nickel dominates with more than 60 percent of the sales revenue.

Crust operations are basically cobalt mining activities. As shown in Table 5.8, with manganese recovery, cobalt and manganese would each contribute about 43 to 45 percent of total gross sales revenue. Without manganese recovery, sales revenue from cobalt rises to almost 80 percent of total revenues. Potential investors, therefore, would be very dependent on the small, unstable cobalt market to justify crust operations. This leads to the conclusion that without some form of market and price guarantees, it seems unlikely that a commercial firm would accept the perceived risks associated with a marine mining operation so dependent on cobalt for its commercial success.

Known sulfide deposits of substantial size are either copper rich, with copper representing more than 90 percent of the sales revenue, or silver-zinc rich, with zinc representing more than 70 percent of the sales revenue (Table 5.8). From a marketing perspectave, sulfide deposits face less risk in metal markets than either nodules or crusts. One sulfide operation would account for no more than 5 percent of any metal market and would be heavily dependent on the large zinc market—which is more than two hundred times as large as the cobalt market.

FUTURE OUTLOOK FOR OCEAN MINERALS

It is generally agreed among analysts that no commercial development of nodules, crusts, or sulfides will be undertaken by private industry in the foreseeable future. The main constraining factors are low metal prices, excess capacity from land-based mines, and forecasts of relatively low growth rates in metal consumption to the end of the century. However, our understanding of the complex interaction of changing technologies, economies, and politics with respect to long-term metals supply and demand remains quite imperfect. It is impossible to predict with a high level of confidence whether or not commercial mining will occur in the next two decades. The recent discoveries of extensive cobalt-rich crust deposits and polymetallic sulfide deposits is a clear indication that major changes in our knowledge of the size, grade, and distribution of marine resources and the economics of their development are still occurring. Given the above caveats, the following are our views about the future role of marine nodule, crust, and sulfide deposits over the next twenty years.

Nodules

With respect to ocean floor mining of nodules, the present United Nations Law of the Sea Treaty is technically workable; however, it substantially increases the perceived risks to private investors. The consequence is that private investors will continue to seek a higher rate of return on the portions of investment that fall under this Treaty.

The move by the United States to establish legislation to allow American mining consortia to mine nodules in countervention of the U.N. Law of the Sea Treaty is unlikely to reduce perceived risks to acceptable levels. Nations choosing to encourage the development of nodules in countervention of the Treaty may have to face condemnation by most of the nations of the world. The political costs may be substantial. There also could be costs to private companies involved in any such consortium, such as worldwide restrictions on investment opportunities in countries that are signatories to the Law of the Sea Treaty. Possible solutions to the dilemma above are either to (1) revise the mining provisions in the Treaty to meet the key concerns of the major private investment consortia, or (2) accept the terms of the Treaty.

A number of countries have already applied for "pioneer" mining sites under the U.N. Law of the Sea Treaty. To date, claims have been filed by France, India, Japan, and the Soviet Union. This raises the pos-

Table 5.8
Gross Revenues From Marine Mining Operations (One Commercial Operation)

METAL	NODULES (Mn[a] Recovery)		NODULES (No Mn Recovery)	
	Million US$[b]	Percent	Million US$	Percent
Cobalt	90	11	90	21
Copper	68	8	68	16
Manganese	393	48	–	–
Nickel	276	33	276	63
TOTAL	827	100	434	100

METAL	CRUSTS (Mn Recovery)		CRUSTS (No Mn Recovery)	
	Million US$	Percent	Million US$	Percent
Cobalt	135	45	135	79
Manganese	131	43	–	–
Nickel	33	11	33	19
Platinum	4	1	4	2
TOTAL	303	100	172	100

METAL	SULFIDES (Type 1)		SULFIDES (Type 2)	
	Million US$	Percent	Million US$	Percent
Copper	140	96	28	6
Silver	4	3	105	22
Zinc	2	1	344	72
TOTAL	146	100	477	100

a. Mn = manganese
b. Assumed constant 1984 US dollar prices as follows: Cobalt $8.00/lb., copper $1.00/lb., nickel $3.50/lb., platinum $350/oz., ferromanganese $0.28/lb. contained manganese, zinc $0.41/lb., and silver $8.50/oz. (Johnson and Clark, 1985).

sibility that one of the governments above may provide subsidies and guarantees that would result in a commercial development sooner than would have occurred by majority private sector consortia operating under "free market" conditions.

To date, none of the countries mentioned has made financial commitments at levels that would indicate they are going to establish a full-scale mining operation in the foreseeable future. However, France, Japan, and the Soviet Union have both the financial resources and technical capability to establish a commercial operation if such a decision were made for "political" reasons.

Overall, the writers believe there is a 25 to 50 percent chance of a commercial-scale nodule mining operation within twenty years.

Crusts

Crusts may represent a major source of competition for nodules; therefore, commercial development of nodules may be further delayed. Major deposits of crusts occur within the 200-mile EEZ of some Pacific nations, including the United States. The deposits are located at only one-quarter of the depth of nodules and could be developed under more favorable national legislation at lower risk than would apply outside of the 200-mile EEZs under the U.N. Law of the Sea Treaty. The possible disadvantages of crust mining are that the crusts may prove to be relatively costly to separate from the hard underlying rock substrate, and the high share of total value accounted for by the small cobalt market increases market risks.

However, as of early 1985, most research interest with respect to ocean minerals is focused on crusts. Governments including the United States, Federal Republic of Germany, Japan, and various small Pacific island nations are interested in the potential of crust deposits within the EEZs of Pacific nations. Although companies will need to meet strict environmental guidelines to mine in American waters, a stable legal environment can be established and lenders will probably view mining within U.S. waters as much less risky than under the Law of the Sea Convention. It is possible that an American-led consortium might be given preferential access to the large U.S. market, thereby enhancing further the overall economics of a crust mining project. As previously noted, nodules have been noted locally on seamounts and mineable quantities may exist. The authors believe that there is a 40 to 60 percent chance of a commercial crust and/or associated seamount nodule mining operation within the EEZ of Pacific nations within twenty years.

Sulfides

Based on existing information, the longer-term outlook for private sector commercial development of sulfide deposits appears less likely than for either nodules or crusts. This view could change if substantially larger or higher-grade deposits are discovered or if deposits are discovered in much shallower water. The major metals in sulfides rank quite low on the U.S. list of strategic minerals and therefore are probably less likely to receive any form of government support. The authors believe there is a 10 to 30 percent chance of a commercial development within twenty years.

CONCLUSIONS

The previous discussion is intended to summarize the admittedly sketchy evidence about the three most commercially interesting marine metal resources. To summarize, the following observations are made:

(1) There is no evidence to suggest that nodule, crust, or sulfide mining is likely to become commercially viable in the 1980s;

(2) Given the lead time required to develop a full-scale mining and processing operation, it is reasonable to conclude that no full-scale, private-sector financed commercial operation is likely to occur before approximately 2000;

(3) Crusts have a number of physical and locational characteristics that may make them more likely candidates for commercial development than deep ocean nodules. This may further delay commercial development interest in deep ocean nodules;

(4) Sulfide deposits do not appear to have the size and grade characteristics necessary for commercial development during this century;

(5) The only market that would be influenced significantly by one mining operation would be the cobalt market, with cobalt-rich crusts having the largest impact. Indeed, more than one crust-mining operation could substantially depress cobalt prices in the year 2000;

(6) As shown in Table 5.2, the EEZs of the Hawaiian Archipelago and a number of U.S. Trust and Affiliated Territories are known or expected to have major crust deposits. Selected other Pacific nations are also likely to contain important crust deposits within their EEZs. The potential economic importance to small island nations is so large, and the present state of knowledge about the extent of crust resources is so limited, that

priority is justified in evaluating the crust potential of the EEZs of all Pacific countries and territories known to contain seamounts of about twenty-five million years or older;

(7) A single nodule or crust operation could significantly reduce the supply vulnerability for cobalt, manganese, and nickel of even the largest consumer countries;

(8) The U.N. Law of the Sea Treaty increases the perceived risks of private mining consortia and private lending institutions. This may delay commercial developments by private consortia;

(9) Recent interest by some governments in obtaining "pioneer" minesites under the U.N. Law of the Sea Treaty suggests that a commercial development might occur for political reasons.

REFERENCES

Arthur D. Little, Inc., (1979) *Technological and Economic Assessment of Manganese Nodule Mining and Processing*, prepared for the U.S. Department of the Interior, 75 pp.

Arthur D. Little, Inc., (1984) *Technological and Cost Analyses of Manganese Nodule Processing Techniques and Their Significant Variations*, prepared for the U.S. Department of Commerce, Contract No. NA83-SAC-00637.

Broadus, J.M., (1984) "Economic Significance of Marine Polymetallic Sulfides," *Offshore Marine Resource Proceedings,* Group d'Etude et de Recherche de Minoralisations Au Large, pp. 559-75.

Callies, D.L., and C.J. Johnson, (1985) *A Summary of Land and Environmental Laws and Business/Economic Factors Applicable to the Siting of a Manganese Nodule Processing Plant in the Pacific Basin/Rim: Australia, Canada, Colombia, Ecuador, Fiji, and the Philippines*, prepared for the U.S. Department of Commerce, University of Hawaii Sea Grant No. NA81AA-D-00070.

Clark, A., P. Humphrey, C. Johnson, and P. Chinn, (1984) "A Resource Assessment of Cobalt-rich Manganese Crust Potential Within the Exclusive Economic Zones of U.S. Trust and Affiliated Territories in the Pacific," prepared for the U.S. Minerals Management Service by the Resource Systems Institute, East-West Center, Honolulu.

Clark, A., C. Johnson, and P. Chinn, (1984) "Assessment of Cobalt-Rich Manganese Crusts in the Hawaiian, Johnston and Palmyra Islands' Exclusive Economic Zones," *Natural Resources Forum*, Vol. 8, No. 2, pp. 163-74.

Halbach, P., (1984) Personal communication.

Halbach, P., D. Puteanus, and F.T. Manheim, (1984) "Platinum Concentrations in Ferromanganese Seamount Crusts from the Central Pacific," *Naturwissenschaften* 71, S. 577.

Hein, J.R., et al., (1985) "Geological and Geochemical Data for Seamounts and Associated Ferromanganese Crusts in and near the Hawaiian, Johnston Island and Palmyra Island Exclusive Economic Zones," U.S. Geological Survey Open File Report 85-292, 129 pp.

Johnson, C. and A. Clark, (1985) "Potential of Pacific Ocean Nodule, Crust, and Sulfide Mineral Deposits," *Natural Resources Forum,* Vol. 9, No. 3, pp. 179-86.

Malahoff, A., (1982) "A Comparison of the Massive Submarine Polymetallic Sulfides of the Galapagos Rift with Some Continental Deposits," *Marine Technology Society Journal*, Vol. 16, pp. 38-45.

McKelvey, V.E., N.A. Wright, and R.W. Bowen, (1983) *Analysis of the World Distribution of Metal-Rich Subsea Manganese Nodules*, U.S. Geological Survey Circular 886, 55 pp.

McKelvey, V.E., (1980) "Seabed Minerals and Law of the Sea," *Science*, Vol. 209, 25 July, pp. 464-72.

Nyhart, J.D., M.S. Triantafyllou, J. Averback, A. Bliek, B. Sklar, M. Gillia, D. Kirkpatrick, J. Muggerridge, R. Nakagawa, J. Newman, and A. Will, (1983) *A Pioneer Deep Ocean Mining Venture*, Massachusetts Institute of Technology Sea Grant 83-14, 255 pp.

Roskill Information Services, (1982) *Roskill's Metals Databook*, 2 Clapham Road, London SW9 0JA, 283 pp.

U.S. Bureau of Mines, (1983 and 1981) *Minerals Yearbook*, Vol. 3., Washington, D.C.: Government Printing Office.

U.S. Bureau of Mines, (1984, 1983, and 1982) *Mineral Commodity Summaries*, Washington, D.C.: Government Printing Office.

U.S. General Accounting Office, (1982) *Impediments to U.S. Involvement in Deep Ocean Mining Can Be Overcome*, Washington, D.C., Government Printing Office, EMD-82, 31, 57 pp.

World Bureau of Metal Statistics, (1984) *World Metal Statistics Yearbook 1984*, 41 Doughty Street, London WC1N 2LF, 64 pp.

6

China and Japan in the New Energy Era

VACLAV SMIL

"Shu tu tong gui"
Different roads reach the same end
(Chinese saying)

At first glance it would seem that China and Japan, the two leading economic powers of Asia's Pacific Rim, have so little in common that introducing this essay with an old Chinese saying about different roads converging on the same goal is an obvious error.

Indeed, the basic socio-economic differences are enormous. China, on the one hand, is the world's most populous nation—its 1.04 billion people account for more than one-fifth of the world's population. It has a totalitarian regime, tumultuous history, and an overwhelmingly rural and poor society in urgent need of industrial modernization. Its average GNP is a mere $330 (1983 US$) per capita. On the other hand, with a population of only one-tenth that of China, Japan is a vibrant yet disciplined democracy with one of the world's most stable social environments, a largely urbanized and prosperous country, generally seen as one of the top three nations in advanced technology, with a GNP averaging $9,700 (1983 US$) per capita.

The differences between China's and Japan's energetics, or system-wide pattern of energy utilization, are equally fundamental: in fact, the two countries have such idiosyncratic patterns of energy use that it is impossible to find any close analogies even among the nations selected from the best generally matching categories.

The disparity of resource endowment is overwhelming. China's coal reserves are the world's third largest after the United States and the U.S.S.R., and its total resources of solid fuel may be second, if not first. The country's hydroenergy potential, of which less than 5 percent has been harnessed, is by far the world's largest. In comparison with these riches, hydrocarbon reserves are still relatively modest—in 1984 China was no larger than 11 to 13th in worldwide ranking of these reserves—but there is a considerable potential for large onshore discoveries. Verified deposits of fissionable materials can support a capacity of 15 gigawatts (GW) for three decades at full load. And, finally, China's location and size provide it with one of the world's largest geothermal potentials as well as with abundant opportunities for direct conversion of solar energy and wind-powered generation.

Japan's energy patrimony consists of a very limited quantity of poor coals, a mere trace of crude oil or natural gas in spite of decades of diligent search; a helpful bit of hydroenergy which provided 20 percent of all primary energy supply in 1955, but has since fallen to just about 5 percent; and some locally useful geothermal fields. Inevitably, post-World War Two Japan had to become even more dependent on imports while, at the same time, the People's Republic of China has been developing its rich resources to achieve self-sufficiency and then emerging as a relatively small but potentially much more important exporter of both coal and crude oil.

At the time of OPEC's first round of large price increases in 1973-74, the Chinese were just starting to export their waxy crude oil, and although volumes were small, they were growing rapidly, with 1974 shipments being double those of 1973. At the same time, the Japanese were buying nearly 90 percent of their primary energy abroad and these imports were dominated by crude oil purchases which covered almost 70 percent of the country's energy needs. No steam coal was imported at that time, and liquefied gas imports from Alaska and Brunei accounted for less than 2 percent of the total.

Japan's inordinate addiction to crude oil emerged naturally—and unavoidably. Crude oil became the principal energizer of the world's economic dash during the 1950s and 1960s owing to its ease of transportation, the widespread utility of its refined products and, until 1972, a steadily declining real price. Other import choices would have been either uneconomical, such as coal, or technically impossible, such as reliance on renewable energies or large scale imports of liquefied natural gas.

Still, Japan's share of primary energy consumption covered by crude oil was in 1973 much higher than in any other rich industrialized country.

Among the Big Seven, France came closest with 59 percent, followed by Italy with 54 percent. In contrast, China's search for oil was rewarded by the first big find only in 1959 and production from the giant Daqing oil-field in Heilongjiang started to make a difference only in the late 1960s. By 1973, when Daqing was producing half of the country's total output, crude oil still covered no more than one-fifth of China's primary energy consumption. The country's dependence on coal—a bit over 70 percent of the aggregate demand—was at that time matched or surpassed only by three European Communist nations with traditionally high coal extraction—Poland, East Germany and Czechoslovakia.

The fundamental differences between Chinese and Japanese energetics extend beyond supply—resource endowment, degree of self-sufficiency, and make-up of the fuel deliveries—to utilization. The fourth crucial, and qualitatively the most telling, disparity between the two countries has been in conversion efficiency. No other advanced industrialized nation has been able to best Japan's overall first thermodynamic law efficiency, of about 57 percent, for primary energy consumption—the result of the country's inordinate reliance on liquid fuels, its relatively small shares of household and private transportation, and its efficient industries. In contrast, China's record, just short of 30 percent, was unenviable even in comparison with the average performance of other large poor industrializing economies of Asia and Latin America.

This large divergence in energy conversion efficiency was mirrored in the great disparity between China's and other countries' average energy intensity of national product. China's orthodox, Stalinist stress on heavy industry and chronic neglect of consumer goods made this difference even worse. In 1973 China needed no less than 80 megajoules (MJ) of primary energy for each 1983US$ of its GNP, while Japan could do with just over 20 MJ! For comparison, Canadians needed at that time about 35 MJ and Americans about 33 MJ for each 1983US$ of their respective GNPs.

When OPEC's sudden action ended the availability of low-priced crude oil in the winter of 1974, Japan was affected immediately and painfully: for the first time since 1945, GNP fell and inflation rose sharply. In yet another contrast, the Chinese expanded their crude oil extraction by 27 percent in 1973 and by another 20 percent in 1974 and, to attract Japanese investment, started rumors about a new "Saudi Arabia" in the making. Top Japanese officials, including the current Prime Minister Mr. Yasuhiro Nakasone, were returning from China offering predictions of Chinese annual crude oil production surpassing 400 million tonnes within a decade and Japan buying as much as 100 million tonnes of this huge extraction.

However, the first decade of the new energy era did not bring such changes to Chinese and Japanese energetics. Soon, Chinese crude oil output started to stagnate; new onshore discoveries, with the exception of a relatively rich Zhongyuan oilfield, were bringing only smallish additions in production capacity. And offshore exploration, even after foreign oil companies were finally invited for geophysical exploration and eventual drilling in 1979, proceeded slowly, with only one significant natural gas find and no big crude oil discoveries in the south China Sea by the end of 1984. True, Japanese crude oil imports from China increased from just 1 million tonnes in 1973 to 7.9 million tonnes in 1975, but afterwards they stagnated around 7.5 million tonnes and even by 1985 they did not surpass 10 million tonnes.

But other changes took place: shifts of surprising similarity which have demonstrated several essential commonalities guiding the development of energy systems in otherwise very disparate societies. OPEC did us all a great service in making crude oil a much more valued commodity. Although infrastructural inertia and the renewed decline of crude oil's real cost after 1974 kept the consumption of refined products rising for several years, the high prices of the second, Iranian, round of increases eventually made the difference. Japan strove to lower its crude oil consumption in order to reduce its huge import costs; while China embarked on a nationwide program of oil savings to relieve, at least partially, chronic shortages of liquid fuels needed for farm machinery and industrial production, and to make more of the fuel available for exports. Crude oil was a main source of the country's foreign exchange earnings—bringing in about one-fifth of the total in the early 1980s.

The savings have been impressive. Japan's 1983 crude oil consumption was 16 percent below the 1973 level and 19 percent less than the all-time peak reached in 1979. Chinese crude oil use went up sharply from forty-two to ninety-one million tonnes between 1973 and 1983; but all of this growth occurred before 1979 when the output of 106.15 million tonnes was a shade higher than in 1983. Since then, stagnating production has provided more useful energy in every year.

The Japanese reduced their consumption of refined fuels by improving their already high conversion efficiencies, while in China the biggest performance boost came from a gradual withdrawal of the direct combustion of unrefined crude oil in power plants. Declining Japanese use of crude oil brought, inevitably, a substantial slowdown in growth rates of aggregate energy consumption, another common point shared with Chinese energetics. Between 1950 and 1973 Japanese primary energy rose about 9.3 times, but the 1983 total was virtually identical with the 1973 aggregate, and the 1979 peak was just 9 percent above the 1973 level. This represented a change from an exponential increase of almost 10 percent a year to no growth rate at all. Chinese energy consumption kept growing fairly vigorously after 1973 but its annual exponential rise of 4.6 percent between 1973 and 1983 is in marked contrast to the average 1950-73 growth rate of almost 11 percent. Moreover, since 1979, the annual growth has averaged just over 1.5 percent.

This great slowdown of annual consumption increments, shared not only by China and Japan but also by virtually all of the world's economies, translated into impressive declines in the energy intensity of the national product. Unlike many poor Asian, Latin American and, above all, African countries, as well as most rich European nations, both the Japanese and the Chinese economies continued to grow at a relatively fast pace, so their efficiency gains look even better than those achieved elsewhere.

As already noted, in 1973 Japan and China needed about 20 and over 80 MJ for each 1983US$ of their respective GNPs; a decade later, the Japanese needed just 15 MJ and the Chinese consumed about 65 MJ per 1983US$. The Japanese improvement of about 27 percent has been a most remarkable achievement as the initial intensity was already the lowest in the whole industrialized world. It was made possible by a combination of numerous technical changes and process adjustments—for example, the chemical industry saved about 20 percent of all energy by greater recovery of waste heat, while the cement industry's new efficient kilns brought roughly the same percentage savings. There were also important structural shifts, most notably a decline of the steel industry.

The Chinese have reduced their energy use by finally adopting conservation techniques common elsewhere for decades, but their still dismally high energy intensities leave a huge potential for further improvement. For example, the iron and steel industry, China's single largest sectoral user of commercial energy, reduced total energy needs per ton of crude steel by nearly 30 percent in just three years between 1977 and 1980, but its average consumption is still close to two tonnes of coal equivalent compared to Japan's 0.6 t per tonne of steel. Merely through proper recycling, China could save another fifteen million tonnes of coal equivalent as its pig iron/steel ratio is still 0.95 compared to 0.78 for Japan.

Similarly, structural shifts have very far to go in China: adjusting the proportions of light and heavy industry to the level of the first Five Year Plan (1953-1957) would save about thirty million tonnes of coal equivalent. This is a stunning fact which shows that the Chinese economy has been recently even more Stalinist than during the years when it was supervised by Soviet Stalinist planners! The trend toward more labour-intensive light industries has been encouragingly strong since 1980 and, together with the rationalization of heavy industrial production including the closing of many small, highly energy-intensive enterprises, it should keep bringing further improvements in the energy intensity of China's economic product.

The third most notable common trait of post-1973 Japanese and Chinese energetics has been the increased stress on coal. More than just the direction, the two countries also shared an experience of initial overly grandiose plans followed by much modified realities. During the 1960s Japan became a large importer of coking coal with 1970 shipments of 50.7 million tonnes. Nevertheless, small deliveries of steam coal started only in the late 1970s. Japanese energy planners turned to coal in a major way only after the Iranian revolution, which represented a near-total loss of Japan's formerly single largest source of crude oil—32 percent in 1973, and still 13 percent by 1978.

Steam coal imports grew rapidly to 7.2 million tonnes in 1980 and 12.3 million tonnes in 1981—but then the stabilization of crude oil prices and much slower overall growth rates of energy consumption started to exert a strong moderating effect on future expansion. Forecasts of 1990 steam coal imports rose from the Institute of Energy Economics' estimate of 22 million tonnes in late 1976 to the Ministry of International Trade and Industry's projection of 56 million tonnes in 1981. Development of an enormous "coal chain" was to ensure these large deliveries.

The Japan Coal Development Company foresaw a mixture of develop-and-import contracts, straight long-term purchases and spot buys involving projects on four continents, deals with a dozen major coal producers, and trading, banking and research arrangements spanning the globe. Sanwa Bank prepared an estimate of the huge costs required to meet this switch to coal: about (1981) yen 7 trillion, dominated by 5.6 trillion yen for 22 to 23 gigawatts (GW) in new coal-fired power plants, nearly one trillion yen for 110 large coal carriers, and .16 trillion yen for investment in overseas coal development.

But already in 1982 there were clear signs of lower expectations; most striking of all being the nearly 40 percent cut in MITI's budget for the promotion of coal-fired power generation. The Japanese negotiators abroad started to show much less urgency and began to demand what Australians, Americans and Canadians perceived as unreasonable conditions for participation in large-scale coal development. Foreign coal producers noted increasing disparity between Japanese talk about long-term security of energy supplies and investment decisions based on the lowest fuel price.

Simply put, Japan, as the world's largest importer of energy, faces a situation where foreign producers of crude oil, steam coal and natural gas are all eager to sell and where the composition of Japanese consumption makes it possible to engage in major fuel substitutions. Unlike Americans, who consume some three-fifths of all liquid fuels for transportation, Japanese convert only a little over one-fifth of their crude oil into transport fuel. Under these circumstances, there is no urgent need for long-term commitments to develop open-cast mines producing tens of millions of tons of steam coal a year for decades. The switch from oil to coal is very much on, but its rate will be more moderate than predicted at the beginning of the decade.

The Chinese, with their already very high dependence on coal, found the further promotion of this fuel appealing on many grounds. The readily accessible reserves of high gravity bituminous coals assure a possibility of rapid and relatively cheap development. In Shanxi province, for example, reserves of 201 billion tonnes are found in seams with an average thickness of 2.3 meters. Additional benefits to the Chinese of coal development include savings of valuable crude oil and export earnings from steam coal shipments, mainly to Japan, whose money was expected to flow into the opening of large coal mines. However, the initial expansion plan announced by the Ministry of Coal Industry in 1978 of doubling the 1977 output in ten years to 1.1 billion tonnes and then doubling it again by the year 2000, was quite unrealistic.

Fast forgotten, the 1978 fantasy was replaced in 1982 by a more realistic but still highly strenuous program of producing 1.2 billion tonnes a year by the end of the century. Although the Chinese argue that this goal requires annual growth of just 3.4 percent between 1963 and 2000, compared to an average of 10 percent recorded during the previous thirty years, they conveniently ignore the fact that successive production doublings always get more difficult. Both the U.S.S.R. and the United States have been finding their push toward extraction of one billion tonnes a year much slower than anticipated in spite of their superior technical and investment capabilities.

The best signs of a serious Chinese commitment to higher reliance on coal will be the widespread upgrading of existing primitive capacities rather than a stress on large output of inferior quality. Only about one-third of extraction and tunnelling is mechanized, less than one-fifth of all coal is cleaned and sorted before combustion, and there are no unit coal trains. One comparison says it all: should they continue to produce their coal as they do today—with average Chinese raw coal output containing 30 percent rocks and clays—and should they reach the goal of 1.2 billion tonnes by the year 2000, no less than 360 million tonnes of the total they would ship and use would be uncombustible waste!

Again, a greater role for coal makes much sense in China's economy of the late 1980s and 1990s, but many inherent limitations of such a higher reliance, ranging from exorbitant investment needs to environmental consequences, have already lowered the most excessive plans — and they will almost certainly moderate the current ones.

The last shared experience worth stressing here concerns the decidedly marginal role of non-fossil energies. Japan is, perhaps, the best example of the very limited practical appeal of both renewable energy conversions and nuclear generation. More than any other nation, Japan should be expected to push innovative solar, wind, wave and geothermal processes and to pursue a vigorous program of fission generation. True, with 16.6 GW installed in its nuclear stations in 1984, Japan had the world's fourth largest fission capacity after the United States, France and the U.S.S.R. But in relation to the size of its population and economy — leaving aside the import vulnerability concerns — just about every Western European country has a larger share of nuclear power than Japan.

As in all other OECD nations, with the exception of France, Japanese nuclear forecasts have been steadily decreasing. In 1973 it was thought that over 30 GW would be in operation and under construction by 1980. The MITI 1977 forecast for 1990 was 60 GW; by 1981 this dropped to 51 GW and, in 1982, the total was lowered yet again, to 43 GW. The slowing growth in demand for electricity, a series of leakages of radioactive waste water from the Tsuruga station in 1981, and the country's well-known emotional ambivalence about nuclear generation are easy explanations of the declining trend whose end is not yet in sight, although MITI's calculations still show fission as the cheapest way to generate electricity. During the 1979-83 period, the increase in demand was a mere 2.2 percent.

As for renewable sources, Japanese interest has been, by any measure, only a fraction of American and West European effort. Even geothermal generation, where the Japanese potential of up to 30 GW of installable capacity is among the world's highest, has been neglected; and, at the beginning of this decade, the Philippines produced as much geothermal electricity as Japan — leaving aside the United States or Italian achievements. Plans for 3.5 GW by the year 1990 will not be met and foreign critics have charged the Japanese with deliberate delays to let other countries do the expensive development work and then to buy licences for workable technology at a low price.

Should this be the real Japanese intent, then the country's research expenditures and commercialization efforts in solar and wind conversion would be even better examples. In both cases, the outlays and tangible gains since 1973 have been negligible. Even the director of the Sunshine Project admitted that MITI is spending money just to show the willingness to look at new ideas. Any serious student of energy conversion must realize the major obstacles to large-scale commercialization of renewable technologies and should deplore the many questionable schemes which have received extensive funding in post-1973 North America and Western Europe. Nevertheless, the Japanese lack of pioneering spirit is still surprising.

In contrast, the Chinese have tried much harder—but the results have been similarly marginal. Their efforts were born of necessity, aimed at improving inadequate urban supplies and, above all, at reducing massive rural energy shortages. Various Chinese sources claim that between 40 and 60 percent of all rural families are short of fuel for up to six months each year. The biogas program was by far the largest such effort, starting in Sichuan in the early 1970s and culminating in construction of more than seven million units by 1979.

As methanogenic fermentation of animal and human wastes and crop residues requires strict anaerobicity, the slightest leak in the structure turns it into a waste pit. A number of factors tarnished the program with high failure rates: haste; shoddy construction of digesters; shortages of feedstocks; lack of careful management; and the mobilizational approach to popularization of the technology where the country had to build a specified number of digesters by a certain date. Nearly three million digesters were abandoned and large numbers of those remaining do not generate enough biogas to cook three meals a day even during summer. In the winter it is too cold for fermenting bacteria to survive.

Since 1980 the Chinese have been encouraging planting of family fuelwood lots as a part of their de facto privatization of farming. This is hardly an innovation; however, it represents a return to a traditional renewable source of energy which should fill an important need for cooking and heating energy but which can hardly be a base for rural modernization. Among other alternatives, solar water heaters are used in some northern cities and in rural areas of sunny interior provinces, where several tens of thousands of portable solar stoves have been introduced since the late 1970s. Nevertheless, the total contribution of these devices is negligible on a national scale.

No advances worth mentioning have been made in harvesting wind energy. Exploration of the country's rich geothermal resources consists of a single, relatively small, 7 megawatt (MW) station in Tibet and six tiny experimental installations in various parts of China. Of course, one can easily argue that with so much hydroenergy yet to be tapped, the Chinese really have no need to waste their efforts on other renewable alternatives—but the huge hydro potential is very unevenly distributed and will be expensive to develop.

SUMMARY

Lessons from this brief review of surprisingly similar experiences between China and Japan, the world's third and fourth largest energy consumers respectively, are simple indeed, but worth summarizing. The post-1973 emergence of many energy analysts with a poor understanding of energetics and other fundamental energy-related factors resulted in the diffusion of numerous misplaced ideas. None of these was more incorrect than the belief in the impenetrable complexity of energy futures.

It is true that forecasting efforts have been overwhelming failures, but the record would improve if more attention were paid to truisms of modern energetics which are so well illustrated here by post-1973 developments in the world's archetypal poor nation and its leading rich modernizer.

First, when prices rise enough, impressive conservation efforts and efficiency increases will follow. Our real energy needs are clearly much lower than was thought for decades. The most encouraging finding in this respect is that the slack in the system is large enough even in the world's most energy-efficient economy. Second, the right prices trigger substantial fuel substitutions, and on this continent only the excessive attachment to the gasoline-fueled private car precludes the realization that crude oil, the fine and flexible fuel it is, can be replaced to a surprising extent by higher efficiency coals, gases and, later, other sources. Third, coal is the obvious first choice, but the switch should be a gently-paced one. Only then will its goal be achievable and its undesirable side-effects eliminated or minimized. Fourth, while conservation, efficiency increases, and fuel substitutions are desirable and necessary realities, large-scale introduction of alternatives is not a sensible choice for at least the remainder of this century. New energy sources and conversions have always had slow penetration rates, and infrastructural inertia makes the established sources and processes preferable even after their costs rise drastically and their supply reliabilities become questionable.

The experience of Chinese and Japanese energetics during the first decade of the new energy era is thus clearly encouraging. There is still much room to do more with less, to deploy new mixtures of old sources, and to bring in new supplies gradually. The neo-Malthusian tones of many energy projections of the last decade seem inappropriate.

Ku jin gan lai—bitterness gone, sweetness arrives, goes another Chinese saying. How one wishes that such would be a lasting lesson of the first decade of the new energy era—and not only in China and Japan!

INFORMATION SOURCES

China's energy developments since 1973 can be followed in detail by consulting the following chronologically listed publications:

Smil, Vaclav, (1976) *China's Energy*, New York: Praeger.
Smil, Vaclav, (1978) "China's Energetics: A System Analysis," in *Chinese Economy Post-Mao*, Washington, D.C.: U.S.G.P.O.
Woodward, Kim, (1980) *The International Energy Relations of China*, Stanford, Ca.: Stanford University Press.
Smil, Vaclav, (1981) "Energy Development in China," *Energy Policy*, Volume 9, pp. 113-26.
Smil, Vaclav, (1984) *China's Energy Advances and Limitations*, Ottawa: IDRC.

Japanese developments are conveniently summarized, among many others, in the following contributions:

McKean, Margaret A., (1983) "Japan's Energy Policies," *Current History*, Volume 82, pp. 385-89, 392, 395.
Matsui, Ken-ichi, (1977) "Perspectives on Energy in Japan," *Annual Review of Energy*, Volume 2, pp. 387-97.
Oshima, K., T. Suzuki, and T. Matsuno, (1982) "Energy Issues and Policies in Japan," *Annual Review of Energy*, Volume 7, pp. 87-108.
Surrey, John, (1974) "Japan's Uncertain Energy Prospects," *Energy Policy*, Volume 2, pp. 204-30.

7

Petroleum Resources in the Pacific Rim: The Roles Played by Governments in Their Development and Trade*

CORAZON MORALES SIDDAYAO

I. INTRODUCTION

It is generally observed in investment circles that the Asia-Pacific region is a growth area and, except for pockets of instability, a generally stable area for investments. Because the region is a growth area—implying an increasing demand for modern fuels, especially petroleum[1]—some of these investments will be in the oil and gas sector. Furthermore, structural changes in the petroleum industry which principally originated with the sharp oil price increases in the 1970s, plus the accompanying technical improvements and institutional changes, have made the region attractive to risk investors. The petroleum resource potential of the region has generated increased intra-regional and extra-regional trade and investment opportunities. The importance assigned by national governments to energy as consumption and production inputs has, in the process, increased their involvement in petroleum production and trade. Although the traditional view of the nature of public enterprises has been that of utilities providing the public with electricity, gas service, water, transport, etc. (see, for example, Turvey, 1968), this is no longer the case. National oil companies and other government bodies with oversight responsibility over the petroleum industry abound.

The increasing involvement of the public sector in traditionally pri-

* I wish to acknowledge with thanks the contributions of Barbara McKellar to Tables 7.6 and 7.7.

vately run economic activities raises many issues concerning allocative efficiency. This trend allows analyses of such developments in the context of applied microeconomics (especially in the areas of industrial organization and public economics), international trade, and capital theory. It is not the author's intention to dwell on these theories. Rather, using the basic notions of this body of knowledge, this paper will first look briefly at the petroleum potential in the region and the determinants of its trade and related investment flows (the discussion will cover the flow of petroleum in both its primary and processed form). It will then inquire into the implications of existing or emerging government involvement in both upstream and downstream operations,[2] directly and indirectly.

This study finds that the diversity in the endowments of nations in the Pacific Rim has resulted in a significant flow of oil and capital between the countries in the region as well as into the region from elsewhere. Responses to the 1973-74 price changes in the petroleum market have included the creation of new institutions to deal with the problem of energy security. These institutional changes have increased public sector involvement affecting the development and trade of oil and gas.

II. FRAMEWORK FOR ANALYSIS AND SCOPE

Basic Premises

(1) Energy is regarded as a critical input in socioeconomic progress. Petroleum is now technologically the most economical—and, therefore, the most desirable—energy resource, with oil preferred to gas. Because petroleum accumulations are not located in all countries in amounts or at costs that will meet local demand, an international market for this commodity exists. There are thus net oil exporters and net oil importers.

(2) The development, processing, and transportation of petroleum require significant amounts of capital investment. The volume of capital or investment flows (defined as flows of physical, human, and monetary assets) is determined by the yield from such investments, measured in terms of the investor's desired positive net present value or internal rate of return (IRR). The IRR, which may also be viewed as the cost of capital or the measure of an investor's opportunity cost, is at least equal to but may be higher than the real interest rate. The IRR will, however, differ among stages in the industry as well as among economic units, projects, and environments because of variations in the parameters chosen, for example, variations in the levels of acceptable risks.

(3) Each economic agent is assumed to want to maximize the benefits

and minimize the costs from the decisions it makes in the oil and gas sector; that is, each decision-maker "optimizes." The measures for optimality are not assumed to be identical for each decision maker, nor are the goals or the time frames against which each agent measures such optimality. Hence, private investors are assumed to seek, where possible, to maximize profits by generating the maximum revenues attainable and minimizing direct costs to themselves within their own sets of time frames. The investment-receiving country is assumed to act similarly with respect to revenues and costs to the state, according to the priorities it sets and according to its own time frame.

(4) Attitudes towards risk differ, but it is assumed that investors are basically risk-averse. Given the availability of various investment opportunities, foreign investors will rank areas according to expected income streams and the stability of those streams. Thus, the revenues from and the costs of the venture are principal determinants of project choice, *given equal technical risks*. The stability of the institutional framework within which a project will be operated influences final choice; the stability factor includes what is often referred to as "political risk" (as opposed to technical risks— associated with hydrocarbon search—and economic or commercial risks).

(5) The institutional framework is defined as including: (a) the contractual framework delineating the relationship between economic agents, (b) government policies affecting the net gains from sanctioned behavioral relations among economic agents, and (c) other institutional factors that may inhibit or enhance perceptions of the attractiveness of such relationships. This framework affects both commodity and financial flows in the petroleum sector in the region. Hence, the role of government in influencing such flows will be given principal attention.

(6) Government is assumed to be only one among several institutions of social control. Government is the agent, the mechanism, by which the ends of the people associated in a state are pursued. The state is only one of many human associations in a society. Governments may change, but the people living in a definite territory, with some kind of government, make up a continuing association. The state is legally supreme, but this does not mean—unless the form of government is a dictatorship—that it is all-powerful and that it controls *every* activity. And if it attempts to do so, individual economic units with the freedom to make economic choices will reflect their choices in the elasticities of demand and supply.

Additional Premises

The basic purposes for setting up a state-owned or national oil company (NOC) are assumed to be the following:

(1) In a situation where private investments are available for the operation of an oil enterprise engaged in the usual activities that the oil industry has been experienced in conducting, the establishment of a publicly owned national enterprise can be economically justified under the following set of circumstances (which is not complete): (a) a suspicion that severe market imperfection exists with regard to the operation of privately owned oil enterprises; (b) the national oil company is used as a yardstick against which the performance of privately owned companies will be measured; (c) the establishment of a national oil company will not severely hamper the operation of the market, by worsening a distortion in the allocation of the nation's resources, if such already exists; (d) the market imperfection that initially justified the creation of the national oil company is seen as a possible source of national insecurity in the provision of energy goods considered vital to the operation of the economy.

(2) Where a national enterprise is created to serve as a yardstick for measuring private performance, the national enterprise is required to operate and be managed under the usual efficiency conditions required of a privately owned enterprise. That is, least costs and maximum revenues remain the guiding principles in management decisions. Profits generated would be used: (a) to expand capital bases where necessary, as in a private enterprise; and (b) to increase government revenues, in the same way that a private enterprise would be expected to pay corporate taxes. "Dividends" would accrue to the national treasury.

The foregoing justifications will not always hold true, but they are provided as the starting points for discussion.

Scope and Approach

This paper will focus on the nations on the western rim of the Pacific Basin. To keep the analysis within manageable bounds, the discussion will be limited to the following countries: Japan, South Korea, the Philippines, Thailand, Malaysia, Brunei, Singapore, Indonesia, Australia, and New Zealand. References will be made to Burma, China, and the Indochinese countries where appropriate. The United States will also be referred to since it is an important buyer of petroleum and supplier of capital.

The discussion will cover government involvement in both the upstream and downstream segments of the industry. Treatment will be uneven; developments of a more recent nature will be given more space because the implications of such events may not have received as much attention as earlier ones. Data availability will also be a constraint.

This chapter will not provide econometrically based analyses to support the inferences that it draws. Rather, the paper will raise policy-oriented research issues about such government involvement which need to be addressed more carefully and in depth in a systematic way.

III. THE FLOW OF OIL AND GAS IN THE REGION

The region has a market for crude oil and natural gas as well as for the products processed from these two basic sources. In the countries under review, the nature of the market depends on the capability of the buyer to receive crude oil and to refine products for domestic use, as well as the ability of the buyer to receive natural gas in liquefied form. Gas is less easily transportable than oil; but with improvements in technology and cost-price ratios, an expanding overseas market for gas has also developed.

Current Dependency, Resource Bases, and Trading Patterns

Notwithstanding the sharp changes in oil prices that have occurred over the period between 1972 and 1982, there have been only slight changes in levels of dependency on hydrocarbons as a group, with a shift in favor of natural gas occurring in some countries in the region.

Table 7.1 shows the flow of oil to and from the Western Pacific Rim countries. The table indicates that Japan and other Southeast Asian countries receive some petroleum from Canada and the United States and that Japan and the United States are currently the major markets for Southeast Asian output. Overall, however, the Middle East remains the principal source of oil supply for Japan, Australia, and Southeast Asia as a whole.

The continued large dependence on Middle Eastern supply is not surprising, of course. The principal reason is that the Middle Eastern reserves and production levels are several times larger than those of the whole region; see Tables 7.2 and 7.3. The type of crude produced in the region and the existing product demand patterns also encourage that flow.

The following patterns were reported in early 1984 (*Petroleum News,* May 1984, p. 25):

(1) Persian Gulf crudes moving to East Asia amount to around three million barrels per day (b/d), with Japan accounting for 90 percent, Singapore for 3 percent, and the balance to the others;

(2) Of approximately 0.5 million b/d of Indonesian crude exports to the region, 95 percent goes to Japan, and the balance to Australia;

(3) China exports around 0.2 million b/d to Japan and a smaller amount to the Philippines; and

Table 7.1
Oil Flows Into and From the Western Pacific Rim, 1983 (Thousand B/D)

TO: FROM	USA	CANADA	SOUTHEAST ASIA	JAPAN	AUSTRALIA
US	–	80	80	105	15
Canada	540	–	–	5	–
Latin America	2,160	125	5	180	5
Western Europe	550	15	5	–	5
Middle East	575	60	1,615	2,750	120
North Africa	280	25	–	40	–
West Africa	475	15	–	5	–
East and Southern Africa	–	–	5	–	–
South Asia	–	–	25	15	10
Southeast Asia[a]	345	–	–[b]	780	85
USSR, Eastern Europe, China	60	–	240	235	5

Source: British Petroleum Company (1984).
a. Southeast Asia is defined as: Brunei, Hong Kong, Indonesia, Malaysia,
Philippines, Singapore, South Korea, Taiwan, and Thailand.
b. Trade occurs among Southeast Asian countries, but this matrix does not report intra-regional trade.

(4) Of Brunei's exports of about 0.08 million b/d, about 96 percent goes to Japan, with the rest going to Australia.

The above says nothing about Malaysia, which produces low-sulphur crude. Hoffman (1984, Table 2) shows that in 1979 and 1980 Malaysia exported over 0.2 million b/d. Its major markets were—and should continue to be—Japan and the United States, with shares of over 40 and 25 percent, respectively. Small amounts go to the Philippines, Singapore, Thailand, and New Zealand. (Hoffman did not specify if the flows to Singapore include those sent for processing and for re-export to Malaysia.) Taiwan is reported to be considering doubling oil imports from Malaysia, from 1984 levels of five thousand b/d (*Petroleum Economist*, August 1984, p.39). Thailand was reported to have signed an agreement to import five thousand b/d from Indonesia for a one-year period beginning in April 1984, and there is little reason at this point not to expect this to continue (*Bangkok Post,* 8 May 1984).

The imports of the Philippines—a net oil importer—are shown as coming from East Asian producers as well as from the Persian Gulf (Hoffman, 1984). China and Indonesia are the country's major Asian sources of crude imports; Saudi Arabia supplies most of the balance.

Japan is the principal importer of liquefied petroleum gas (LPG)[3] in

Table 7.2

Western-Pacific Rim: Oil and Gas Reserves and Resources, January 1984

COUNTRY	Estimated Proved Reserves[a] (Jan 1984)		Ultimately Recoverable Resources[b]			
			OFFSHORE		TOTAL	
	OIL (mmb)[e]	GAS (bcf)[f]	OIL	GAS	OIL	GAS
EAST AND SOUTHEAST ASIA						
Brunei	1,390.0	7,050	D	E	D	D
Burma	30.0	180	D	C	C	C
China	19,100.0[d]	30,300[d]	D	C	C	B
South Korea			D	D	D	D
Japan	58.0	900	D	D	D	D
Indonesia	9,100.0	30,200	C	C	C	B
Malaysia	3,000.0	48,000	D	C	C	C
Philippines	16.3	14	D	C	C	C
Taiwan	6.2	550	D	D	D	D
Thailand[c]	45.0	8,500	D	D	D	C
AUSTRALASIA						
Australia	1,622.1	17,768	C	B	C	B
New Zealand	169.0	5,545	E[g]	C	E	C
MIDDLE EAST	370,100.8	775,047	NA[g]	NA	NA	NA

Sources: Reserve data are from the Oil and Gas Journal (26 December, 1983). Resource data are from Albers et al. (1973). Oil (1 billion bbls.) and gas (trillion cu.ft.) categories as follows: A = 1,000 - 10,000; B = 100 - 1,000; C = 10 -100; D = 1 - 10; E = 0.1 - 1.
a. "Reserves" are defined as deposits recoverable under existing or foreseeable legal, economic, and technical conditions.
b. "Resources" are defined as deposits believed to be present in sedimentary rocks in unexplored or partly unexplored areas.
c. Thailand's potential resources have been upgraded in light of new information. New onshore discoveries also changes total basin data.
d. negligible or zero.
e. mmb = million barrels.
f. bcf = billion cubic feet.
g. NA = not available on a regional basis from comparable estimates.

Table 7.3

Western Pacific Rim—Oil and Gas Production, 1981 and 1983

COUNTRY	OIL PRODUCTION 1983 Total (mbd)b	OIL PRODUCTION 1983 % Offshore	OIL PRODUCTION 1981 Total (mbd)	OIL PRODUCTION 1981 % Offshore	NATURAL GAS PRODUCTION 1983 Total (mmcfd)c	NATURAL GAS PRODUCTION 1983 % Offshore	NATURAL GAS PRODUCTION 1981 Total (mmcfd)	NATURAL GAS PRODUCTION 1981 % Offshore
EAST AND SOUTHEAST ASIA								
Brunei	160	76.0	156	75.9	942	95.5	909	96.3
Burma	22	0.0	23	0.0	67	–	56	–
China	2,100	0.0	2,010	negl.	5,500	–	5,184	–
Indonesia	1,420	30.9	1,620	34.9	1,813	36.2	1,620	39.0
Japan	8	0.0	8	12.6	NA	–	150	20.0
Malaysia	383	100.0d	258	96.5	723	99.9	234	–
Philippines	14	100.0	5	100.0	–	–	–	–
Taiwan	2	NA	3	NA	140		170	–
Thailand	13	52.4	3	0.0	183	96.6	98	100.0
AUSTRALASIA								
Australiaᵃ	405	84.2	382	96.4	1,350	45.2	1,060	52.0
New Zealandᵃ	15	44.4	10	45.0	243	73.0	177	47.4
MIDDLE EAST	11,711	30.9	15,694	33.8	5,450	11.8	5,020	20.0

Source: Production data for all but the Middle East and 1981 Australia and New Zealand data are from Association of Petroleum Geologists (1984). Other oil data are from the Oil and Gas Journal (25 December,
1981 and 26 December, 1983). Offshore data are from Offshore (20 July, 1984). Middle East natural gas
data are from Petroleum Economics (August 1983, August 1984).
a. Natural gas annual data originally reported in cubic meters for Australia and New Zealand were converted to mmcfd by multiplying by a factor of [(37.3/365)1,000].
b. mbd = thousand barrels per day.
c. mmcfd = million cubic feet per day.
d. As reported, but questionable offshore/total relationship.

the region (*Oil and Gas Journal*, 26 March 1984, p. 58). LPG is imported in bulk refrigerated form from Australia, Indonesia, and from the Persian Gulf countries. Australia ships about 90 percent of its LPG to Japan, with the rest going to ASEAN countries. Indonesia's exports go mainly to Japan and the United States, with about 20 percent going to other Asian markets.

Prospective Shifts

As the domestic production of oil or gas, or both, increases in several net oil importers, the pattern described above will change for some countries. For example, Thailand's natural gas production is expected to supply about 70 percent of its primary source for power generation by 1986 and 62 percent by 1991 (Thailand, National Energy Administration, 1983). New Zealand's natural gas production is also expected to displace oil by 1987 (government source, as reported in *Petroleum News*, January 1984, p. 85). Japan's gas reserves have increased considerably from 720 bcf at the beginning of 1983 to 900 bcf at the start of 1984; see Table 7.2. Deliberate policy strategies adopted by national governments to switch away from oil not only to indigenous resources of all types, but also to coal imports and nuclear power as well, could eventually reduce intra-regional demand.

Market pressures may, however, slow down this shift. Already China's fields are touted as the source of new production in Asia after 1986 (Mooradian, 1984; *Offshore*, May 1984). Even at 1984 output levels, China was reportedly marketing its oil in Asia at prices below those of Indonesia (at US$28.45/bbl. in October 1984 versus the official US$29.53/bbl. price for Minas crude, Indonesia's major export), a strategy which could open up markets in Japan, Singapore, and Korea. Iran was also reportedly flooding Asia with low-priced oil, as other Persian Gulf prices began falling in mid-1984 (Ibrahim, 1984; Toner, 1984). With the October 1984 decrease in North Sea oil prices followed by a drop in Nigerian prices that led to an OPEC pricing meeting in Geneva a few days later, trading among western Pacific Rim countries —including Australia, which approved limited crude oil exports in 1983 (*Oil and Gas Journal*, 5 September, 1983)—was negatively affected.

These pressures may not affect the shipment of liquefied natural gas (LNG) where projects have already been committed. LNG contracts run for around twenty years and are associated with a deposit's project development. Malaysia's first shipment of LNG left in January 1983 to supply Japanese utilities. Similar agreements between Thai and Japanese companies may not be affected, nor will those signed between Japanese companies and Indonesian or Australian suppliers, nor that between South

Korea's Electric Power Corporation and Indonesia's Pertamina (*Petroleum News*, January 1984, p. 83, and August 1984, pp. 29-30; *Asian Wall Street Journal*, 22 May 1984, p. 3; *Petroleum Economist*, November 1984, p. 415).

The weight given to energy security in energy policy planning may, however, dampen the true effect of market pressures on the flow of oil into the region from the Persian Gulf; Asian oil importers have not forgotten the 1973 embargo and how some of them were indirectly affected by an act that was intended to cripple the United States. Hence, the notion of energy security will continue to constitute a significant factor in the oil importers' determination to diversify not only the type of energy used but also the geographical source of imported energy. In this respect, OPEC oil would continue to be taken with caution by most countries. Indonesia may be spared from this bias, even though it is an OPEC member, because it is a party to the ASEAN emergency supply agreement (the effectiveness of this agreement has not, of course, been put to the test to date). There is strong evidence that a premium associated with developing alternatives to oil is acceptable to most countries in the interest of assuring the security of a stream of oil supplies for their economies. The Iran-Iraq war makes short-term contracts at low prices attractive, but long-term contracts continue to be treated with caution. Emergency plans have become standard policy in the region.

Additional shifts have also been occurring in the petroleum product flow in the region. Singapore has long served as the principal refining center for the region, although each country has its own set of refineries. Until Indonesia upgraded its refining capability, the bulk of Indonesian oil not exported as crude was refined in Singapore; this contract was cancelled in April 1984 (*Asian Oil and Gas*, April 1984, p. 5). Singapore has also served as a processor for Malaysian crude; excess capacity in Korea and the Philippines was also utilized by other Southeast Asian countries when required. All this is changing, as producing countries achieve their goals to confine processing within their boundaries and complete their refinery construction programs (Fesharaki, 1984).

IV. CAPITAL FLOWS INTO THE REGION'S PETROLEUM INDUSTRY

Just as oil as a commodity flows into and out of the region, the capital funds required to initiate and develop upstream and downstream petroleum activities in the countries under review have been generated both within the home countries and elsewhere.

Table 7.4

Forecast of Capital Expenditures for Petroleum Exploration and
Development in Asia-Pacific Countries (1983–90) (US $ Million in 1983
Current Values)

COUNTRY	1983	1984	1985	1987	1990	GROWTH RATE 1983–90[a]
(PERCENTAGE)						
EAST AND SOUTHEAST ASIA						
Brunei	480	390	410	500	960	9.90
Burma	200	220	260	300	500	13.09
China (Offshore)	700	1,100	1,600	3,000	5,500	29.45
Indonesia	3,900	3,900	3,600	4,200	4,300	1.39
Japan	400	420	400	550	530	4.02
Malaysia	1,500	1,400	1,600	1,900	2,500	7.30
Philippines	360	310	390	450	550	6.05
Thailand	560	650	520	500	950	7.55
AUSTRALASIA						
Australia	2,200	1,800	1,600	2,800	4,100	8.89
New Zealand	240	300	310	350	450	8.98
OTHERS[b]	3,000	3,450	4,300	6,400	7,900	13.83
TOTAL[c]	13,540	13,940	14,990	20,950	28,240	10.50

Source: Based on data in Resources Asia (December 1983), Figure 1, p. 4.
a. Computed using the formula $Y_t = Y_0 e^{rt}$.
b. Includes India.
c. The total capital expenditure for petroleum exploration and development in Asia-
Pacific countries for 1982 was US$16.5 billion.

Investment Expenditures

Using Chase Manhattan Bank (1979, 1984) data, capital and exploration expenditure changes in the Far East for the period 1967-77 and 1977-82 can be analyzed.[4] Growth rates for the ten years that include the first sharp oil price increases can be compared against the succeeding five years, which include the second set of increases and the beginning of their decline to current levels. Both periods showed high and increasing growth rates for exploratory geological and geophysical expenses at 11.0 and 25.4 percent, development and production investments (crude oil and natural gas) at 23.0 and 31.2 percent, and refinery investments at 14.4 and 17.0 percent (see Siddayao, 1985, Table 4.1(a)).

Table 7.4 shows a projection of exploration and development expenditures in individual Asia-Pacific countries to 1990. This shows Australia, Indonesia, and China (offshore) as areas where the bulk of these new investments will occur.

Table 7.5 lists some commercial financing in the oil and gas sector in some countries in Asia for the years 1982 and 1983. The amounts and the rate bases are also shown. The commercial loans shown are limited to the development stage of oil and gas projects.[5] Five of the six loans involved governments.

Risk capital flows to areas where the prospects of acceptable returns to investments are reasonable. The expected revenues from the sale of the commodity or service[6] are only one side of the equation; the other side consists of expected costs. These costs will include fiscal elements such as taxes, bonuses, output or profit-sharing, and royalties. The net revenue would, however, always be discounted for uncertainty over the future stream of returns.

In the petroleum industry, the risks associated with the upstream stage are generally acknowledged to be higher than those downstream. The size of this difference is influenced, in part, by the institutional framework of the country in which the investment is made. Hence, in addition to the technical and economic risks associated with hydrocarbon search, the type of risk often referred to in the foreign investment literature as "political risk" cannot be ignored. The investor's profit function may thus be expressed in the following form:

$$P = \int [R(t) - C(t)]e^{-rt}dt$$
$$R(t) = R(P, Q)$$
$$C(t) = C(T, M, V, K, G)$$
$$r = r(X_1, X_2, X_3)$$

where P = profits, R = revenue, C = costs, t = time, P = selling price, Q = output, T = costs associated with technical difficulty, M = raw material or geological costs, V = other variable costs, K = capital costs, G = government costs (e.g., taxes, royalties, etc.), r = the discount rate, X_1 = geological risks associated with petroleum search, X_2 = economic and technical risks associated with ordinary venture capital (such as unexpected changes in the market), and X_3 = "political risk."

The Fiscal Regime

The general economic and political framework is the usual starting point for investment risk-ranking of a country. The level of government revenues derived from the taxation of labor and capital returns has no apparent relation to judgments of the stability rankings of a country for investment purposes. Aggregate data provide almost no guidance on the indirect influence of the general tax structure of the countries on the attractiveness of a country, tax-wise, to the petroleum investors (see Siddayao, 1985). One can only seek explanations for variations in the country rankings in the specific variables that characterize the institutional framework of each country and influence investment behavior.

Table 7.6 shows that corporate tax rates applicable to petroleum investors in the different countries under review range from a low of 40 percent (the Philippines) to a high of 60 percent maximum (Thailand), where applicable. Most tax rates are in the area of 45 to 55 percent. (Burma's national oil company is reported to assume the costs of all taxes imposed on petroleum contractors; the foreign companies that operated in Burma in the 1970s were not successful in their exploration, and this approach is therefore academic at this point.)

Attempts by the Indonesian government to simplify its tax laws in 1983 have created concern over the effects of such changes on the net income and cash flows of both foreign employers and employees. Among other things, these new laws provide for elimination of the tax deductibility of employee fringe benefits as expenditures by a company; this means that such benefits would be treated as income for the employee. The revisions also provide for a withholding tax arrangement that is seen as cutting into available operating funds (*Petroleum News*, May 1984, pp. 61-63).

Other aspects of an investor's operation influence the profitability of a venture. These are the physical or monetary shares of the output from a project that must be turned over to the state, either in the form of royalties, output sharing, or profit-sharing. Royalties range from 1 percent (Japan) to 12.5 percent (Korea and Thailand) with variations and

Table 7.5

Major Petroleum Loans in the Western Pacific Rim, 1982–83

COUNTRY	BORROWER	TOTAL AMOUNT (US$MILLION)	INTEREST RATE BASE	PURPOSE
Australia	Private	3,481.4	Libor[a]	Cooper Basin development and gas pipeline.
Indonesia	State and private	199.0	Libor and fixed	Term loans, aromatics plant.
Malaysia	State and private	688.0	Libor	LNG project and oil storage terminal.
New Zealand	Private and state	2,720.0	Libor	Methanol plant, synthetic gasoline plant, refinery expansion.
South Korea	State	38.0	Libor, USP[a]	Drilling rig.
Thailand	State	257.4	Libor, LTP[a]	Drawdown, gas separation plant.

Source: Euromoney Syndication Guide as published in Far Eastern Economic Review (1984).
a. Legend: Libor = London inter-bank offered rate. USP = US prime rate. LTP = Japanese long-term prime rate.

Table 7.6

Western Pacific Rim — Miscellaneous Revenue Determinants, Upstream and Downstream Petroleum Industry

COUNTRY	CORPORATE, INCOME AND OTHER RELEVANT TAXES	ROYALTY, OR OUTPUT SHARING ON PRODUCTION[a]	COST RECOVERY BY CONTRACTOR	BONUSES TO BE PAID	PRICE REGULATION
Australia	+/- 46 percent, levies on "old" and "new" oil, resource rent tax (RRT) on "greenfields" offshore	R = Onshore: 10 percent. Offshore: 10-12 percent (may be reduced by government). Abolition proposed with use of RRT.	Allowable exploration and development costs.	Not specified.	Prices set by government.
Brunei	50 percent or rate in effect at time of agreement.	R = 8-12.5 percent	Normal allowable.	Not specified.	None.
Burma	Myanma Oil Corporation assumes all taxes imposed on contractor.	PS, sliding scale.	Variable, up to 40 percent.	Yes.	Prices set by government.
China	50 percent (on net income).	R = 17.5 percent per field (includes taxes[b]	49 percent minimum.	US$1 million (signature plus variable offer).	Not available.
Indonesia[c]	45 percent (plus 20 percent dividend tax).	PS: variable; latest at 88/12.	Accounting depreciation according to field productivity, double declining method.	Variable	Graduated. Domestic prices set by government.
Japan[c]	56.4 percent.	R = 1 percent.	Normal accounting procedures.	Not specified.	Not on crude output. Ceiling on products pre-1980 and spot purchase.
South Korea	50 percent[d]	R = 12.5 percent	Assumed to follow normal accounting procedures.	Variable (all stages).	Ceiling on petroleum products.

Malaysia	45 percent plus 25 percent on revenues from exports (imposed in 1980).	R = 10 percent	20 percent on oil, 25 percent on gas (1976); 30 percent on oil, 35 percent on gas (1982).	Variable.	Prices set by government.
New Zealand	45 percent.	R = Negotiated on individual contracts.	Assumed normal.	Not specified.	Set by government.
Philippines	39.875 percent*.	PS: variable.	55-70 percent.	Variable.	Crude at world prices. Product prices controlled.
Thailand	50-60 per cent (maximum).	R = 12.5 percent.	Assumed normal.	Not specified.	Primary output prices negotiated; product prices controlled.

Sources: Siddayao (1980), Barrows (1983), Petroleum Economist/PetroConsultants (1981), U.S. Department of Energy (1981), Oil and Gas Journal (3 September, 1984), Petroleum News (July 1984), and World Oil (1 August, 1984).
a. Legend: R = royalties; PS = product-sharing.
b. In addition to output-sharing under terms of PSC or variant.
c. Modified terms apply to Joint Development Zone with Korea.
d. All other taxes, duties, and other charges are waived.
e. Corporate tax = 35 percent; profit remittance tax = 75 percent x 7.5 percent = 4.875 percent. Tax total = 39.875 percent.

qualifications. Output-sharing rates range from 70/30 in favor of the state to Indonesia's latest agreement with Caltex of 88/12 in favor of the state.[7] Cost recovery allowances in production-sharing contracts (PSCs) and their variants affect the net share accruing to investors. The sizes of these allowances range from 20 to 30 percent (Malaysia) to 49 percent upwards (China and the Philippines). The effective output share—when corporate tax rates, royalties, and cost recovery allowances are taken into account—will differ significantly among countries according to the sizes of these variables.[8] Bonuses further add to the cost factor, while any type of control on the manner in which prices are set upstream or downstream affects the sizes of the net revenues.

As Table 7.6 shows, a significant amount of intervention exists in the pricing of either crude oil or petroleum products in the countries reviewed. Directives related to the fiscal regime (such as those connected with the use of Batam Island instead of Singapore for importing oil exploration and development equipment) also affect costs if such directives result in less efficient handling, time loss, or higher lifting/loading rates; this could, in turn, affect the net revenue to the government if such costs increase the amount recoverable under the terms of the production sharing contract. Some of these features will be expanded upon in a later section.

The overall investment environment—including the stability of this environment—determines the investor's IRR. To a certain extent, the direction of the flow of commercial loans and direct investment in the upstream and downstream stages is an indicator of investors' perceptions of the economic viability of projects in these environments.

Investment Types

Table 7.7 shows the sources of petroleum investment funds in the countries reviewed. Foreign investments are shown in every country listed; details on the number of investing companies or the amounts of the investments are given elsewhere.[9] The Korean government is reported to encourage Korean companies to seek joint ventures and explore for petroleum in the offshore areas of Korea. Brunei was also reported to be seeking foreign investors in oil exploration (*Petroleum News*, January 1984, Supplement).

These foreign investments are not always solely from private companies. State-owned companies (such as the Japan National Oil Company and the Korea Petroleum Development Corporation) are involved in overseas ventures in the region and elsewhere. The state-run Chinese Petroleum Corporation (CPC) of Taiwan is reported to have entered a joint

Table 7.7

Western Pacific Rim—Ownership and Contractual Form, Upstream and Downstream Petroleum Industry (Selected Countries)

COUNTRY	NATIONALITY OF OPERATORS	UPSTREAM CONTRACTUAL FORM	DOWNSTREAM TYPES OF OWNERSHIP
Australia	F, P.	Onshore: varies with state. Offshore: exploration permits and production licenses.	F, P. 50% Australian required.
Burma	F, G.	Concession and PSC.	G.
China	F, G.	PSC variant offshore.	G.
Indonesia	F, G.	PSC.	G.
Japan	F, G.	Exploration permits and production licenses.	F, P. 50% Japanese equity required. State assistance provided.
South Korea	F, G.	Concessions.	F, P, G.
Malaysia	F, G.	PSC with royalty payments.	F, G.
New Zealand	F, P, G.	Prospecting and mining licenses.	F, P, G.
Philippines	F, P, G.	PSC variant (risk service).	F,P,G, and joint F-G.
Thailand	F,G.	Concession.	F, P and joint F-P-G.

Sources: Siddayao (1984), Barrows (1983), Oil and Gas Journal (7 May 1984) p. 76, Petroleum Economist/Petroleum Consultants (1981), Petroleum News (January 1984), Resources Asia (December 1983), World Oil (1 August 1984).
a. Legend:
F = foreign companies, both private and state-owned.
P = domestic private companies.
G = domestic state-run agencies.
PSC = production-sharing contract.

venture with the PNOC Exploration Corporation in the Philippines in 1984 (*Petroleum News,* September 1984, p. 17). Japan's Burma Petroleum Development Company is reported to have financed the exploration that led to the discovery of offshore gas fields in Burma's Gulf of Martaban, although no indications exist at this writing that similar financing will be arranged for the development of those fields (*Petroleum Economist,* November 1984, p. 428).

Japan's drilling level in Asia in all phases of the upstream stage is more than half its total worldwide. In some cases, drilling participation comes as funds provided for exploration programs, rather than participation as operator or technical partner. The returns to such investments or loan repayments are received in the form of oil or natural gas as profit shares (*Offshore,* 20 July, 1984).

Other forms of innovative financing are reported. For example, a scheme identified as an "evergreen revolving hydrocarbon credit" is reported to be already in use in Asia. A highly discounted value is assigned to proven production reserves and a company can borrow against it on an ongoing basis. The funds received can then be used for exploration (*Petroleum News,* March 1982, p. 14).

A significant amount of direct state involvement occurs in upstream and downstream operations in the region in the form of direct investments and subsidies to state-owned companies. These companies may be engaged in exploration for or in developing petroleum resources, or they may be involved in transporting oil or gas from Asian countries to the investor's home countries. Direct state involvement does not necessarily mean that such funds are from internally generated revenues. China, the Philippines, and Thailand, for example, have received World Bank loans for oil and gas development projects.[10] Some funds are also borrowed at commercial rates; see Table 7.5 again.

Capital inflows are also required to address shifts in the market. A good example is Singapore, which has to upgrade its refinery facilities to cope with the loss of processing arrangements with Indonesia and the influx of petroleum products from the Middle East, especially Kuwait. Term contracts signed with China may offset the lost market. In any case, Singapore's refining industry is switching over from producing low-value fuel oils into higher-value middle distillates such as kerosene and diesel. A new hydrocracker will help the Singapore Refining Company, for one, compete with similar refineries recently completed in Indonesia (*Asian Oil and Gas,* April 1984). In Singapore's case, its economic stature provides it with relatively easy access to capital investments for its downstream operations.

Domestic capital is generally not easily available for petroleum projects. Except for Japan, which provides a significant amount of the capital flows within the region, most countries—including Australia and New Zealand—which seek the development of indigenous oil and gas (both for domestic consumption and for export) are aware that domestic capital sources are inadequate to meet current financing demands. Yet, as the following sections show, certain aspects of the institutional framework in many of these countries suggest that policy planners may not recognize the limitations of their respective frameworks in terms of achieving both national goals and overall allocative efficiency.

V. GOVERNMENT INVOLVEMENT IN OIL AND GAS IN THE REGION

Government intervention levels vary by country and by industry stage. The country with the least amount of private sector involvement is Burma, where all types of foreign investment in the petroleum industry are allowed only according to specific targets set by the government with reference to a specific activity, upstream or downstream. All other countries have different (and sometimes parallel) types of intervention and involvement. The degree of such intervention is implied in Table 7.8. The agency or agencies involved in supra-operational as well as in operational capacities are listed.[11]

To appreciate the degree of intervention by the state in the oil and gas sector of the western Pacific Rim countries and to appreciate the arguments presented in this chapter, a summary of the important features of such intervention in selected countries is given below.[12]

Australia

The Australian government increased its role in the management of Australia's natural resources with the election of a new government in 1972. Pricing and ownership policies affecting the petroleum sector were adopted, and new institutions were created.

Current fiscal arrangements include the following: (1) excise taxes on oil discovered before September 1975 continue; (2) a higher levy on "new oil" (discovered post-September 1975) onshore and offshore is in effect; and (3) a "resource rent tax" (RRT) was introduced in 1984 that would apply to "greenfields" offshore which had not reached the development stage. (The RRT will be analyzed more closely in a later section, together with the cost-recovery allowance in the production-sharing type of contracts introduced by Indonesia.)

Table 7.8

Western Pacific Rim — Government Involvement in the Petroleum Industry

COUNTRY	AGENCY(IES)	AREAS OF INVOLVEMENT[a]
Australia	Various state governments. Federal: Department of National Development and Energy; Prices Justification Tribunal (PJT)	State: U, leases; D, pricing. Federal: U, taxation policies ownership ratios, pricing, etc. PJT: D, on,pricing.
Brunei ported	Brunei	Policy only. New legislation re- which requires state partnership in ventures.
Burma	Ministry of Industry and Myanma Oil Corporation.	U, D.
China	State Energy Commission, Ministry of Petroleum Industry, National Oil and Gas Exploration and Development Corporation, China National Oil Corporation (CNOC). China Petrochemical Corporation (SINOPEC)	U, D.
Indonesia	Ministry of Mines and Energy; Pertamina	Ministry: U Pertamina: U, D including petrochemicals and LNG.
Japan	Ministry of International Trade and Industry (MITI), Agency for Natural Resources (ANRE), Japan National Oil Company (JNOC).	U, D.

South Korea	Ministry of Energy and Resources Korea Petroleum Development Corporation (PEDCO), Korean Oil Development Company (KODECO), Korean Electric Power Company (KEPCO).	PEDCO: U and overseas purchases. KODECO: D. KEPCO: D (LNG).
Malaysia	Ministry of Energy, Telecom and Post Petrolieam Nasional Bhd. (Petronas), Petronas Carigali, and Malaysian LNG Bhd. (MLNG).	Ministry: Policy only. Petronas et al.: U, D.
New Zealand	Ministry of Energy (MOE), Petroleum Corporation of New Zealand (Petrocorp), and Liquids Fuels Trust Board (LFTB).	MOE: U. Petrocorp: U, D. LFTB: gas
Philippines	Ministry of Energy, Bureau of Energy Development Philippine National Oil Company	U.D.
Thailand	Department of Mineral Resources, Defense Energy Department (DED), Petroleum Authority of Thailand (PTT), and Thai LNG Company (TLNG, semi-govt.).	DED: U, northern onshore area. PTT: U, D. TLNG: D.

<u>Sources:</u> Siddayao (1984), <u>Petroleum News</u> (January 1984), <u>Oil and Gas Journal</u> (7 May, 1984, 27 August, 1984), <u>Petroleum Economist</u> (November 1984), U.S., Department of Energy (1981), and Woodward (1985).

a. U = upstream; D = downstream.

Indonesia

The nucleus of the petroleum sector in Indonesia is Pertamina (which is short for Perusahaan Pertambangan Minyak dan Gas Bumi Negara), formed in 1971. Pertamina is responsible for all petroleum activities, upstream and downstream, including supervisory control over the operations of foreign companies. It is obliged to make available to the public unlimited quantities of eight fuel products at prices which are set by the government. If revenues from the sale of those products do not cover costs (crude, refining, storage, transportation, and distribution), the government makes direct payment to Pertamina to cover the loss.

Japan

Japan's Basic Petroleum Law of 1962 gave the Ministry of International Trade and Industry (MITI) control over petroleum operations. It limits the role of foreign oil companies by curtailing their equity shares and the growth of refining and marketing operations. By the 1970s the refining sector was close to 50 percent Japanese-owned.

MITI's mandate includes providing assistance to independent Japanese companies in expanding their activities domestically and overseas by: (a) offering low-interest loans to both upstream and downstream operations; (b) giving these companies preference in domestic refinery applications and favorable marketing quota allocations for service stations; (c) providing diplomatic assistance to enable these companies to obtain favorable foreign exploration agreements; and (d) providing them with assured access to the Japanese market for foreign petroleum developed under such arrangements. In response to cutbacks on third-party sales by the majors in 1979, MITI encouraged domestic oil companies to secure crude directly from oil-producing states and raised the price ceiling for spot market purchases.

The Japan National Oil Company (JNOC), originally called the Japanese Petroleum Development Corporation (JPDC), was created to serve as a catalyst for Japanese overseas petroleum exploration and development initiatives and is responsible for Japan's strategic oil reserves. Its functions include the provision of financial incentives (loans and equity capital) for petroleum stockpiling by both private companies and joint government/industry ventures. JNOC also guarantees the financial overseas projects of Japanese companies.

JNOC acts as an agent for the direct acquisition of overseas petroleum rights but this is predicated on the transfer of such rights to a private party. The government was reported to have increased its subsidy for domestic exploration in 1984 by 19 percent over the 1983 budget, for a total allocation of US$14.2 million. Higher taxes on crude oil imports and new taxes on LNG and LPG were also reported to have been imposed in 1984 to replenish the tax-based fund for the development of new energy sources that had been depleted as oil prices fell in the 1980s (*Oil and Gas Journal,* 26 March 1984, p. 58, and 27 August 1984, p. 58).

Korea

The Korea Petroleum Development Corporation (PEDCO) is a 100-percent government-funded enterprise responsible for petroleum exploration and development and for the management of production and refining facilities. PEDCO is responsible for overseas purchases and is also in charge of the emergency petroleum reserve intended to improve Korea's energy supply security. This responsibility includes government-to-government deals with oil-producing nations. PEDCO is also heavily involved in providing the country with LPG (*Petroleum Economist,* November 1984, p. 413). As part of its policy of diversifying its oil supply sources away from the Middle East, the Korean government also subsidizes the transportation of crude imports from Mexico, Ecuador, Libya, and Egypt.

Malaysia

The national oil company, Petroleum Nasional Berhad (Petronas), has responsibility for implementing oil and gas policies, including pricing and oversight of foreign contractors. Petronas Carigali Sdn. Bhd., a subsidiary, is responsible for government-funded exploration. Malaysian LNG Bhd. (MLNG) is a joint venture between Petronas, Shell Gas B.V., and Mitsubishi, to build and run an LNG plant.

New Zealand

The government is directly involved in exploration through the government-owned Petroleum Corporation of New Zealand (Petrocorp), which has sole or part interest in at least nineteen of a total of about fifty permits, mostly offshore. The state shares ownership with Mobil of several petrochemical and natural gas plants.

A tax policy change in 1979 was expected to stimulate hydrocarbon exploration by foreign and domestic investors. As part of the policy shift, Petrocorp now has to fund its operations and the government's 51 percent share in development projects from retained earnings; it has to do this by borrowing in the open market and farming out of some of its acreage interests instead of depending on direct government outlays. Interest payments and loan repayments come from the government's share of output revenues (*Oil and Gas Journal*, 10 December 1984, p. 55).

The Philippines

The Philippine National Oil Company (PNOC) is directly involved in the country's petroleum refining, marketing, transportation, and development activities. PNOC (which bought out the Esso marketing and refining subsidiary in the Philippines in the early 1970s) controls about 60 percent of the Bataan refinery; this refinery was jointly owned with Mobil until 1983, when Mobil sold its share to Caltex, reportedly below book value (*Asian Wall Street Journal*, 23 September, 1983; *Petroleum News*, July 1984).[13] PNOC controls about 40 percent of the domestic product market. Over half of Philippine oil imports are purchased on a government-to-government basis by PNOC and distributed to all refineries (including those privately owned). PNOC also has developed an ocean transport capability, owning as many as three tankers in 1981 and controlling 90 percent of product tanker lifting capability and all barge lifting capabilities.

The Bureau of Energy Development (BED) monitors upstream and downstream activities. However, the distinction between the status of the BED and the Bureau of Energy Utilization (BEU) staff relative to those of PNOC is fuzzy at times. Whereas PNOC is run as a profit-making corporation and pays industry-competitive salaries, BED and BEU are technically government bureaus (which places them within the oversight of the government's Civil Service Commission). Some BED and BEU staff are, however, PNOC-appointees seconded to these government bureaus. The boundary separating the policy-making and monitoring area from that of serving as a supplier of oil services (or the supra-operational versus the operational aspects of government intervention) is thus a gray area.

Thailand

The Thai government has traditionally allowed the private sector to be principally responsible for oil and gas exploration, development, refining, and marketing. With commercial discovery of natural gas in the Gulf of Thailand in 1977, however, the Natural Gas Organization (NGOT) was formed. In 1978 the Petroleum Authority of Thailand (PTT) took over NGOT and the small government marketing outlet called Oil Fuel Organization, which had been formed earlier to complement private sector activities. PTT exercises control over crude purchases and product distribution.

In December 1979 the government decided to take a 49 percent share in the Thai Oil Refinery Company Ltd. (TORC). The remaining 51 percent is owned by Shell, Caltex, and other private companies. A semigovernmental enterprise called the Thai LNG Company was also reported to have been formed, with 60 percent capital provided by the Thai government and 40 percent by four major Japanese trading companies (*Asian Wall Street Journal,* 22 May, 1984, p. 3).

VI. THE INSTITUTIONAL FRAMEWORK: SOME ALLOCATIVE IMPLICATIONS

The foregoing sections raise many allocative issues, and it is not possible to discuss all of them here.[14] It will be useful, therefore, to concentrate on a few topics, with emphasis on more recent developments; these are associated with (1) the role of national companies, upstream and downstream, in domestic and foreign operations, and (2) the fiscal regime in the upstream stage.

State Intervention in the Form of National Oil Companies

Various explanations have been provided to justify the role of government in the petroleum sector and the formation of national oil companies.[15] This author's view of the roles of government and, where necessary, of a state-owned or national oil company (NOC) was outlined in Section II of this paper. As Section V shows, however, the NOC roles are varied. In the producing developing countries, the NOC can be both a regulator of other companies and an active participant in upstream and/or downstream activities; examples are Pertamina, Petronas, PNOC, and PTT. The reasons for their existence may have nothing to do with the conditions outlined in Section II. In both the lower-income and higher-income oil importing countries, government-to-government deals and stockpiling are part of the NOC's responsibilities.

Active participation by the state raises no allocative issues if the NOC does not draw upon a state's resources to survive in competition with other investors. The same is true if state intervention does not hinder the efficient operation of other economic units through unfair practices; such practices include preferences received in markets where the NOC would not otherwise survive. Because economic activity involves an element of risk—in varying degrees—it is not clear that it is in a society's best interests that state resources be deployed in risk-laden activities, unless it can be shown that the private sector is not available to undertake activities that are considered socially necessary. It can thus be argued that in the upstream stage of the industry, use of a state's limited resources to undertake the risks of exploring frontier areas raises allocative issues. Yet, as a proliferation of unorganized data will show, public sector involvement occurs frequently in the region.

To reiterate that exploration is risky and that the discount rate for risk changes inversely with knowledge about a prospective area is not to overstate one's case. The Mukluk "dry hole" was a US$1.6 billion loss, one of the biggest exploration investment losses in recent history. It is a timely reminder that to date the only known method to establish the true potential of an area is by drilling, despite significant advances in exploration technology.[16]

The overseas operations of NOCs is another area of interest. Some NOCs actively engage in the upstream phases of the industry overseas or, at the minimum, provide assistance to private national firms attempting to invest in the upstream sector in producing countries. Where subsidies are involved to promote the home country's energy security goals, the premium paid may be justified by the state in terms of the future security of supply. It is not clear, however, whether the producing country or the rest of society is well served and that investments are, in fact, efficiently allocated in this manner.

That is, when an enterprise's funds are provided at interest below the opportunity costs of the normal investor or where "diplomatic assistance" is provided by the NOC to its nationals, no effective competition for investment opportunities exists. Does such subsidy promote the optimal development of the region's petroleum resources? Is the receiving country truly benefitting from this exchange where inequality exists in bargaining positions among those competing for the right to develop the host country's petroleum? Are the investing country's taxpayers well-served by the loss of revenue from such concessionary loans?

The answer is not clearly negative or positive. All we know is that a significant amount of upstream and downstream investments are emanating from NOCs in the region, that these investments will eventually result in the movement of petroleum from the producing countries to the investing country, and that some investors are left out by the arrangement. At issue is imperfect information with respect to alternatives.

The proliferation of NOCs also exacerbates the information problem. That buyers and sellers must deal with uncertainty in real life is not arguable. To be partly responsible for increasing that uncertainty is another matter altogether. The multiplication of such uncertainty, given the complexity of petroleum trading in the region, and its implications for investment decisions are highlighted by the observation of Fesharaki (1984) that the entry of NOCs has reduced individual awareness of changes occurring within and outside the region which affect their operation. It is tempting to suggest at this point that multinationals, having to address a larger scale picture, may be better able to deal with this problem; the evidence for a categorical statement is not available in this respect,[17] but again the overall efficiency implications and costs of the recent increase in refineries that are state-owned cannot be overlooked.

Government investments in and control over refining or marketing facilities may be justified if private investors are not available within the country. Undue advantage in the domestic marketing of products can raise issues of efficiency in the use of state resources if no clear benefits result from such ownership or control, especially where the efficiency of such operations is impaired owing to lack of competition. Casual observation and some of the popular literature suggest that this is the case. At this writing, reports are that refining capacity in the region significantly exceeds processing requirements (*The Economist*, 28 July 1984; *Petroleum News*, March 1984, pp. 60-61). Where NOC investment in refineries precludes its taking advantage of the economies of scale in the home country or the region and, in the process, increases overall unused capacity, allocative efficiency issues on a global level are pertinent.

The desire of a home country to capture the value added in processing or the economic rents[18] from the sale of petroleum products needs to be weighed against the costs of such investments. It is not clear that such trade-offs were the primary consideration in the construction of new refineries in producing countries or in new state investments in others. Because of the highly capital-intensive nature of the industry, a question could be raised with respect to the opportunity cost of reallocating those funds away from other industrial activities that might have larger proportions of domestic value added and a higher multiplier-accelerator effect on income and employment. What is clear is that trading and investment patterns are changing, and so are the relationships among the buying and selling countries.

An increase has also been noted in government-to-government deals involving NOCs or small domestic companies in the importing country to procure petroleum supplies; where the NOC is involved, it becomes the supplier of crude to other domestic refiners. The Japan National Oil Company, for example, was created as a result of growing concern on the part of the government over the security of Japanese oil supplies if it continued to depend on the international companies. There was concern over the ability of these companies to deal with OPEC and a desire to have greater control over Japan's supply security.

Country-to-country deals do not guarantee the best price for the country concerned. After all, NOCs or individual companies are small buyers and, therefore, have relatively less bargaining power in dealing with a supplier than the large integrated, multinational company the government mistrusts. Furthermore, a multinational's bargaining power is enhanced by its access to a variety of sources not necessarily open to small buyers. Again, however, the perceived security associated with such deals may outweigh the true social costs of such arrangements. There is no guarantee that large buyers will pass their savings on to their customers in pricing refined products. The low prices to customers preceding OPEC's dominance of the market suggest, however, that this is not unlikely.

To what lengths can one stretch the security basis for government intervention? The severity of the costs associated with errors in judgment associated with NOC purchasing may not be passed over lightly. It is well known among petroleum analysts and market observers that spot market prices were partially driven up in 1979 by panic-buying on the part of the Japanese government, which decided to increase its stockpile to levels far above its usual 90-day minimum (stockpiles were reported to have gone as high as 140-day levels). It is also known in industry circles that they later had to sell some of these stocks at a loss (of about US$4/bbl.) because of storage problems.

What is the optimum social premium to be paid for energy security? Is this a luxury that Japan can afford? Can less affluent countries afford the costs of similar errors? What was the cost to the rest of the world of this error? For, indeed, the high prices were paid for not only by the Japanese but also by other oil importers, including the developing countries.

The move in the Western Pacific countries towards increased use of state resources for activities that are normally undertaken by private funds contrasts with the increasing commercialization in formerly non-market economies like Burma and China.

The Fiscal Regime

For the purposes of this chapter, the fiscal regime will be defined as the deliberate choice of taxes and tax-type elements to influence economic activities in the petroleum sector. The usual intention of fiscal policy is to raise general revenues for operational purposes; general corporate taxes fall in this category. The incidence of such taxes on the buyer is determined by the demand/supply elasticities; that is, treated as costs, they may be passed on in whole or in part by the seller.

In the extractive sector an additional intention of fiscal policy is to capture part of the economic rents that are associated with the production and supply of output. Thus, cost recovery allowances, royalties, output sharing ratios, bonuses, the pricing and marketing clauses, and—more recently—resource rent taxes form part of the fiscal regime. In this chapter, only the cost-recovery clause in production sharing contracts (PSC) and the resource rent tax (RRT) introduced effective 1 July 1984 in Australia (which grants licenses to exploration companies) will be discussed.[19] These features of two different fiscal regimes have been chosen because of a clear similarity in the restrictive nature of their application: (a) the cost-recovery clause of the PSC precludes recovery of losses by an operator in an unsuccessful (or "dry") contract area from the returns of a successful contract area; and (b) the RRT is to be applied separately to each individual project and not to aggregate company results.

The resource rent tax has been proposed as an optimal way of capturing the benefits from developing a resource while at the same time avoiding initial disincentives to investors.[20] This tax is collected only after a specified "threshold" discounted-cash-flow internal rate of return (IRR) on total cash flow has been realized. The "threshold" was defined by the Australian government as the "long term bond rate . . . plus 15 percentage points," and the RRT rate was set in 1984 at 40 percent (Australian Government, 1984). The final version for initial implementation in late 1984 was expected to have a threshold of 30 percent (on the rate of return from a project), this threshold still tied to the bond rate (*Petroleum News*, July 1984, p. 61). The RRT is levied prior to company tax; payments of RRT are a deduction for company tax purposes.

The RRT's proponents suggest that this tax precludes the need to predict the inherently uncertain future profitability of a project, since the actual tax liability adjusts automatically and progressively to the outcome. It is claimed that risk in a project is actually shared by both investor and government when the RRT is adopted. Because the RRT starts only after the threshold IRR has been earned on the investment, it has been argued that the RRT will not act as a deterrent to investments that are marginal in nature (Garnaut and Ross, 1983). The strong interventionist nature of the RRT raises many related questions, however.

Assessing a rent tax based on the IRR of a company for a specific project assumes that such information is easily available. To assume this information is available for one project or even more for an investor's overall operations is to be highly optimistic. Garnaut and Ross (1983) implicitly assume that cash flows represent economic rent. Since dividends do not represent the IRR where cash is set aside for reinvestment in expansion or in new ventures, then an RRT on cash flows would be taxing a portion of what the authors call "the supply price of capital" or part of what economists generally refer to as a "fair return on investment."

Linking the threshhold to the bond rate is obviously an effort to deal with the heroic ideal of determining the appropriate threshold without knowing a company's IRR. There is no reason to believe that an exploration investor's IRR is close to the prevailing bond rate in a country. To appreciate this, one only needs to recall the notions of technical, economic, and "political" risks that are part of the foreign petroleum investor's discounting process.

The project-by-project basis for the RRT also suggests that the tax may be more conveniently tried in a small developing country, or a country with few petroleum projects. A problem arises in the application of this approach to a large country with many deposits, where a project-by-project calculation of a rent taxation scheme of the nature proposed would be administratively costly and could be socially counterproductive. Even if such a scheme were inherently free of other problems, there remains the question of simplicity in administering the tax and monitoring it effectively and efficiently in a country where many projects exist. Consider the administrative costs of allocating resources to determining the resource rent tax for individual projects in Indonesia, for example, with its many fields. A new bureaucracy would be required to handle such a complex task. Proponents may implicitly assume—heroically—that bureaucracies can be designed to enhance a society's welfare; yet as Norgaard (1984) points out, to argue that this is so is mythology. It may further be argued that bureaucracies do not generally work well, whether in industrialized countries or in those less so.

It is generally acknowledged that a significant proportion of capital investments for both upstream and downstream activities comes from internally generated corporate sources. Keenan (1981) estimated that for downstream capital needs alone—where risks are relatively lower—as much as 73 percent normally comes from internal corporate sources. Even with the new schemes available (for example, the "evergreen" hydrocarbon revolving credit already mentioned), one can expect that, in general, at least that proportion will come from internal funds for the riskier upstream operations, especially for oil and gas. By focusing on projects rather than on overall operations within a country, the RRT reduces that source of funds and can thus serve as a disincentive to risk-bearing.

Garnaut and Ross (1983) recognized that the RRT has a "bias towards under-investment under conditions of uncertainty... " (p. 136). This shortcoming is, however, not sufficiently stressed in their book, nor is it treated at all in the *Outline* which served as the basis for the RRT's adoption in Australia. The petroleum exploration and development stage represents one of the best examples of a venture involving a high degree of uncertainty with regard to outcome. Siddayao (1980) argued that the Indonesian PSC, where losses in a dry contract area cannot be recovered from profits in successful areas, would influence risk-averse investors to restrict the search for new sources to areas where sufficient information exists that would lead to expectations of a higher probability of success than failure. The RRT would, it may also be argued, elicit the same response and would result in under-investment in frontier areas.

Game theoretic models have suggested that a government's share of economic rent increases in some direct proportion to the amount of information an interested investor has on a prospective exploration area (Norgaard, 1977). Since definitive information on potential cannot be obtained without drilling, the RRT thus appears to have all the demerits associated with the U.S. "windfall profits tax" and more.[21] Observations made in 1984 that the continued high levels of drilling activity in Australia suggested that the feared negative industry response had not materialized failed to specify the nature of the activities that were continuing. The same popular observation was made of Indonesian activity in the late 1970s where unilateral changes were made that reduced the output share of investors; yet the current concentration of contracts in Indonesia to areas already known to be successful is evidence of the rational investor's response to the risk component of the PSC.

The implications of the contractual framework for the behavioral response of profit-maximizing or cost-minimizing rational enterprises may also be gleaned from the number of operators in Indonesia and Malaysia, for example, that bear the names of major oil companies (Sabah Shell and Sarawak Shell in Malaysia are typical). One might well ask if this multiplication of subsidiary companies is an efficient way of organizing economic activity and if the costs that might accrue to society as a result could very well have been spent more effectively on another economic activity.

VII. CONCLUDING REMARKS

Several inferences may be drawn from the preceding sections:
(1) The countries of the region may be grouped into four categories: (a) those that produce oil sufficient to meet most of their requirements; (b) those that produce all, or slightly more than, they want to use; (c) those that produce more than they can use; and (d) those that produce

negligible amounts relative to their total energy requirements. This diversity has resulted in a significant flow of oil among these groups of countries.

(2) Geologically, although no one thinks of the region in terms of its potential for giant discoveries, the region's oil and gas resources are still far from fully developed. Hence, in addition to direct state involvement, the region is still seen by investors as a growth area for exploration, development, and production. The flow of capital into the projects comes from both within and outside the region.

(3) Security of petroleum supply is a priority in the agenda of most net-oil-importers. Their responses to the instabilities created by the 1973-74 and 1979-80 threats to petroleum supply have varied according to geological endowments and financial capabilities for reducing the degree of such insecurity. Such responses have sometimes appeared to be socially costly, especially where the impacts of errors extend beyond national borders.

(4) Among the responses to the market upheavals has been the creation of new institutions to deal with the problem. In addition to strictly policy-making and implementing bodies, national oil companies have proliferated. Such national companies occasionally serve as both competitor and regulator in the industry. They also engage in international activities in competition with private foreign investment. The social value of this competition with respect to societal efficiency is not immediately clear because of special privileges accorded national companies that are not available to private investors.

(5) Recognition of the changing structure of the relationship between investors and resource owners plus the desire to capture as much of the associated rent from such ownership have given rise to new fiscal regimes and shifts in investment and trading patterns.

(6) Although most countries are not capable of tapping domestic capital sources for the development and marketing of indigenous petroleum resources, the institutional framework does not always appear to recognize this need. Directives affecting the way business is conducted, price controls, and the like affect the investment climate.

(7) The existence of some elasticity is observed in the demand and supply of hydrocarbons, even that of the critical liquid commodity; this elasticity is reflected in the behavior of buyers and sellers. Responses vary according to differing attitudes toward risk; such variation is observable both in the private and public sectors.

Overall, a general assessment suggests that present arrangements are far from optimal. To date this situation has not been aggravated by potential conflicts that could arise from boundary problems in the process of developing these traded resources. There is no guarantee, however, that the present amicable situation, or at worst dormant hostility, will prevail and that countries will always see the benefits of settling disputes amicably.[22]

NOTES

*This paper was completed in 1984 and revised in 1985 while the author was resident at the East-West Center.

1. For purposes of this paper, the term "petroleum" will be used in the accepted industry terminology that includes both liquid and gaseous hydrocarbons. The terms "oil" and "gas" will be used where a distinction is necessary.
2. The *upstream* stage involves exploration (or the location of producible reserves), development (or the delineation of the discovered resources), and production (or the actual lifting of the resources from the traps). The *downstream* stage includes transporting, refining, and marketing of the discovered resource in crude or processed form.
3. LPG is the generic term for propane, butane, and mixtures of both. It is produced from two sources: (1) as a by-product in refineries and chemical plants; and (2) as a result of the extraction of such liquids from natural gas streams or crude oil at or close to the point of production.
4. Chase Manhattan does not specify the countries covered, but one assumes that the term "Far East" includes the traditional group of Asian and Australasian countries.
5. Some loans by India in April 1983 given in the reference material were for exploration and development, and two short-term loans were shown for Bangladesh for the payment of oil imports.
6. Oil companies sometimes want to refer to themselves in this era as management companies in the upstream stage because of the nature of the current contractual arrangements.
7. The Indonesian version of the 85/15 split—and presumably of the 88/12 split, for which no details are available to this author at this writing —includes corporate and other taxes due the government in the 85 percent state share of "profit oil." The true split after cost-recovery, therefore, may be close to or even better than the 70/30 split of Malaysia and the Philippines. See pages 65, 89, and 105 in Siddayao (1980) for a detailed explanation.

8. See Table 5.5 in Siddayao (1980) which shows how these variables affect the net "take" of governments and companies.

9. The interested reader may find a perusal of the annual exploration issues of the *Petroleum News* informative.

10. See Appendix C in Siddayao (1984) for a summary of the details of some of these loans.

11. Supra-operational activities are defined, for the purposes of this chapter, as policy interventions (licensing procedures, contract determinations, price setting) and government activities that are of a general oversight nature. Operational involvement is defined as engaging in actual exploration, production, refining, purchasing, and marketing activities.

12. The summary that follows draws from the references cited in Table 7.8, except where otherwise noted. The author has provided additional insights from personal knowledge of the framework in the Philippines. More detail is found in Siddayao (1985).

13. Mobil reportedly also sold its retail outlets and distribution system for industrial customers to Caltex.

14. Furthermore, some of the issues peculiar to the region's upstream and downstream institutional framework (including contracts, subsidies, and pricing policies) have already been discussed by this author in depth elsewhere. See, for example, Siddayao (1980, 1981, 1985a, b).

15. See, for example, Bell (1983).

16. Those interested in the historical details of this loss may consult *Oil and Gas Journal* (12 December 1983, 16 January 1984, 30 January 1984), *Offshore* (January 1984), and *Wall Street Journal* (19 April 1984, 23 August 1984).

17. This author's personal experience in the industry and in dealing with Singapore marketers in the late 1970s provides an impression that conflicts with those suggested by Fesharaki (1984).

18. The term *economic rent* is used to refer to the difference between production costs (which include a minimum, or reasonable, return on investment) and selling price. Other authors use the term "net price."

19. The interested reader is referred to Siddayao (1980, 1981, and 1985) for an analysis of the allocative implications of the other elements of the fiscal regime in Asia.

20. For details on this tax, see Garnaut and Ross (1983) and *Outline of a "Greenfields" Resource Rent Tax in the Petroleum Sector* (April 1984) prepared for the Office of the Prime Minister, Canberra, Australia.

21. See Eck (1983) for an analysis of the "windfall profits tax."

22. These issues are discussed by the author elsewhere. See Siddayao (1978 and 1984).

REFERENCES

Alberts, J.P., M.D. Carter, A.L. Clark, A.B. Coury, and S.P. Sweinfurth, (1973) *Summary Petroleum and Selected Mineral Statistics for 120 Countries, Including Offshore Areas*, Geological Survey Professional Paper 817, Washington, D.C.: U.S. Government Printing Office.

American Association of Petroleum Geologists, (1984) *AAPG Bulletin*, "World Energy Developments, 1983" issue, Vol. 68, No. 10.

American Embassy, (1984) *Indonesia's Petroleum Sector*, Jakarta.

Asian Oil and Gas, (April 1984) "Energy Update," pp.5-6.

Asian Wall Street Journal, (23 September 1983) "Mobil Signs Accord to Sell Its Manila Unit," p. 14.

Asian Wall Street Journal, (22 May 1984) "Japan Trading Firms to Develop Thai LNG," p. 3.

Asian Wall Street Journal, (11 May 1984) "Asia Is Called a Reasonable Risk for Firms," pp. 1, 14.

Australian Government, (1984) "Statement by the Treasurer the Hon. P.J. Keating, MP and the Minister for Resources and Energy Senator The Hon. Peter Walsh - 27 June 1984", Canberra, Australia.

Bangkok Post, (8 May 1984) "Thailand Signs Oil Deal," p. 1.

Barrows, G.H., (1983) *Worldwide Concession Contracts and Petroleum Legislation*, Tulsa, Oklahoma: PennWell Publishing Company.

Bell, J., (1983) "Government Oil Companies: 'Quo Vadis'?" In P. Nemetz (ed.), *Energy: Ethics, Power, and Policy*, Special Issue of the *Journal of Business Administration*, Vol. 13, Nos. 1 and 2 (Vancouver: University of British Columbia).

British Petroleum Company, (1984) *BP Statistical Review of World Energy*, London.

Chase Manhattan Bank, (1979, 1984) *Capital Investments of the World Petroleum Industry*, New York.

Eck, T.R., (1983) "Energy Economics and Taxation," *Journal of Energy and Development*, Vol. 8, No. 2 (Spring), pp. 293-304.

Far Eastern Economic Review, (1984) *Asia Yearbook*, "Asia-Pacific Principal Energy Financings," pp. 96-97.

Fesharaki, F., (1984) "The Singapore Story: A Refining Center in a Transitory Oil Market," Manuscript, OPEC Downstream Project, Resource Systems Institute, Honolulu: The East-West Center.

Garnaut, R., and A.C. Ross, (1983) *Taxation of Mineral Rents*, Oxford: Clarendon Press.

Hoffman, S.L., (1984) "The ASEAN Refining Industry: A Preliminary Survey and Analysis," Draft manuscript for the OPEC Downstream Project, Resource Systems Institute, Honolulu: The East-West Center, April.

Ibrahim, Y., (1984) "China Pushing Oil on Asian Markets at Cut-rate Prices," *Wall Street Journal* (15 October), p. 34.

Keenan, P.J., (1981) "Financing the Petroleum Industry 1980-1990: $3.17 Trillion," *Ocean Industry* (October).

Mooradian, A.H., (1984) "Asian Oil Production outside China is Expected to Decline after 1986," *Asian Wall Street Journal* (9 April 1984), p. 3.

Musgrave, R.A., and P.B. Musgrave, (1973) *Public Finance in Theory and Practice*, McGraw-Hill.

Norgaard, R.B., (1977) "Uncertainty, Competition, and Leasing," Manuscript, Energy Resources Group, University of California, Berkeley.

Norgaard, R.B., (1984) "Bureaucracy, Systems Management, and the Mythology of Science," Giannini Foundation of Agricultural Economics Working Paper No. 297, May (first draft).

Offshore, (January 1984) "Drillers Seek Alaska Supergiant," Vol. 44, No. 1, pp. 29-39.

Offshore, (May 1984) "Offshore China Offers Great Potential," Vol. 44, No. 5, p. 122.

Offshore, (20 July 1984) "Japan Provides Funds, Encourages Worldwide Search," Vol. 44, No. 8, pp. 90-94.

Offshore, (20 July 1984) "Offshore Crude, Gas Production Increases," Vol. 44, No. 8.

Oil and Gas Journal, (18 December 1981 and 26 December 1983).

Oil and Gas Journal, (5 September 1983) "Australia Approves Crude Oil Exports," Vol. 81, No. 36, p. 54.

Oil and Gas Journal, (12 December 1983) "Mukluk Test Appears to Be Dry Hole," Vol. 81, No. 50, pp. 66-67.

Oil and Gas Journal, (26 December 1983) "Worldwide Oil and Gas at a Glance," Vol. 81, No. 52.

Oil and Gas Journal, (16 January 1984) "Apparent Mukluk Wildcat Failure Doesn't Dim North Slope Outlook," Vol. 82, No. 3, pp. 45-48.

Oil and Gas Journal, (30 January 1984) "Beaufort Lists Strike; Mukluk Plugged," Vol. 82, No. 5, pp. 74-75.

Oil and Gas Journal, (26 March 1984) "LPG International Trade Seen Rising," Vol. 82, No. 13, pp. 58-59.

Oil and Gas Journal, (7 May 1984) "Changing Times Alter the Way State Oil Firms Do Business," Vol. 82, No. 19, pp. 73-78.

Oil and Gas Journal, (27 August 1984) "Asia/Pacific Oil Flow Up, Exploration Down," Vol. 82, No. 5, pp. 55-62.

Oil and Gas Journal, (3 September 1984) "Thai Concessions Carry Revamped Terms," Vol. 82, No. 36, pp. 50-51.

Oil and Gas Journal, (10 December 1984) "Indonesia Presses Oil Companies to Use Its Ports," Vol. 82, No. 50, p. 54.

Oil and Gas Journal, (10 December 1984) "New Zealand Energy Changes to Open Acreage," Vol. 82, No. 50, p. 55.

Petroleum Economist, (August 1983) "World Survey: Natural Gas," Vol. 50, No. 8, pp. 293-96.

Petroleum Economist, (August 1984) "News in Brief: Taiwan," Vol. 51, No. 8, p. 39.

Petroleum Economist, (August 1984) "World Survey: Natural Gas," Vol. 51, No. 8, pp. 286-88.

Petroleum Economist, (August 1984) "South Korea: "Economic Boom Continues," Vol. 51, No. 11, pp. 413-15.

Petroleum Economist, (August 1984) "News in Brief: Burma," Vol. 51, No. 11, p. 428.

Petroleum Economist and Petroconsultants, (1981) *Far East Oil and Energy Survey*, London.

Petroleum News, (March 1982) "Asia's Finance Business: How Does Energy Tap In?" Vol. 12, No. 12, pp. 14-15.

Petroleum News, (July 1983) News Supplement: "Philippines," Vol. 14, No. 4.

Petroleum News, (January 1984) Exploration Annual, Vol. 14, No. 10.

Petroleum News, (March 1984) "Tracking Energy Demand: Malaysia Sets up New Unit," Vol. 14, No. 12, p. 26.

Petroleum News, (March 1984) "Map of the Month," Vol. 14, No. 12, pp. 60-61.

Petroleum News, (May 1984) "Map of the Month: Major Crude Flows to East Asian Countries," Vol. 15, No. 2, pp. 24-25.

Petroleum News, (July 1984) "Compromise Reached on Australia's RRT," Vol. 15, No. 4, p. 61.

Petroleum News, (August 1984) "NW Shelf Gas Flows to Perth," Vol. 15, No. 5, pp. 29-30.

Petroleum News, (September 1984) "Taiwan Moves to Total Import Reliance," Vol. 15, No. 6, p. 17.

Resources Asia, (December 1983) "Outlook for 1984."

Siddayao, C.M., (1978) *The Off-shore Petroleum Resources of South-East Asia: Potential Conflict Situations and Related Economic Considerations*, Kuala Lumpur: Oxford University Press.

Siddayao, C.M., (1980) *The Supply of Petroleum Reserves in South-East Asia: Economic Implications of Evolving Property Rights Arrangements*, Oxford University Press.

Siddayao, C.M., (1981) "Petroleum Resource Development Policies: Implications of the Southeast Asian Contractual Framework," *Energy*, Vol. 6, No. 8 (August).

Siddayao, C.M., (1984) "Oil and Gas on the Continental Shelf: Potentials and Constraints in the Asia-Pacific Region," *Ocean Management*, Vol. 9, pp. 73-100.

Siddayao, C.M., (1985) *The Development and Trade of Petroleum Resources in the Pacific Rim: The Roles Played by Governments*, Resource Systems Institute Working Paper Series WP-85-2, Honolulu: The East-West Center.

Siddayao, C.M., (1985a) "Capital Investment Requirements for Oil and Gas Development: Constraints in Developing Countries," In R.K. Pachauri (ed.), *Proceedings* of the International Conference on "Global Interactions" of the International Association of Energy Economists, Delhi, India, 4-6 January 1984, Delhi: Allied Publishers.

Siddayao, C.M. (ed.), (1985b) *Criteria for Energy Pricing Policy*: A Collection of Papers Commissioned for the Energy Pricing Policy Workshop, Bangkok 8-11 May 1984, London: Graham & Trotman Ltd.

Thailand Government, National Energy Administration, (1983) *Thailand Energy Master Plan*, Bangkok.

Toner, A.J., (1984) "Iran's Crude Oil Floods East Asia as Prices Plunge," *Wall Street Journal* (26 June), pp. 1, 3.

Turvey, R., (ed.), (1968) *Public Enterprise*, Baltimore, Md.: Penguin Books, Inc.

U.S., Department of Energy, (1981) *Energy Industries Abroad*, Prepared by the Office of International Affairs, Doc. No. DOE.IA-0012, September.

Wall Street Journal, (19 April 1984) "After Mukluk Fiasco, Sohio Strives to Find, or Perhaps to Buy, Oil," pp. 1, 24.

Woodard, K., (1985) "Development of China's Petroleum Industry: An Overview," Paper prepared for the China Energy Workshop, East-West Center, Honolulu.

World Oil, (1 August 1984) "Offshore China: High Risk, Potential," Vol. 199, No. 2, pp. 59-60.

8

Factors Affecting Steam Coal Trade In Asia and The Pacific

TOUFIQ A. SIDDIQI

INTRODUCTION

During the forty years since the end of World War II, trade in energy has meant mainly trade in oil—at least in Asia and the Pacific. It was primarily following the sharp increases in the price of oil during 1973-74 that coal, liquefied natural gas, and uranium also became important components of trade for the countries surrounding the Pacific Ocean. Even in this relatively short time span, many coal producers have already been through a complete cycle of "boom and bust." In many countries, infrastructure including port-handling capacity has been built to handle volumes that have failed to materialize. Is this situation likely to persist, or will there be another boom in coal trade in the near future?

The record of forecasts in the energy area during the last fifteen years has been pretty dismal. Rather than add one more forecast to the pool, an attempt is made in this paper to identify the major factors affecting steam coal trade in Asia and the Pacific, and some of the trends likely to be important.

As background material, the current production and consumption of coal in the Asia-Pacific countries is given in Table 8.1. Exports and imports by country are presented in Table 8.2. Data for steam coal and metallurgical coal are given separately where available; otherwise the figures are aggregates.

In the following sections, we discuss each of the major factors expected to affect steam coal trade in the region:

Table 8.1
Current Production and Consumption of Coal in Asia and the Pacific

COUNTRY	PRODUCTION (IN MILLION TONNES)	CONSUMPTION (IN MILLION TONNES)	COAL AS A PERCENTAGE OF COMMERCIAL ENERGY USED, 1983[b]
Afghanistan	0.17	0.17	17.9
Australia	149.00(L) (1983/84)	70.30(L)	43.3
Bangladesh	0	0.16	3.0
Burma	0.04	0.22	9.6
Canada	44.70(L)	44.00(L)	15.3
China	772.00 (1984)	710.10(L)	79.3
Taiwan	2.01 (1984)	7.97 (1982)	n.a.
Fiji	0	0.02	11.1
Hong Kong	0	4.46 (1984)	31.5
India	147.50 (1984/85)	144.10(L)	70.7
Indonesia	0.49	0.33	0.9
Japan	16.80 (1984/85)	91.70	20.8
North Korea	49.00(L)	49.40(L)	86.3
South Korea	21.20 (1984)	29.70	39.6
Malaysia	0	0.55 (1984)	1.0
Nepal	0	0.07	28.6
New Zealand	2.42(L)	2.22(L)	15.2
Pakistan	1.87 (1983/84)	2.38	8.3
Philippines	1.20 (1984)	1.20 (1984)	7.1
Singapore	0	0.01	0.0
Sri Lanka	0	0.03	1.6
Thailand	2.25(L)	2.76(L)	4.9
US	712.00(L)	670.60(L)	25.4
Vietnam	6.00	5.00	70.0

Source: Newer Coal Technologies: Implications for Energy and Development Policies in Asia and the Pacific. Edited by Toufiq A. Siddiqi and Shen Shihua. New York: Pergamon Press, 1986.

a. In million tonnes, except for E = million tonnes of coal equivalent, L = substantial amount of lignite included. The data are for 1983 unless otherwise indicated, and include both steam and coking coal.

b. Data in this column have been calculated from UN - 1983 Energy Statistics.

c. N.A. = Not available.

Table 8.2
Coal Exports and Imports in the Asia-Pacific Region[a]

COUNTRY	IMPORTS (QUANTITY)	IMPORTS FROM	REFERENCE[b]	EXPORTS (QUANTITY)	EXPORTS TO	REFERENCE[b]
Afghanistan	0			0		
Australia	0.174			82 (1984/85)	Japan, Korea, United Kingdom, Taiwan, Hong Kong, India, Others	QER
Bangladesh	0.262	China, India, Indonesia		0		
Burma	0.202	Australia, China		0		
Canada	15.8	US		17.0	Japan, Mexico, Korea, Sweden, Brazil, Chile, Germany, US, Others.	
China (PRC)	2.19(E)			6.51 (1983)	Japan, North Korea, Belgium, Bangladesh, Hong Kong, Macao	EA
-Taiwan	7.8	Australia, South Africa, US	QER	0		
Fiji	0.023			0		
Hong Kong	4.46	Australia, South Africa, China		0		
India	1.24(E)			0.129(E)		
Indonesia	0.028			0.211	Malaysia, Thailand, Bangladesh	
Iran	0.06					
Japan	67.3(1984, coking), 17.2 (1984, steam)	Australia, Canada, US, South Africa, USSR, China, Australia, South Africa, China USSR, Canada, US	QER	1.59		
Korea-North	0.72			0.050		
-South	8.4 (coking) 2.5 (steam)	Australia, US, Canada, South Africa, China	NCT	0		
Malaysia	0.55 (1984)			0		
Nepal	0.020			0.315(1984)		QER
Pakistan	0.487		NCT	0.023		
Philippines	0.42			0.001		
Singapore	0.010			0.008		
Sri Lanka	0.033			0		
Thailand	0.08			0.005(E)		
US	0.77			95.5	Japan, Canada, EEC, Others	
Vietnam	0.013			1.00		

Source: Unless indicated otherwise, the data are from *Coal Transportation in Asia and the Pacific: Infrastructure and Environmental Considerations*. Edited by T.A. Siddiqi, H.H. Webber, and E. Winternitz-Russell, Arlington, Virginia: Pasha Publications, 1985
a In million tonnes, except where indicated with E = million tonnes of coal equivalent. The data are for 1982 and include both steam and coking coal, unless otherwise indicated.
b QER = Quarterly Energy Review, 1983, 1984; EA = Energy Asia, 1984, 1985; UN = Energy Statistics Yearbook, 1982; NCT = Newer Coal Technologies, 1986 (see References).

    i.   the overall increase in energy use,
    ii.   the share of coal in energy consumption,
    iii. the domestic production of coal,
    iv. the relative costs of imported coal from different countries,
    v.   environmental considerations,
    vi. technological changes, and
    vii. international relations.

The concluding section of this chapter summarizes some of the earlier discussion, and assesses the trends in steam coal trade in Asia and the Pacific.

THE OVERALL INCREASE IN ENERGY USE

The extent to which coal will be used in a country depends to a considerable extent on the total energy use and the rate at which that use is increasing. Until about a decade ago, there was a general impression that the relationship between the Gross Domestic Product (GDP) and energy use was linear. One could then make projections of the rate of increase in energy use by looking at the expected increases in national GDP. Following the increases in energy prices during the 1970s, a number of countries took steps to use energy more efficiently and discovered that this did not result in a corresponding decrease in economic activity.

The rate of growth of the GDP, as well as changes in the GDP/Energy Use ratio, will have to be taken into account in projecting expected increases in overall energy use in the Asia Pacific region. Both of these numbers show considerable variation amongst countries (World Bank, 1983, 1984), and this situation is not likely to change soon, given the wide differences in the level of industrialization. The recent past may be used as an approximation for the immediate future. For this reason, national rates of growth of GDP and energy use are given in Table 8.3.

THE SHARE OF COAL IN ENERGY CONSUMPTION

The proportion of energy supply of a country that is provided by coal is changing, and the extent of that change will be a major factor affecting coal trade in the Asia-Pacific. The two most populous countries of the region, China and India, will continue to depend mainly on coal for their supply of commercial energy. The percentage contribution of this fuel is expected to remain at roughly the same level (70 percent) for China and to increase somewhat for India. The *amount* of coal used in each country

Table 8.3
Annual Rates of Increase of the Gross Domestic Product (GDP) and Energy Consumption in Some Asian Countries (1970–80)

COUNTRY	RATE OF INCREASE IN GDP (PERCENT)	RATE OF INCREASE IN ENERGY USE (PERCENT)
China	5.8	5.4
India	3.6	4.6
Indonesia	7.8	8.8
Korea, Republic of	9.5	9.9
Malaysia	7.8	3.9
Nepal	2.3	2.2
Pakistan	4.7	3.8
Philippines	6.4	4.1
Singapore	8.5	8.7
Sri Lanka	4.4	0.1
Thailand	7.2	8.2

Source: World Bank, 1983

is expected to increase considerably over the next two decades.

The most notable changes in the relative contribution of coal to energy supply are for countries that were heavily dependent on the use of oil at the beginning of the 1970s. Following the quadrupling of oil prices, many of them decided to diversify their energy supply system by making greater use of coal, natural gas, and geothermal, hydro, and nuclear power. Even an oil-exporting country like Indonesia chose to make much greater use of domestically available coal in order to save dwindling oil reserves for maintaining stable oil exports in the future.

For uses like electric power, where a variety of energy sources can be utilized, cost considerations obviously play an important role. The relative cost of electricity generated from different energy sources, in Japan, for example, is given in Table 8.4.

The relative cost of electricity from different energy sources will vary from country to country. In India and Pakistan, for example, hydropower has generally supplied electricity at costs lower than that from other energy sources. An interesting trend evident from Table 8.4 is the closing of the gap between the cost of electricity from coal and nuclear power. In most countries, coal may be a cheaper source for generating electricity than nuclear fission reactors.

In several countries, the projected contribution of coal to future energy supply was much larger at a time when it was expected that oil prices were going to continue increasing. The actual decline in the price of oil during the past three years has led to the postponement of some of the more expensive schemes to convert oil-based energy facilities to coal.

Table 8.4
Cost of Generating Electricity in Japan From Different Energy Sources (in yen per kilowatt hour)

	1980	1982	1984
Hydro	17.5	20	21
Oil	17.1	20	17
Coal	11.3	15	14
LNG	15.6	19	17
Nuclear	8.4	12	13

Source: Coal Report (Energy Asia), 25 January 1985.

THE DOMESTIC PRODUCTION OF COAL

The ability of countries in the region to increase the domestic production of coal has had significant impacts on coal exports as well as imports. Australia, Canada, and the United States are countries where production capacity at present greatly exceeds domestic demand, and there is consequently considerable incentive to look for additional export markets. In Japan and South Korea, production of domestic coal may have reached its peak, and increments in coal use will have to be supplied by imports.

The production of coal is expected to increase approximately 50% in China and to double in India by the end of this century. The domestic demand for coal in these countries still exceeds the supply, and very little of the production is likely to be exported. China is exporting some coal, primarily to Japan, to earn foreign currency for other imports, and such exports may increase somewhat during the next few years. They will, however, constitute only a small percentage of the 1.2 billion tonnes per year expected production by the year 2000.

Indonesia, starting from a relatively small level, is expected to build up coal production rapidly and could become an exporter during the 1990s. During the next few years, it is likely to import coal to meet the demand for new coal-based power plants. The Philippines also has substantial coal resources, and domestic production is likely to show large percentage increases.

Thailand and Pakistan have low-quality coal resources. They have been using these for several years and expect domestic coal production to increase substantially during the next few years. These resources are generally not suitable for export.

Table 8.5
Projected Coal Production and Consumption in the Asia-Pacific 1990, 2000[a]

COUNTRY CONSUMPTION	1990 PRODUCTION	1990 CONSUMPTION	2000 PRODUCTION	2000 CONSUMPTION
Australia	248 (L)	118 (L)	293-460 (E)	113-170 (E)
Bangladesh		0.15 (E)		
Burma		0.22 (E)		
Canada		55-72		100.0
China	850	840	1200	1180
Taiwan	2.6	25.6-34.7	2.6	
Fiji	0			
Hong Kong		11.0		
India	225-274 (1992/93)	225-274 (1992/93)	300-427	300-427
Indonesia	15.9	16.8		
Japan	17.0	107-113		
Korea-North				
Korea-South	19.8 (1991)	44.6 (1991)		
Malaysia	2.0	2.5		7-14
Nepal		0.098 (E)		
New Zealand	5.0-5.3 (1990/91)	4.5-4.8 (1990/91)	6.2-7.3 (2001/02)	5.7-6.8 (2001/02)
Pakistan	5.8	7.1	11.7	14.0
Philippines	4.00 (1987)	4.98 (1987)		
Singapore	0			
Thailand	9.6 (L)	10.0 (L)		
US	1218	1122		

Source: Siddiqi et al., 1985.
a. In million tonnes, except for E = million tonnes of coal equivalent. L = substantial amounts of brown coal (lignite) are included.

The expected production and consumption of coal in several major countries of the region is summarized in Table 8.5. The projections are for 1990 and 2000, unless indicated otherwise.

THE RELATIVE COSTS OF IMPORTED COAL FROM DIFFERENT COUNTRIES

Whereas the total amount of foreign coal purchased by the importing countries is influenced by the other factors mentioned in this chapter, the relative share of the market supplied by each of the coal exporting countries in the region depends strongly on the delivered price of the coal in the importing country if the quality of the coals is roughly comparable. The three major components of the delivered price of coal are:

i. the price of the coal at the mine;
ii. the cost of transporting coal overland to an exporting terminal, and handling at the terminal; and
iii. the cost of shipping from the exporting terminal to a port in the importing country.

In the Asia-Pacific region, the total cost of transporting coal from the United States to major importers like Japan and the Republic of Korea is almost half of the total price of the delivered coal in many cases. The prices of steam coal imported into Japan from the major coal exporting countries are listed in Table 8.6. Although the prices shown are for 1981, the relatively higher cost of American coal is still maintained primarily because of higher overland transportation costs. Strikes in Australia curtailed coal shipment from that country in 1981, but it has increased its share since then.

Australia, Canada, and the United States each have adequate export capacity to meet the present steam coal importing needs of Japan, South Korea and Taiwan. The need to diversify sources and the price premium that importing countries are willing to pay for such diversification will determine the relative share of imports from each of the countries.

The location of coal mines in relative proximity to ports gives a competitive edge to Australian coal. This has provided a strong incentive to other countries such as Canada, China, and the United States to examine ways of reducing the costs of transporting coal overland. Coal slurry pipelines were proposed by a number of groups as one way of lowering transportation costs, but none is presently under construction. The only such pipeline in operation, the Black Mesa, transports coal from one in-

Table 8.6
Steam Coal Imports Into Japan, 1981, 1983

| COUNTRY | 1981 | | AVERAGE CIF PRICE | 1983 | |
	MILLION TONNES	% OF TOTAL	SEPTEMBER, 1981 ($/tonne)	MILLION TONNES	% OF TOTAL
Australia	5.68	(49)	66.5	7.65	(55.0)
South Africa	1.26	(11)	66.6	2.62	(18.8)
China	1.19	(10)		1.71	(12.3)
US	2.12	(18)	75.9	0.93	(6.7)
Canada	1.14	(10)	68.5	0.55	(4.0)
USSR	0.26	(2)		0.42	(3.0)
Others				0.04	(0.3)
TOTALS	11.65	(100)		13.92	(100.0)

Source: Energy Quarterly, 1984.

land point to another within the United States, rather than for export. Interestingly, it is operated by a railroad holding company—the Santa Fe Southern Pacific.

ENVIRONMENTAL CONSIDERATIONS

In a number of the more industrialized countries, the move away from coal to oil and gas during the 1950s and 1960s was influenced by a number of factors including environmental problems associated with mining, transporting, and burning coal. These considerations still affect the extent to which coal is likely to be used, particularly in densely populated areas and other sensitive locations such as those with historic monuments or other tourist attractions. Japan, for example, is using liquefied natural gas in some locations, even though it would be cheaper to use coal, because the air quality in those areas was already considered inadequate and additional use of coal would have led to unacceptable levels of air pollution.

Another example of environmental considerations affecting coal trade is provided by the limitations placed on the expansion of coal exporting capacity at the port of Los Angeles. These were based on concerns arising from the existing poor air quality in the area and the expectation that a large number of trains every day carrying coal would lead to further deterioration in air quality (Webber et al., 1986; Wiebe et al., 1986).

Many countries in the region, including China and India, have recently announced air quality standards (Siddiqi, 1984). These are likely to restrict the use of coal in specific locations but allow the countries to increase the use of coal in industrial areas. This is facilitated by the use of ambient air quality standards which differ by area. (See Tables 8.7 and 8.8 for two major air pollutants, particulates and sulfur dioxide.)

TECHNOLOGICAL CHANGES

Changes in technology could work for, as well as against, the increased use of coal. Examples of technologies that could result in the increased use of coal are:

  i.   cheaper ways of mining deeper coals;
  ii.   use of coal-water mixtures instead of fuel oil;
  iii. removal of sulphur from coal before combustion;
  iv.   cheaper ways to remove sulphur dioxide after combustion;

Table 8.7

Ambient Air Quality Standards for Total Particulates in China, India, Japan, and the United States (in micrograms per cubic meter; μ g/m³)

	DAILY AVERAGE	EIGHT-HOUR AVERAGE	ONE-HOUR AVERAGE	ANNUAL AVERAGE	MAXIMUM ALLOWED AT ANY TIME
CHINA[a]					
Class I	150				300
Class II	300				1000
Class III	500				1500
INDIA[b]					
Area C		100			
Area B		200			
Area A		500			
JAPAN	100		200		
US					
Primary	250			75	
Secondary	150			60	

a. China has also established standards for particulates that are less than 10 microns diameter. The permitted daily averages are: Class I areas (daily average 50, max. 150), Class II areas (daily average 150, max. 500), and Class III (daily average 250, max. 750). All of the above numbers are in μ g/m³.

b. In this and the following table, the standards given for India are defined as follows: ``When monitored uniformly over the 12 months of a year with a frequency of not less than once in a week with a sampling time of eight hours for any sample, and analysed according to procedures specified by the Central Board, the concentrations for the following pollutants shall be 95% of the time within the limits prescribed.''

Table 8.8
Ambient Air Quality Standards for Sulphur Dioxide in China, India, Japan, and the United States ($\mu g/m^3$)

	DAILY AVERAGE	ANNUAL AVERAGE[a]	EIGHT-HOUR AVERAGE	THREE-HOUR AVERAGE	ONE-HOUR AVERAGE	MAXIMUM ALLOWED AT ANY TIME
CHINA						
Class I	50	20				150
Class II	150	60				500
Class III	250	100				700
INDIA						
Area C			30			
Area B			80			
Area A			120			
JAPAN[b]	100				250	
US						
Primary	365[c]	80				
Secondary				1300[c]		

a. Arithmetic mean. In the case of China, the mean is of the measurements taken daily.
b. Japanese standard given as parts per million. Converted here to facilitate comparison.
c. U.S. standard not to be exceeded more than once a year.

v. use of slurry pipelines that do not require large quantities of water;

vi. new ways of using ash and other coal-combustion residues; and

vii. ways of using lower-quality coals.

In the preceding sections, we have looked at some of the economic and environmental factors affecting coal use. The reduction in oil use is a high priority in many countries. If fuel oil could be replaced with coal-water mixtures, for instance, without very expensive modifications to the boilers, coal use could increase substantially. Also, if the use of slurry pipelines for transporting coal becomes economic, possibly as a result of newer technologies using liquids other than water, there could be substantial changes in the patterns of coal trade. The high levels of sulphur in some coals limit their use in many locations. If technologies such as fluidized-bed combustion become economical, there could be changes in the patterns of coal use.

Other technologies that could result in a lowering of coal use are those associated with the development of other energy sources. If the costs of generating power from photovoltaic sources, or from wind, for example, become competitive with power from coal, many communities are likely to prefer the former because of the relative cleanliness of those energy sources when compared to coal.

INTERNATIONAL RELATIONS

The impact of international relations on coal trade has been less visible than for some of the other major sources of energy. The price of oil traded in the world market was set mainly by the Middle-Eastern members of OPEC and was greatly influenced by political and military events in the Middle East during the 1970s.

The encouragement of nuclear power during the 1950s and 1960s and its discouragement during the 1970s and 1980s were also largely the result of international considerations. Many of the nuclear research reactors and power plants supplied to Third World countries by Canada and the United States, for example, were considered a part of ''development assistance'' to friendly countries. More recently, rising concern in North America and Europe about the possible implications of nuclear weapons proliferation has led to controversy regarding the supply of additional nuclear power plants or the honoring of previous contracts for fuel and equipment.

The use of coal has been promoted both because of the increase in the price of oil and because of the concerns about nuclear proliferation. International relations have had a direct effect on coal trade in the Asia-Pacific region. Labor strikes in Poland and Australia during the early 1980s gave a boost to coal exports from Canada and the United States, and provided a strong incentive to several companies in Japan to make direct investments in coal supply systems in a number of countries. Japan also made a conscious decision to diversify the source of its coal, even if it cost somewhat more, rather than buy all of it from the lowest cost supplier.

The international relations between South Africa and a number of countries also led to the decision by several nations to import coal from Australia or other suppliers even in cases where coal from South Africa may have been cheaper.

More recently, the balance of payments advantage enjoyed by Japan vis-à-vis Canada and the United States has led to a re-examination of the possibilities for importing more coal from those countries.

CONCLUSION

The discussion in the preceding sections has pointed out a number of factors that presently affect, and are likely to continue affecting, steam coal trade in Asia and the Pacific. The one thing we can be sure about is that, unlike oil, there appears to be no danger of our running out of coal resources even during the 21st century. Except for temporary shortages caused by strikes or other disruptions, there is unlikely to be a shortage of coal available for international trade. The duration of booms in the price of coal are likely to be of a few years duration, at the most, determined alternately by the time it takes to open up new mines, or to develop the infrastructure to transport the coal to the ports and to build loading/unloading systems.

The prolonged availability of coal sets an upper limit on the price of other fuels used for electricity generation—such as fuel oil and natural gas—and cost escalations that countries may be willing to accept in the price of electricity from nuclear fission reactors.

The major patterns of coal trade in Asia and the Pacific, shown in Figure 8.1, are not expected to change dramatically during the next decade. It is more likely that the "minor" movements of coal, shown in Figure 8.2, may show greater change. New Zealand, for example, is already exporting a small amount of this commodity. The volume of exports from Indonesia are likely to increase, as are exports from China to other countries in addition to Japan.

Probably the largest uncertainties affecting the use of coal beyond the next decade are those associated with the effect of carbon dioxide on the

Figure 8-1
LARGER VOLUMES OF COAL
TRADED IN THE ASIA-PACIFIC REGION

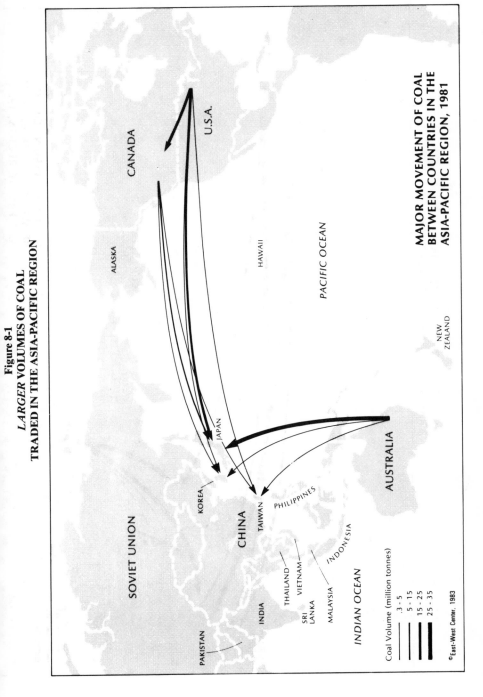

**MAJOR MOVEMENT OF COAL
BETWEEN COUNTRIES IN THE
ASIA-PACIFIC REGION, 1981**

Coal Volume (million tonnes)

.3 - 5
5 - 15
15 - 25
25 - 35

©East-West Center, 1983

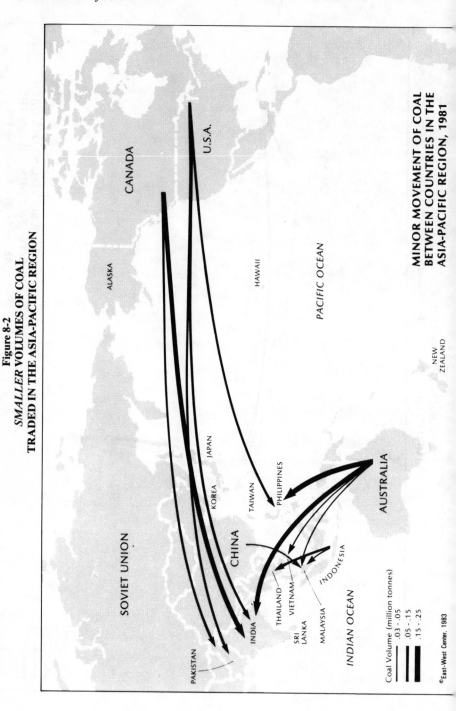

Figure 8-2
SMALLER VOLUMES OF COAL
TRADED IN THE ASIA-PACIFIC REGION

**MINOR MOVEMENT OF COAL
BETWEEN COUNTRIES IN THE
ASIA-PACIFIC REGION, 1981**

©East-West Center, 1983

Coal Volume (million tonnes)
.03 - .05
.05 - .15
.15 - .25

world's climate. The general view at present is that increases in carbon dioxide in the atmosphere could lead to a gradual warming of the earth, with possibly severe implications for food production and coastal populations. The largest contribution to a buildup of carbon dioxide in the atmosphere is from the use of fossil fuels and, during the 21st century, this is likely to be coal. The most promising alternative to the use of coal for generating electricity was nuclear fission. With nuclear power having run into major economic, political, and safety problems, the development of cleaner energy sources that are also price-competitive is likely to be a very major factor affecting coal use and coal trade in the decades ahead.

REFERENCES

Energy Asia, (1984, 1985) Published by Petroleum News Southeast Asia. Hong Kong.

Quarterly Energy Review, (1983, 1984) Published four times a year by The Economist Intelligence Unit Limited. London.

United Nations, (1984) *Energy Statistics Yearbook, 1982.* New York.

Siddiqi, Toufiq A., (1984) "Environmental Standards and National Energy Policies," *Annual Review of Energy,* Vol. 9, 81-104.

Siddiqi, Toufiq A., and Shen Shihua (editors), (1986) *Newer Coal Technologies: Implications for Energy and Development Policies in Asia and the Pacific.* New York: Pergamon Press.

Siddiqi, Toufiq A., Herbert H. Webber, and Elizabeth Winternitz-Russell, (editors), (1985) *Coal Transportation in Asia and the Pacific: Infrastructure and Environmental Considerations.* Arlington, Virginia: Pasha Publications.

Webber, Herbert H., et al., (1985) *Environmental Guidelines for Overland Coal Transportation.* Nairobi: United Nations Environment Programme, 1986 (in press).

Wiebe, John D., et al., (1986) *Environmental Guidelines for Coal Port Development.* Nairobi: United Nations Environment Programme (in press).

World Bank, (1983) *The Energy Transition in Developing Countries*. Washington, D.C.

World Bank, (1984) *World Development Report*. New York: Oxford University Press.

9

The British Columbia Coal Industry

HAROLD HALVORSON

This chapter examines the British Columbia coal industry and the importance of Pacific Rim markets. Before this can be done, however, some general comments about the types of coal and their role in world trade are of value.

TYPES OF COAL

There are various grades of coal, ranging from very low grade lignite or brown coals through the better quality bituminous or black coals to the highest rank or anthracite coals. Lignite coals have low heat values (6300 to 8300 btu per lb.), low fixed carbon content (approximately 30 percent) and high moisture content (25 to 35 percent). Anthracite coals have high heat content (over 12,000 btu per lb.), high fixed carbon content (over 86 percent) and low moisture and volatile contents. The bituminous coals have properties between those of lignite and anthracite.

Western Canada possesses all grades of coal; however, only the bituminous coals are of interest here since these dominate world trade. Considerable lignite is mined in Saskatchewan, but it is used locally (in Saskatchewan and Manitoba) for power generation. A large quantity of a similar quality coal (sub-bituminous) is also mined in Alberta, but it is all consumed in "mine-mouth" power plants. No anthracite is produced in Western Canada although one such mine is under study in the northwestern British Columbia Groundhog coal formation. All the coal exported from western Canada is bituminous coal mined in the Rocky Mountains of B.C. and Alberta.

Another common nomenclature used for coals divides them into thermal and coking types. Thermal coals, sometimes referred to as steam coals, are used for their heating value only, and their main use is for electricity generation. Other significant uses are as fuel in cement kilns and for generating steam for industrial purposes. All three ranks of coal, lignite, bituminous and anthracite, can and are used as thermal coals. What determines which type of coal is used in a specific application at a given location is the delivered cost of a btu of energy. Also important are the volatile matter and the sulfur content, the latter for environmental "acid rain" reasons. A good quality thermal coal contains about 0.5 percent sulphur and volatile matter approaching 30 percent. B.C. coals meet the sulfur specification but generally contain too little volatile matter.

Coking coals, also called metallurgical coals, are used to make coke, virtually all of which is used in steel-making. Small quantities are used in foundries. Coking coals require rigid physical and chemical properties. To make coke, coking coals are heated in the absence of air until the fixed carbon in the coals "melts and fuses" producing coke with correct strength, porosity and other physical properties. Only the better bituminous coals produce quality coke. Coking coals are premium coals and command a higher price than do thermal coals. For example, the current world price for good coking coal is roughly $70 per tonne loaded on a ship while that of thermal coal is about 30 to 40 percent less.

WORLD TRADE

Nearly all countries in the world have exploitable coal deposits and most of the coal consumed does not cross international borders. For example, in 1981 the world production of coal was reported to be 3.8 billion tonnes while trade between countries was 271.6 million tonnes or only 7 percent of the total. Coal involved in world trade is largely bituminous plus a small amount of anthracite. In 1981, of the coal traded, approximately 65 percent was coking and 35 percent thermal.

The number of countries involved in supplying coal to world trade is small and the number in ocean trade even smaller. Table 9.1, summarizing world trade in 1981, demonstrates that the U.S., Australia, South Africa and Canada supplied over 90 percent of the total ocean-borne trade. The remainder came from China, the U.S.S.R., Poland, West Germany, and a variety of smaller shippers. Japan and Western Europe are the principal recipients of ocean-borne trade.

In summary, only a small fraction of the total coal consumed in the world is traded between nations. There are two big consumers, Japan and the industrial nations of Western Europe, and four big suppliers, the U.S., Australia, South Africa and Canada.

Table 9.1
World Coal Trade in 1981 (Million Tonnes)

EXPORTER	NORTH AMERICA	OECD EUROPE	JAPAN	EAST EUROPE	ALL OTHERS	TOTAL	EXPORT SHARE
A) LOCAL TRADE: RAIL, BARGE							
US	14.8					14.8	20%
West Germany		11.5			0.1	11.6	16%
UK		9.1				9.1	13%
USSR		1.9		18.7		20.6	28%
Poland		6.6		7.1		13.7	19%
Czechoslovakia		1.1		1.9		3.0	4%
Subtotal	14.8	30.2		27.8		72.8	100%
Share (percentage)	20%	42%		38%		100%	
B) OCEAN TRADE							
US		48.2	23.8	2.4	12.9	87.3	44%
Australia		8.5	34.6	0.4	7.5	51.0	25%
South Africa	0.7	20.2	4.3		4.0	29.2	15%
Canada	0.2	1.7	10.5		3.3	15.7	8%
China		0.2	2.8		3.5	6.5	3%
USSR			1.4			1.4	1%
Poland			0.1		1.2	1.3	1%
West Germany					0.4	0.4	0.2%
All others		2.5	0.5	1.9	1.1	6.0	3%
Subtotal	0.9	81.3	78.0	4.7	33.9	198.8	100%
Share (percentage)	0.5%	41%	39%	2%	17%	100%	

Source: IEA/OECD Coal Statistics

Thermal Coals

The principal importers of thermal coals are the countries of Western Europe:

Share of 1981 OECD Imports (percentage)

Western Europe	74
Japan	14
Canada	11
U.S.	1

The principal supplier is the U.S. (eastern U.S. mines) with South Africa and Australia being distant second and third:

Share of 1981 OECD Exports (percentage)

U.S.	55
South Africa	19
Australia	12
Canada	6
Poland	4
U.S.S.R.	2
China	2

In 1981 Canada had 6 percent of the world trade. Canadian coal exports are from Cape Breton, Nova Scotia, sold in Europe, and from B.C. and Alberta, sold in the Far East and Europe.

Western Canada is a minor factor in the world trade of thermal coal. B.C. exports offshore of thermal coal commenced in the early 1970s with the first oil shock but did not expand significantly through the 1980s, unlike exports from B.C.'s main competitors. This is demonstrated in Table 9.2 where B.C.'s growth in exports is compared to those of Australia, South Africa, and the U.S. Over the period 1975 to 1981, B.C.'s exports held static at about 0.5 million tonnes per year (tpy) while the combined exports of the four nations increased by a factor of 4.2. In the period 1982-84 new mines in the province and contracts, primarily with South Korea, increased B.C. shipments significantly. However, even with this improvement, B.C.'s growth in exports has not kept pace with those of Australia and South Africa. In fact, over the period 1975-84, combined shipment from Australia, South Africa, the U.S., B.C. grew at a rate of 18 percent per year while B.C.'s share only grew at a rate of 4 percent per year.

Table 9.2

Comparison of B.C. Thermal Coal Exports With Those of Major Competitors (Million Tonnes)

	1975	1976	1977	1978	1979	1980	1981	1982	1983	1984	GROWTH 1975-84 PERCENTAGE PER YEAR (compounded)
Australia[a]	3.4[b]	3.0	3.7	5.4	5.5	8.9	10.5	11.6	17.7	29.2[c]	27%
South Africa	2.5	4.8	10.3	13.1	20.9	26.4	27.1[d]	26.0[d]	24.4[d]	29.2[d]	32%
US[a]	12.8	10.5	10.7	9.8[e]	12.8	26.0	42.9	37.8	24.8	21.7[f]	6%
BC[d]	0.6		0.6	0.2	0.2	0.4	0.6	1.5	1.5	3.6[g]	22%
TOTAL	19.3		25.3	28.5	39.4	61.7	81.1	76.9	68.4	83.7	18%
BC Share (percentage)	3.1%		2.4%	0.7%	0.5%	0.6%	0.7%	2.0%	2.2%	4.3%	4%

a. IEA/OECD Coal Statistics.
b. Europe 90 percent, Japan 7 percent, other Asia 3 percent.
c. Europe 30 percent, Japan 40 percent, other Asia 30 percent.
d. Estimated.
e. Canada 89 percent, Europe 1 percent, Japan 5 percent, other 5 percent.
f. Canada 51 percent, Europe 32 percent, Japan 3 percent, other 14 percent.
g. South Korea 60 percent, Japan 25 percent, Europe 15 percent.

Data for Japan presented in Table 9.3 also demonstrate that Western Canada (B.C. and Alberta) has not fared as well in the important Japanese market as have our competitors. Japan commenced importation of significant quantities of thermal coal in the late 1970s. Australia is its major supplier (with 64 percent of the 1984 total) while Canada in 1984 supplied only 4 percent of Japan's imports. Since 1980, Canada's exports to Japan have doubled while all Japanese imports have increased by a factor of 3.3.

The B.C. thermal coal producers, their published capacities and estimated 1984 offshore shipments, are summarized in Table 9.4. In 1984 the B.C. producers operated at roughly 75 percent of design capacity. Most of the exports come from three new mines, Greenhills, Line Creek and Quintette. Balmer and Fording, while having low production rates, have had and continue to have the capability to supply large amounts from waste coal not suitable for sale as coking coal. Consequently, the capacities in Table 9.4 are understated.

B.C. thermal coals obviously have not enjoyed wide acceptance in export markets. They are expensive because of the long rail haul and do not have volatile contents most desired by power plants—the biggest market by far. B.C. coals are and will continue to be purchased as a diversification strategy by major consumers. Little, if any, growth in exports over the 1984 level is likely this decade. In fact, a decline could occur because of major increases in South African exports and the start-up of a huge (fifteen million tpy) thermal coal project in Colombia. In any event, thermal coal is and will continue to be a minor component of the B.C. coal industry. This will be in spite of a likely good growth in the world trade of thermal coals.

Coking Coal

The dominant factors in the B.C. coal industry are coking coal and the Japanese steel industry. Coal production in B.C. started to supply thermal coal in the last century. With the passing of the steam locomotive, the B.C. industry essentially collapsed. It was revived in the early 1970s with the opening of the Balmer and Fording mines built to supply coking coal to Japan.

The world's largest importer of coking coal is Japan. In 1981, of a total of 117 million t of coking coal imported by OECD countries, Japan accounted for 56 percent. Western Europe purchased 40 percent and Canada the remaining 4 percent. Outside of the OECD countries, only South Korea, Taiwan, and Brazil purchase significant but comparatively small quantities.

Table 9.3
Growth in Japanese Thermal Coal Imports (Calendar Years)[a]

	SOURCE OF COAL						
	AUSTRALIA	CHINA	CANADA	SOUTH AFRICA	USSR	US	TOTAL
IMPORTS (million tonnes)							
1971				0.001			0.001
1972	0.0005					0.002	0.0025
1973	0.0006						0.0006
1974	0.074	0.035			0.062	0.012	0.183
1975	0.213	0.123			0.040		0.376
1976	0.248	0.105			0.209		0.562
1977	0.433	0.190		0.021	0.231	0.004	0.879
1978	0.685			0.025	0.144		1.024
1979	1.000	0.256	0.013	0.021	0.117		1.407
1980	3.529	0.613	0.328	0.238	0.223	0.289	5.220
1981	5.676	1.188	1.140	1.263	0.255	2.119	11.641
1982	6.344	1.483	1.302	2.581	0.213	1.629	13.591[e]
1983	7.442[b]					1.580[d]	15.5
1984[c]	10.866	1.740	0.681	2.358	0.774	0.485	16.967[f]
1984 share (percentage)	64%	10%	4%	14%	5%	3%	100%
Growth 1980-1984 (percentage)	210%	180%	110%	890%	250%	70%	230%

Source: 1983 Coal Manual.
a. Excludes anthracite (a high of 1.6 million tonnes in 1971 and running at about 1 million tpy during the period 1971-1981).
b. IEA/OECD Coal Statistics.
c. Japan Echo News Service Ltd., February 26, 1985.
d. Donaldson, Lufkin and Jenrette.
e. Includes 0.039 million tonnes from Indonesia and others.
f. Includes 0.063 million tonnes from other countries.

Table 9.4

B.C. Thermal Coal Producers

COMPANY	MINE	START-UP DATE	CAPACITY (million tpy)	1984 EXPORTS (million tonnes)
A. SOUTHEASTERN B.C.				
Westar	Balmer	1975 ⎫		0.25
	Greenhills	1984 ⎬	1.6	0.8
Fording		1975	0.3	0.3
Shell	Line Creek	1982	1.1	1.2
Esso	Byron Creek	1974	2.0	0.4 (1.2-1.3[a])
B. NORTHEASTERN B.C.				
Quintette		1984	1.3	0.6
TOTAL			6.3	3.6 (4.4-4.5[a])

Source:

a. Including approximately 0.8-0.9 million tonnes are estimated to have been shipped to Ontario Hydro on long-term contract.

Japan buys a mixture of various hard, medium and soft coking coals and blends them with indigenous coals and non-coking coals to make coke for reducing iron ore to crude steel in blast furnaces. The Japanese steel industry has mastered the blending of diverse coals to maximize coke quality while minimizing coal cost. To assure supply, Japan has encouraged coking coal production in Australia, Canada, South Africa, China, the U.S.S.R., Indonesia, and New Zealand through a combination of long-term contracts and direct mine investment. In the case of China and the U.S.S.R., Japan has invested in rail and/or port infrastructure. By aggressive industrialization policies, Japan has been most successful in building up a major steel industry. Between 1966 and 1974 the production of crude steel in Japan increased by a factor of 2.4 from 48 to 117 million tonnes per year. Over the same period the country's imports of coking coal increased by a factor of 3.4 from 18 to 62 million tonnes per year.

Over the 1966-74 period, Canada (i.e., B.C. and Alberta) successfully captured an increasing share of the growing Japanese imports. In 1966 Canada supplied 0.8 million tonnes or 4.4 percent of the total. By 1974 this had risen to 9.6 million tonnes or 15 percent of total imports. This growth was met by the new Balmer and Fording mines in southeastern B.C. and the McIntyre, Luscar and Coleman mines in Alberta. Over the 1974 to 1983 period, Japanese production of crude steel leveled off as did their requirements for imported coking coal. Western Canada maintained its share of the Japanese market.

As shown by Table 9.5, Canada in the 1974 to 1983 period has supplied a relatively constant tonnage to Japan of about ten million tpy. Australia, Japan's largest source, has also maintained a relatively constant tonnage of approximately twenty-five million tpy. The swing supplier has been the United States. Over the decade the smaller Japanese suppliers, Poland, and West Germany, have been phased out while China, South Africa, New Zealand, and Indonesia have been phased in. The U.S.S.R. has maintained a relatively constant tonnage of approximately two million tpy. Over the period these small suppliers have had 8 to 11 percent of the Japanese business.

The U.S. has been the swing supplier because its coking coal is the most expensive delivered in Japan. This is demonstrated below where the prices landed in Japan during December 1984 for the same grade of coking coal* are compared:

---

* 8 percent or more ash; less than 30 percent volatile matter—the most common material produced in B.C.

US$ per tonne, CIF Japan

U.S.	76.43
Canada	70.35
Australia	60.45
China	51.91
U.S.S.R.	50.25

In the 1980-81 period, decisions were made by all of Japan's supplier nations to expand coking coal capacities. This was encouraged by the Japanese through long-term contracts and direct investment in new mines. This expansion was especially large in Australia and western Canada. By 1985 Australia announced plans to increase capacity by twenty-seven million tpy; Canada, by thirteen million tonnes, or a combined increase of 51 percent. In B.C. four new mines were added to the existing two. One new mine was built in Alberta, bringing that province's total to three. These mines are summarized in Table 9.6.

Based on generally accepted forecasts of Japanese crude steel production and the fraction made with coke, essentially no growth in Japanese demand for coking coals is foreseen for the rest of this decade. Considerable growth in both U.S.S.R. and Chinese shipments to Japan will occur over the next few years. South African sales will hold at present levels. It is expected that the Japanese steel industry will use increasing proportions of weak coking, lower cost coals in their coking feed blend. Other markets for coking coal, South Korea, Taiwan, and South America, will grow but not to the extent that they will make significant inroads into the existing mine overcapacity in the major suppliers, Australia, U.S., and western Canada.

The result of all these factors will be continued overcapacity for at least a decade, downward pressure on prices, and increasing competitiveness to capture other producers' customers. One result in B.C. could be mine closures. If this does not occur, the B.C. industry will likely only operate at about 60 percent of design capacity for the rest of this century—a level that is hardly economic.

What went wrong? Figure 9.1 demonstrates the main error: overly optimistic forecasts of Japanese crude steel production and hence coking coal imports.

The decision to proceed with the northeast B.C. coal project and the expansions in the southeast were made in the 1980-82 period. Figure 9.1 shows that forecasts during that period concluded that Japanese crude steel production would grow to approximately 140 million tonnes per year by 1990, a compounded growth rate of 1 percent per year from the

Table 9.5
Sources of Japanese Coking Coal Imports

CALENDAR YEARS

	1971	1972	1973	1974	1975	1976	1977	1978	1979	1980	1981	1982	1983	1984[a]
A. COAL IMPORTED (million tonnes)														
Australia	16.6	20.6	24.9	22.8	22.8	26.0	26.0	24.5	26.0	25.8	29.1	25.4	25.3	29.8
US	18.5	16.5	16.5	25.4	22.4	17.5	15.2	8.9	13.5	19.2	21.5	23.9	14.1	15.3
Canada	6.6	7.7	10.3	9.6	10.7	10.3	10.8	10.9	10.5	10.6	9.6	9.5	9.6	15.4
South Africa		0.02	0.08	0.1	0.2	0.8	2.3	2.4	2.2	2.9	3.0	3.3	2.9	4.6
China						0.02	0.01	0.3	0.8	1.0	1.2	1.4	1.2	2.0
USSR	2.5	2.5	2.7	3.2	3.1	3.0	2.9	2.3	2.2	1.9	1.1	1.1	1.1	1.7
Other	1.1	1.2	1.3	1.4	1.5	1.5	1.3	0.8	0.9	0.4	0.3	0.3	0.0	0.5
TOTAL	45.3	48.5	55.8	62.5	60.7	59.1	58.5	50.1	56.1	61.8	65.8	64.9	54.2	69.3
B. DISTRIBUTION (Percentage)														
Australia	37	42	45	37	37	44	44	49	46	42	44	39	47	43
US	41	34	30	41	37	30	26	18	24	31	33	37	26	22
Canada	14	16	18	15	18	17	19	22	19	17	14	14	18	22
Other	8	8	7	7	8	9	11	11	11	10	9	10	9	13
	100	100	100	100	100	100	100	100	100	100	100	100	100	100
C. JAPANESE CRUDE STEEL PRODUCTION—MILLION TONNES		119	117	103	107	102	102	112	111	102	100	97[b]	106	

Source: Coal Manual.
a. Japan Echo, February 26, 1985.
b. Vancouver Sun, June 13, 1984.

Table 9.6
Coking Coal Mines in Western Canada

(MILLION TONNES)

OPERATOR	MINE	JAPANESE EQUITY (PERCENT)	START-UP	PLANNED CAPACITY 1984	1985	PRODUCTION 1984
BC						
Westar	Balmer	33.4	1973	6.5	6.5	5.2
	Greenhills	26.7[b]	1983	1.8	1.8	1.8
Fording	Fording	nil	1974	5.2	6.0	3.7
Shell	Line Creek	nil	1983	1.0	1.1	1.0
Denison	Quintette	38	1984	3.5	5.0	2.8
Teck	Bullmoose	10	1984	1.7	1.7	1.4
Subtotal				19.7	22.1	15.9
ALBERTA						
Luscar	Cardinal River	nil	1972	3.0	3.0	2.5[a]
McIntyre	Smokey River	nil	1970	2.0	2.0	1.8[a]
Manalta	Gregg River	40	1983	1.6	2.1	1.8[a]
Subtotal				6.6	7.1	6.1
TOTAL				26.3	29.2	22.0

Source:
a. Alberta Coal Industry Monthly Statistics.
b. 20 percent South Korea.

Figure 9-1

FORECASTS OF JAPANESE CRUDE STEEL PRODUCTION

COMPARISON OF ACTUAL JAPANESE CRUDE STEEL PRODUCTION
WITH FORECASTS BY JAPANESE AGENCIES AND
THE B.C. AND CANADIAN GOVERNMENTS

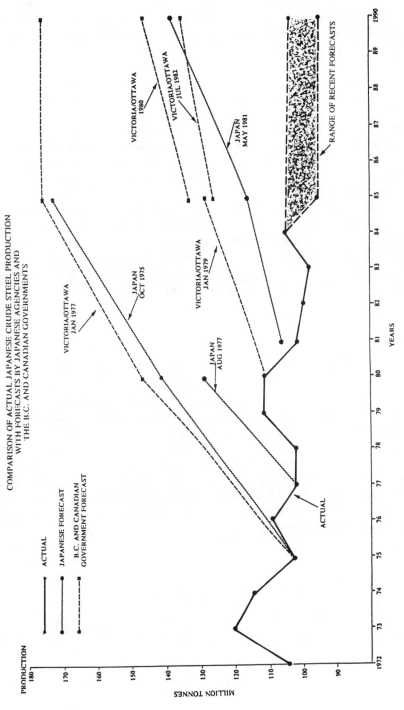

actual 1973 production of 119 million tpy. In fact, production in the period 1973 to 1983 declined at a compounded rate of 2.1 percent per year. Current forecasts call for Japanese crude steel production to be only 95 to 105 million tpy in 1990.

A point to note in Figure 9.1 is that the Canadian/B.C. government forecasts lagged those being made in Japan. For example, the Japanese May 1981 forecast was less optimistic than the Victoria/Ottawa forecast made in July 1982, over a year later. Subsequently, when Japanese companies and government agencies were forecasting crude steel production levels in 1983 in the 100 million tpy range, certain Canadian circles were dismissing such low forecasts as an attempt by the Japanese to effect lower coal prices.

It must be remembered when reviewing the forecast shown in Figure 1 that even had the optimistic forecasts made in the 1980-82 period been realized, there was still too much coking coal capacity built. It was possible as early as 1980 to foresee a glut of coking coal on world markets. The current dismal production levels of steel in Japan simply made what would have been a bad picture into a drastic one.

CONCLUSION

The outlook for the British Columbia coal industry is not optimistic. The principal product, coking coal, will continue to depend primarily on the Japanese steel industry. Little if any growth in steel output by Japan is expected. Consequently, B.C. producers can expect a long period of overcapacity, downward pressure on prices, and increased aggressiveness by competitors to capture the business that exists. Closure of B.C. capacity is a distinct possibility. Thermal coal has been a minor factor in the B.C. industry since the coal industry in the province was revived in the early 1970s. This situation will continue. Because of price and quality, offshore customers will consider B.C. thermal coal only for strategic reasons of diversification.

10

Canada and the Far West

EDWARD ENGLISH

One of the lessons still to be learned by most Canadians about the Pacific region is that the Western Pacific is the land of the setting sun. This is not merely a statement of the obvious consequence of global geography; it proclaims the need to view the Pacific region through North American rather than European eyes. The European today views East Asia primarily as a lost empire and a particularly difficult new economic challenge. Countries such as Japan and Korea are seen as competitive threats to European industry, and Europeans seem unwilling to acknowledge that "Far Eastern" countries are competing on fair terms, succeeding on their ability rather than some ingenious Oriental form of protection and export subsidy.[1] Southeast Asia and China are seen as markets for European capital goods and investment (or joint ventures) and as a source of tropical and other raw materials.

In North America, there are many similar attitudes, but there are also wider perspectives which happily play a significant role in the high levels of political decision in Washington and Canberra, and among a few policy advisers in Ottawa.[2] This perspective includes both political and economic dimensions. The political dimension includes two primary elements. The first is the vital importance of Japan and China as forces for regional stability and deterrence of military adventurism even, and perhaps especially, if they remain relatively limited military powers. The second is the vital role of the region as an exemplar of North-South relations, providing scope for the smooth 'graduation' of advanced developing countries such as South Korea, and for the outward-oriented industrialization of Southeast Asia. If these opportunities for effective cooperation are to be exploited, it is vital that more resources (in time and money) be devoted to Pacific economic relations. This requires not only the best "on the spot" services that can be provided by trade commissioners, and so forth, but also a continuing effort to create a policy environment that is conducive to the trade, technology, and investment flows that reflect the complementarities of Pacific economies and stimulate dynamic efficiency. This includes a willingness to accept and bring about constructive change in the structure of some North American industries.

An appropriate policy environment requires support for the multilateral institutions, such as GATT, and the IMF, in which most Pacific countries wish to continue to operate and indeed to provide leadership. It also requires more specific effort to strengthen bilateral contacts and contracts. The key question is whether there may also be regional initiatives that are complementary to what can be achieved by the traditional bilateral channels and particularly whether such initiatives might be catalytic in sustaining resistance to forces of protectionism and generating new momentum toward multilateral trade liberalization.

The recently established Pacific Economic Cooperation Conference is one initiative designed to identify areas of consensus and possible joint economic action by the Pacific Rim countries. It began in 1980 when the then prime ministers of Australia and Japan (Fraser and Ohira) took steps that brought about the first meeting in Canberra in September of the same year. This was followed by meetings in Bangkok in June 1982, Bali, Indonesia, in November 1983, and Seoul, Korea, at the end of April 1985. At each of these meetings national delegations have included representatives of business, the academic-professional community and government. They have been distinctive in bringing together these different perspectives on international relations. This can contribute to building a constituency reflecting more than particular industrial or bureaucratic interests.

The conference is also distinctive in that it brings together all the developed OECD countries outside Europe (Japan, Australia, New Zealand, Canada and the United States), and at least six of the most dynamic and outward-looking developing countries of the region, the ASEAN countries and South Korea. Others who have been represented at one or more conferences either as observers or "accredited" members include Taiwan, Hong Kong, the South Pacific Islands, Mexico, Peru, and Chile. It thus represents a North-South forum of countries who share a common commitment to international trade and investment as engines of growth in mixed economies. The demonstrated record of success of the developing countries in this group is seen as an example for other developing countries. If the trade and other policies of the region are favourable to the continuation of economic growth, other countries may be attracted to participate, or to emulate the region's approach to North-South co-operation.

This optimistic prognosis will be justified only if there is success with the specific substance of regional co-operative ventures. The identification of issues worthy of regional consensus has progressed over the years through the efforts of business organizations, notably PBEC (the Pacific Basin Economic Council), and by professional economists, through the Pacific Trade and Development Conferences. Both these groups began in the late 1960s at a time when the remarkable growth performance of the Japanese economy was becoming a familiar fact and the need to come to terms with the challenge and opportunity in Pacific trade and investment was increasingly recognized. At the business level, motives for participation in PBEC meetings in early years ranged all the way from the novelty of a visit to the "exotic" orient, or the outposts of Commonwealth in Australia, to more specific bilateral corporate deals. For the business group, as for the economists' conferences, the main focus was at first on the five developed countries of the Pacific (Australia, Canada, Japan, New Zealand, and the United States). But it was not long before developing countries, notably the NICs of East Asia (South Korea, Taiwan, Hong Kong, and Singapore) were represented and also the other nations of Southeast Asia. By the early 1970s there were also participants from Latin America (Mexico and the Andean countries of South America). The Pacific Trade and Development Conference of 1974 was held in Mexico City. There were also Soviet economists present at this and several successive meetings. Economists from the Peoples Republic of China have been invited since 1979.

Meanwhile official dealings continued to be concerned with major political events—the Vietnam war in the late 1960s and early 1970s, and the negotiations leading up to establishment of normal relations between North America and China in the early 1970s. On economic matters, the focus continued to be on multilateral issues (the international monetary adjustments after the "Nixon shocks" in 1971,[3] the efforts to deal with the food and energy crises of 1972-74, and the "Tokyo" round of GATT negotiations beginning about 1974). Bilateral government economic relations in the Pacific were largely related to these matters.

Then in the last half of the 1970s, a number of new priorities began to emerge which pointed to a more complex pattern of regional interactions:

(i) The first is the end of the Vietnam war and the withdrawal of the U.S. from an active military role on the continent, except for South Korea. This led to a more activist ASEAN (the Association of South-East Asian Nations, including Indonesia, Malaysia, the Philippines, Singa-

pore, and Thailand).⁴ Starting with the Bali summit in 1976, this group
began to develop plans for economic co-operation as a means of strength-
ening regional security. At first, it was the People's Republic of China
(PRC) that worried many of the members of ASEAN, since national
Communist parties with ideological or more direct (for example, arms
supply) affiliations with Peking had been major obstacles to the achievement of political stability. Later, the threat has been much more direct,
from Vietnam, allied with the Soviet Union, that has taken over
Kampuchea and violates the eastern boundary of Thailand. As a consequence, China has achieved common cause with ASEAN, though its
partnership is not welcomed by all members with equal enthusiasm.

(ii) The end of the Cultural Revolution in the People's Republic of
China in the late 1970s and the adoption of the economic reforms associated with the "four modernizations" has resulted in opening up of trade,
joint ventures and other economic linkages with Pacific regional developed countries, notably Japan and the U.S. but also Australia and Canada. These as well as the Southeast Asian developments have served to
bring China into closer and, on the whole, more positive association with
almost all the non-Communist states of the Western Pacific region as
well as with North America.

(iii) The role of Australia has been disproportionately strong in generating this sense of community of interest. With a population of about fifteen million largely of European stock, Australia could not expect to play
a leading role in a Western Pacific region dominated by larger Asian
countries. However, since the early 1970s when Britain finally joined the
European Community, Australia has accepted the Western Pacific relations as its top priority. It has pursued this primarily in the context of
Australia-Japan economic links—through export of major primary resource products developed with Japanese capital; but it has also been active in establishing closer relations with its nearest neighbours, the
ASEAN countries, and with China and South Korea. Australia has made
this contribution in more subtle ways, notably through its government's
assignment of resources to the study of Asian language and culture and
the role of East Asia in international politics and economics. One of its
best academic and research institutions, the Research School of Pacific
Studies at Australian National University, is a source of some of thebest
analytical work in the English language on Southeast Asia and the
South Pacific and is on a par with better U.S. centres for East Asian
studies. This and other Australian universities have substantial training
capability in East and Southeast Asian languages.

It is not surprising that it has been the Australians, including their government, who have taken several initiatives to promote Pacific relations.

Unlike Canada, Australia does not have the advantage, and the temptations, of ready access to a large neighbouring market. It has therefore seen the need to build painstakingly a stable economic relationship with its Asian partners. Among those who led the way was Sir John Crawford, senior bureaucrat and trade negotiator, and later vice-chancellor and chancellor of Australian National University. He developed a partnership with Saburo Okita, Japan's best-known international economist, who also served in many senior positions in his government, culminating in the role of foreign minister in the Ohira government. Together these men initiated the Pacific Trade and Development Conferences in 1968. In 1980 they persuaded their prime ministers, Fraser and Ohira, to initiate the Pacific Economic Cooperation Conference series already mentioned. After four meetings of this tripartite group, it has settled down to an effort to identify specific projects on which Pacific regional co-operation would be both constructive and practical. This effort uses a group of inter-conference task forces. Each task force is based at a research institution or university but includes corresponding members from each interested country. Studies are prepared as background to the meetings of the task force at which the various national and professional perspectives are available to help formulate a practical consensus on relevant policy questions.

Two examples are the Task Force on Trade Negotiations which was based at the Korean Development Institute in Seoul and the task force on Pacific fisheries issues based at the University of British Columbia.[5] The former has developed an agenda for trade negotiations that was founded on a survey of national trade officials, business and academic economists in each of twelve countries. This agenda has been accepted by the plenary Pacific Economic Cooperation Conference in Seoul, and with further specification could result in a Pacific regional initiative in a new round of GATT negotiations. The Seoul conference, through its standing committee, reported to the Summit in Bonn a consensus in setting a date early in 1986 for a new round of GATT negotiations. If such negotiations are delayed or likely to be too limited in scope, some of the agenda items could be negotiated by the Pacific Rim countries acting alone.

The task force on fisheries questions has recommended a number of policy moves to support better resource management affecting both the fisheries in international waters, especially tuna, and the fisheries now within the extended jurisdictions of developing countries, particularly those of the South Pacific island countries. It also supported guidelines for mutually advantageous fishing by distant water fishing fleets in coastal waters of Pacific Rim countries as a worthwhile subject for regional negotiation.

Other task forces have suggested a search for better regional consultative arrangements on energy supplies and technology, and for means of harmonizing policies affecting foreign direct investment and technology transfer in the region. More recently, a working group on policies affecting feed grains and livestock trade and development has been established.

CANADA'S PARTICULAR INTERESTS

Canadian activity in the Western Pacific is often characterized as a search for new export markets needing both persistent effort by Canadian business and support by trade commissioners and other governmental and financial services. There can be no doubt that this is a valid Canadian priority. However, it should not be the only concern of Canadians. The exploitation of Pacific trade potentials requires attention to imports and two-way investment as well. And the role of official aid should not be understated.

It has become almost commonplace to note that Canada's trans-Pacific trade has surpassed its trans-Atlantic trade, that Canadian banks have full-time representatives in most of the Western Pacific countries, that Canadian private investment and consulting firm activities, mainly related to resource development, are multiplying in countries which were almost unknown to Canadian business a few years ago. These activities are now receiving substantial support from both the private sector and government. The organizers of the Fourth Pacific Rim Opportunities Conference (the Canadian Chamber of Commerce and the PBEC), 11 to 13 March 1985, stated that this time "We believe that most of the people that are going to attend the Conference do have a basic knowledge of the Asian Pacific," so that more time was spent on highly focused panels using case studies of business experience in the region and opportunities for private consultation with Trade Commissioners and representatives of the governments of the Pacific Rim countries. The business community also has active bilateral councils with businessmen from Japan, Korea and China, and others are being developed.

Government supports these activities not only through its trade commissioner service but also by the Export Development Corporation (EDC) and some of the Canadian International Development Agency's (CIDA) activities, notably its Industrial Cooperation Program. The EDC is reported recently as having over $7 billion in loans outstanding and another $2.5 billion in insurance and guarantees, much of this related to Pacific regional transactions. These include both commercial and concessional loans. The latter are designed to cover political and other risks and to meet competition from other countries' export credit arrangements, especially in those cases where large contracts tempt exporters to seek government-subsidized interest rates. CIDA and EDC engage in "parallel financing" for projects where development support combines appropriately with Canadian export activity. CIDA's Industrial Cooperation Program helps Canadian firms to do "feasibility studies" in developing countries, to set up joint ventures or to explore technical assistance prospects. Of course, most of CIDA's bilateral program involves Canadian goods and services since about two-thirds of such funds are spent in Canada.

Proposals for expanded aid-plus-trade programs are frequently brought forward, but these continue to raise doubts on grounds that the purpose of trade promotion and the administrative arrangements needed to make such activity efficient are rather different from the purpose and administrative requirements of development aid. Among other considerations, the countries most important to Canadian trade potential are not the same as those whose low income levels make them high priority recipients of Canadian aid. However, in the Western Pacific group, there are two countries that have high priority for CIDA *and* potential for trade development—Indonesia and Thailand. Canadian aid to these countries focuses on resource development and related infrastructural assistance that can lead to fuller use of their substantial resource endowments. Canada's endowments are rather well suited to their skill and hardware requirements. It is noteworthy that other developed countries also place a high priority on aid to these two nations so that Canada's interests lie in directing its aid to those sectors for which we do have a comparative advantage in the supply of goods and services. Such an emphasis can lead to an appropriate basis for commercial business, as successful development reduces the need for official aid.

On the trade side, Canadian experience with the Southeast Asian countries also highlights the problems of expanding commercial links. These countries strongly adhere to the principle of export-based development and are particularly anxious to expand exports of two kinds—processed forms of tropical raw materials and labour-intensive manufactures. For the former group of products, a major problem is the existence of escalated tariffs and non-tariff barriers on processed forms of many tropical products—e.g., tropical hardwoods, fruits, and so forth. Most countries have little or no tariffs on raw tropical products but protect early-stage processing in ways that impose high levels of effective protection. Some of the non-tariff barriers on fruit include distinctive and strict quality standards reflecting traditional tastes and methods of preparing food, but

these may also prove conveniently protective. This problem is encountered for exports of many food items to Japan, not only those from
tropical sources.

The restrictions on trade in labour-intensive manufactures are even
more important. They are important to the current major exporters of
such products—South Korea, Taiwan, and Hong Kong; but they are also
important to Thailand and Indonesia, who wish to increase their exports
of such products in the future when they do not expect to be able to rely
as much as in the past on exports of resource industry products. Indonesia, now dependent on petroleum exports for more than two-thirds
of its export earnings, is trying to develop exports of textile and other
manufactures that will embody its plentiful labour resource, now available at wages well below those of most East Asian countries, except the
People's Republic of China. Indonesia must struggle to establish such
exports. One problem is that the foreign exchange value of its rupiah has
in the past decade been raised by Indonesia's substantial oil exports to a
level that makes her other products less competitive than they will be
when oil revenues decline. Another problem is that as Indonesian exports
of labour-intensive clothing have begun to increase from very low past
levels, they have been subject to quantitative import restrictions. Importing countries, including Canada, have sought to apply the minimum import growth levels allowed under the multi-fibre agreement, even though
Indonesian exports of such products are a tiny fraction of those of well-
established exporters. This kind of restriction of the trade of countries
like Indonesia has the effect of making its leaders cynical about the apparent hypocrisy of developed countries that proclaim the advantages of
"free" markets, but at the same time obstruct the export opportunities of
those developing countries that have stressed export-led development.

Indonesia has also demonstrated how a developing country, if it is
large and influential enough, can exercise some bargaining power over
those who might be tempted to restrict its exports. When a country is an
important aid donor, and at the same time ties its aid to the export of its
goods and services, it has a larger stake in maintaining its aid in order to
sustain the jobs that create the goods and services financed by aid. Thus,
when Indonesia informed the Canadian government about two years ago
that it would consider cancelling an important Canadian aid project, it
was able to win concessions on the levels of textile product exports that
would be admitted to Canada. This tough bargaining approach is less
available to developing countries with fewer donor options and less
proven capacity to achieve growth and political stability.

Another Indonesian move has been to adopt countertrade. As a large
net importer of manufactured products, Indonesia decided it should im-

pose on exporters of such products an obligation to accept part payment in Indonesian goods. This is old-fashioned "barter" under another name. It is important to stress that it would not likely have emerged were it not for the slump in world demand and the growth of protectionism, especially that limiting labour-intensive imports. Although countertrade clearly distorts international trading patterns, it is important to stress that it is in large part a reaction to other distortions. The great danger is that it will be adopted by more countries, developed and less developed, to support export activity much less economically justified than that of Indonesian labour-intensive manufactures.

These observations illustrate the need for a policy approach by Canada and other developed countries that supports both the import and export trade of developing countries, a trade which is particularly important for Pacific Rim developing countries. In some cases they have an already demonstrated capacity to achieve impressive and sustained rates of export-led economic growth, and others are on the threshold of achieving similar results. The consequent high and growing levels of income in the Western Pacific are the basis for the sustained growth of Canadian and U.S. exports of goods and services to the region and have already made it our principal overseas market.

Those who point to the possible loss of jobs in certain North American industries that might result from the end of quantitative restrictions have a severe case of "blinders." Our willingness to forego such restrictions is essential to the preservation of our export opportunities. Furthermore, the cost to consumers in North America of maintaining "voluntary export restraints" is substantial. Authorities in Washington recently published estimates of the cost of voluntary export restraints (VERs) on Japanese automobiles. The cost borne by U.S. consumers was estimated at about $160,000 per job, many times the salaries paid. The money saved from having to pay less for cars would have been spent on other goods and services, creating jobs in those sectors. It has also been estimated by two government agencies and one independent econometric analysis that the content legislation recently before the U.S. Congress, seeking to require a minimum U.S. content in all imported cars, would result in a net loss of jobs in the U.S. economy ranging from a minimum of 66,000 to a maximum of 365,000.

Since Canada has also used voluntary export restraints on Japanese car imports and was advised by the Lavalle-White task force to impose content requirements,[6] the above estimates are highly relevant to Canadian policy-makers. Fortunately, the U.S. has decided not to press for continuance of VERs on Japanese cars, and two of the three largest U.S. firms have agreed with this stand. Although Canada has followed this lead, as its VERs expired at the end of March 1985, it is regrettable that many politicians as well as labour leaders have continued to perpetrate the unproven claim that removal of quantitative restraints would result in a net loss of jobs in Canada. At least the auto workers have a right to ask how they will be treated by government if the adjustment falls on them, while other workers receive the main benefits of removal of barriers on automobile trade.

How can the Canadian government ensure that trade in the Pacific takes place in an environment that encourages two-way flows and limits the cost of non-tariff devices such as those described? The answer would appear to be in part through multilateral action, and in part through regional initiatives that go beyond regional bilateral negotiations.

No one can be sure how successful the proposed new GATT round will be. In the present environment of unemployment and investment uncertainty, especially in Western Europe, the willingness of many GATT members, particularly the members of the European Economic Community, to enter into another major GATT round is in considerable doubt.

What Pacific regional strategy can be suggested either as a stimulus to multilateral action, or as a complement to multilateral negotiations, or indeed as a substitute for them if they are indefinitely delayed? The work of the Task Force on Trade Negotiations, already mentioned, suggested an agenda dealing with some of the following:[7]

(i) Reduction or elimination of duties on processed forms of natural products of the Pacific region; for example, many tropical and temperate zone forest products, fruit, fish and non-ferrous minerals;

(ii) Measures for limiting agricultural protectionism, including harmonization, wherever possible, of health and related policies of importing countries, some limitation of agricultural subsidization, and so forth;

(iii) Agreed liberalization of trade in labour-intensive manufactures, either by elimination or reduction of voluntary export restraints and other quantitative controls; agreed targets for imports by developed countries above the minima established under the multi-fibre agreement;

(iv) Agreed limitation and phasing out of similar quantitative restrictions on automobiles and consumer electronic goods exported by Japan and the newly industrialized countries;

(v) Agreed guidelines affecting the property rights (for example, patents, trade marks) that have an impact on trade in technology-intensive products, so that such rights are neither abused nor exploited in ways that restrict competition unnecessarily.

The Pacific area countries could develop a strong and liberal negotiating position embodying the above elements and call for GATT negotiations within the next two years on these and other matters. If little interest is shown by other signatory countries, then the group might proceed on those measures that are of concentrated regional interest and, if there is agreement on liberalization, could choose in each case whether to extend concessions conditionally or unconditionally to other GATT countries. Of course, any conditionality on these matters would involve waivers or compensation if GATT positions affecting them exist, as they would on tariff issues relating to processed forms of natural products. If they do not exist for the particular non-tariff barriers cited, then conditionality could be introduced legally, though it might be unnecessary, especially if the trade concerned would have little implication for the competitive interests of countries outside the Pacific region.

Trade liberalization measures relating to the above list could create some momentum in the multilateral arena and leverage toward liberalization of other countries' trade restrictions in the GATT framework. Canada could have an interest in supporting these efforts as a country that benefits from both export and import trade in the region. As an exporter of primary goods, it has a direct stake in reducing duties on processed natural products, limiting agricultural protectionism, and as the third most important producer of technology-intensive products, in guidelines for patents and trademarks.

CANADA'S SOCIAL AND CULTURAL LINKS WITH THE PACIFIC

Canada's social contacts with the Western Pacific countries have been limited by the lack of financial support. Academic and cultural exchanges with Europe greatly exceed those with Asia, and these contacts that have been established are, with one or two exceptions, not backed by funds dedicated to the purpose. With one notable exception, the Max Bell Foundation, private sources have not yet come forward with substantial resources to support Canadian social and educational endeavours focused on the Western Pacific.

As for governments, until the establishment of the Canada Asia-Pacific Foundation, virtually nothing was done, except as a byproduct of the research program of the International Development Research Centre. IDRC has encouraged some research on problems of the developing countries of Southeast Asia, such as support for research and ASEAN scholar participation in the Pacific Trade and Development Conference of 1981 on "Renewable Resources in the Pacific." Of course, a number of Canadian academics and other professionals have had an opportunity to become acquainted with the region through CIDA assignments and projects relating to the developing countries, and more recently China. Understandably these can have only an incidental bearing on basic research on the problems of the region or critical treatment of Canadian policies.

The Canada Asia-Pacific Foundation has been greeted with a mixture of anticipation and scepticism. The former was a product of the desperate need for more support for all types of linkages, especially given the cost of travel and tooling-up, such as acquiring language and other "access" skills relevant to the very different and complex cultures of the region. The scepticism has resulted from the very slow start that the Foundation has experienced. This can be explained to some degree by the period of fiscal restraint of the last two or three years. The federal government offered matching support for funds gathered from provincial governments and the private sector. This was slow to emerge and is still well below the level originally suggested by both federal and provincial proponents of the Foundation. Eventually the federal government itself committed a basic start-up fund of several millions from CIDA resources, and more commitments by provincial governments have been forthcoming as well.

This atmosphere of austerity has also tended to bias the direction of the Foundation's planning toward immediately "practical" business-oriented programs and to public relations endeavours, some of which are probably necessary to raise public awareness of the Foundation. Academics are wondering if the Foundation at its present level of endowment will be able to devote many resources to the establishment of a longer-term basis for Canadian understanding and involvement in the region. That goal can only be realized with much more extensive facilities for language studies or applied social science research. The lack of representation of academic and professional specialists on the management or board of the Foundation is disappointing. There are only two specialists with Pacific-related research credentials on the board, and none from the principal British Columbia or Ontario universities with the most established staff and research experience on Western Pacific matters.

One can only hope that stronger finances and policy development will eventually enable a better balance between concern for short-term domestic political and commercial concerns and the long-term foundations for Canadian economic, cultural and political relations with the Western Pacific. We should aim to match the Japan Foundation's support to overseas study and cultural exchange in the Pacific region; at least to a level that represents the same proportion of our GNP or our exports to the region. Any comparison of Canadian and Australian performance in these activities is bound to be embarrassing for Canadians for some time to come.

NOTES

1. Following the Bonn summit in May 1985, the British government including Prime Minister Thatcher made rather intemperate statements about the "unfair" methods used by the Japanese in winning a contract to build a bridge across the Bosphorus in Turkey, a contract which the British had hoped to win. The British threatened protectionist action unless the Japanese took actions to reduce their trade surplus, but gave no indication of the relevance of the contract to this issue. The Japanese success was attributed to better credit terms, but British spokesmen admitted that the Japanese "did not appear to have broken any rules covering government support for international contracts."

2. A particularly good analysis of the circumstances which make it difficult for others to compete in Japan's domestic market appeared in a recent *Far Eastern Economic Review* article, "U.S. bites the bullet," May 9, 1985. Many other more technical assessments of the U.S. trade deficit have appeared recently, including those by the Institute of International Economics.

3. This refers to the decision of the U.S. government to impose surcharges on other countries' goods entering the U.S. in order to induce them to revalue their currencies. It resulted in the Smithsonian agreement of December 1971, and the subsequent adoption of a managed fluctuating exchange rate system. In the Pacific, the main outcome was the appreciation of the yen relative to the dollar. In late 1985, the U.S. Congress was again considering surcharges and other trade-related measures.

4. Brunei became independent and a sixth member of ASEAN in 1984.

5. The Reports of the Task Forces are contained in *Issues and Opportunities for Pacific Economic Cooperation*, Korea Development Institute, 1985.

6. These issues are discussed in "The Great Japanese Auto Debate," *Toronto Star*, Section D, March 16, 1985. In the fall of 1985, the emphasis in the position of the parts manufacturers shifted to pressure on Japanese manufacturers to buy Canadian components for their branch plants to be built in Ontario and Quebec.

7. *Issues and Opportunities*, especially page 13.

Notes on Contributors

PETER N. NEMETZ—Associate Professor and Chairman, Policy Analysis Division, Faculty of Commerce, University of British Columbia.

YOKO SAZANAMI—Professor, Department of Economics, Keio University, Tokyo, Japan.

RODNEY TYERS—Research Fellow in Economics, Development Studies Center, The Research School of Pacific Studies, The Australian National University, Canberra.

PRUE PHILLIPS—Coordinator, RSPacS Economic Data Bank, The Research School of Pacific Studies, The Australian National University, Canberra.

THEODORE PANAYOTOU—formerly Faculty of Economics and Business Administration, Kasetsart University, Bangkok, Thailand; currently with the Institute for International Development, Harvard University.

MICHAEL GOLDBERG—Herbert R. Fullerton Professor of Urban Land Policy and Professor of Urban Land Economics, Faculty of Commerce, University of British Columbia.

CHARLES J. JOHNSON—Coordinator, Mineral Policy Program, East-West Resource Systems Institute, East-West Center, Honolulu, Hawaii.

ALLEN L. CLARK—East-West Resource Systems Institute, East-West Center, Honolulu, Hawaii; and United States Geological Survey.

JAMES M. OTTO—Research Fellow, East-West Resource Systems Institute, East-West Center, Honolulu, Hawaii.

VACLAV SMIL—Professor, Department of Geography, University of Manitoba.

CORAZON SIDDAYAO—formerly Coordinator, Energy and Industrialization Project, Resource Systems Institute, East-West Center; and Affiliate Professor, Department of Economics, University of Hawaii, Honolulu, Hawaii; currently on the faculty of the Economic Development Institute of the World Bank, Washington, D.C.

TOUFIQ A. SIDDIQI—Research Associate and Special Assistant to the President, East-West Center, Honolulu, Hawaii.

HAROLD HALVORSON—Resource Consultant, Vancouver, B.C.

EDWARD ENGLISH—Professor, Department of Economics, Carleton University, Ottawa.